JOEL ON SOFTWARE

And on Diverse and
Occasionally Related Matters
That Will Prove of Interest
to Software Developers,
Designers, and Managers,
and to Those Who,
Whether by Good Fortune
or Ill Luck, Work with Them
in Some Capacity

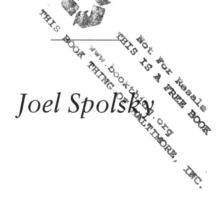

Joel Spolsky

Apress®

Joel on Software: And on Diverse and Occasionally Related Matters That Will Prove of Interest to Software Developers, Designers, and Managers, and to Those Who, Whether by Good Fortune or Ill Luck, Work with Them in Some Capacity

Copyright © 2004 by Joel Spolsky

Lead Editor: Gary Cornell
Editorial Board: Steve Anglin, Dan Appleman, Ewan Buckingham, Gary Cornell, Tony Davis, Jason Gilmore, Chris Mills, Steve Rycroft, Dominic Shakeshaft, Jim Sumser, Gavin Wray
Project Manager: Beth Christmas
Copy Edit Manager: Nicole LeClerc
Copy Editor: Scott Carter
Production Manager: Kari Brooks
Proofreader: Liz Welch
Compositor: Molly Sharp, ContentWorks
Indexer: Ted Laux
Cover Designer: Kurt Krames
Manufacturing Manager: Tom Debolski

Library of Congress Cataloging-in-Publication Data

Spolsky, Joel.
    Joel on software : and on diverse and occasionally related matters
that will prove of interest to software developers, designers, and
managers, and to those who, whether by good fortune or ill luck, work
with them in some capacity / Joel Spolsky.
        p. cm.
    Includes index.
    ISBN 1-59059-389-8 (pbk. : alk. paper)
    1. Computer software--Development. I. Title.

QA76.76.D47S693 2004
005.1--dc22
                                        2004015941

Printed and bound in the United States of America 9 8 7 6 5 4 3 2 1

Trademarked names may appear in this book. Rather than use a trademark symbol with every occurrence of a trademarked name, we use the names only in an editorial fashion and to the benefit of the trademark owner, with no intention of infringement of the trademark.

Distributed to the book trade in the United States by Springer-Verlag New York, Inc., 175 Fifth Avenue, New York, NY 10010 and outside the United States by Springer-Verlag GmbH & Co. KG, Tiergartenstr. 17, 69112 Heidelberg, Germany.

In the United States: phone 1-800-SPRINGER, e-mail orders@springer-ny.com, or visit http://www.springer-ny.com. Outside the United States: fax +49 6221 345229, e-mail orders@springer.de, or visit http://www.springer.de.

For information on translations, please contact Apress directly at 2560 Ninth Street, Suite 219, Berkeley, CA 94710. Phone 510-549-5930, fax 510-549-5939, e-mail info@apress.com, or visit http://www.apress.com.

The information in this book is distributed on an "as is" basis, without warranty. Although every precaution has been taken in the preparation of this work, neither the author(s) nor Apress shall have any liability to any person or entity with respect to any loss or damage caused or alleged to be caused directly or indirectly by the information contained in this work.

Most of the material in this book appeared previously on the Web on www.joelonsoftware.com.

*To my parents, who raised me thinking
that all adults wrote books.*

CONTENTS

part two
Managing Developers 151

part three
Being Joel: Random Thoughts
on Not-So-Random Topics 213

part four
A Little Bit Too Much
Commentary on .NET

part five
Appendix

ABOUT THE AUTHOR

Joel Spolsky, a software industry veteran, writes a weblog called Joel on Software (www.joelonsoftware.com) that is one of the most popular independent websites for programmers. His site has been described as the "anti-Dilbert manifesto." Spolsky has designed and developed software used by millions of people and has worked on a variety of products, from Microsoft Excel to the Juno user interface. He is the founder of Fog Creek Software in New York City.

INTRODUCTION

You never *asked* to be a manager. Like most software developers I know, you would have been much, much happier if they would just let you sit and code quietly. But you're the best developer, and when Nigel, the old team lead, had that *unfortunate* accident with the bungee cord and the laptop computer, it seemed natural to promote you, the team star.

So now, you have your own office (instead of sharing a cubicle with The Summer Intern Who Never Left), and you have to fill out those biannual performance reviews (instead of ruining your eyesight staring happily into a CRT all day), that is, when you're not wasting time dealing with the bizarre demands of prima donna programmers, back-slapping sales guys, those creative "UI designers" (who were hired as graphic designers, for Pete's sake) who want shiny OK/Cancel buttons that *reflect*, I mean, what's the RGB value for "reflective?" And dealing with inane questions from the senior VP who learned everything he knows about software from an article in Delta Airlines In-flight Magazine. "Why don't we use Java instead of Oracle? I heard it's more unified."

Welcome to management! Guess what? Managing software projects has *nothing at all* to do with programming. If all you've done so far is write code, you're probably starting to discover that human beings are perhaps a smidgen less predictable than your garden-variety Intel CPU.

The old team lead, Nigel, had never been particularly good at it, anyway. "I don't want to be one of those managers who spend all their time in pointless meetings," he would say with more than a little bravado. "I think I can still spend about 85 percent of my time coding, and only a little bit of my time *managing*."

What Nigel really *wanted* to say was, "I have no bloody idea *whatsoever* how to manage this project and hopefully if I just keep coding like I did before I was put in charge, somehow everything will work itself out." It didn't, of course, which goes quite a long way to explaining exactly why Nigel was bungee-jumping with an IBM ThinkPad on that fateful day.

Anyway, Nigel has really made a surprising recovery, considering, and is now working as the CTO of a small company he started with his bungee buddies, WhatTimeIsIt.com, and he's only got six months to deliver an entirely new system from scratch, and he can't fake it any more either.

~

Managing software projects is not a well-known art. Nobody has a degree in Managing Software Projects, and there are very few books on the subject. A lot of the very few people who have worked on really successful software projects got rich and retired to trout farms before they had a chance to pass on their accumulated experience to the next generation, and many others just burned out and got less stressful jobs teaching remedial English to inner-city gangsters.

As a result, many software projects fail in some way or another, either overtly or covertly, because nobody on the team has any idea how a successful software project might be run. So too many teams never deliver their product, or take too long to deliver the product, or deliver a product that nobody wants. But the part that really makes me angry is that the people on the team are unhappy and hate every minute of it. Life is just too short to hate your job.

A couple of years ago I posted "The Joel Test," a list of twelve hallmarks of well-run software teams, on my website. Things like keeping a database for tracking bugs, making job candidates write code on the spot, and so on (don't worry, I'll cover all those in detail later). The surprising thing was how many people emailed to tell me that their team only got scores of two or three out of twelve.

Two or three!

It's almost surreal—imagine a bunch of carpenters trying to build furniture when they've never heard of screws. They're relying on nails exclusively, which they stamp into the wood with tap-dancing shoes because nobody told them about hammers.

Managing software projects requires a completely different set of skills and techniques than writing code does; they are two radically different and unrelated fields. Writing code is as different from management as brain surgery is from pretzel-baking. There is no reason to expect that a brilliant brain surgeon, mysteriously transported to a pretzel factory due to a tear in the space/time continuum, would have even the remotest idea of how to make pretzels, even if he *did* graduate from Harvard Medical School. Yet people inevitably assume that it's possible to take a top coder and move them into management without a little bit of readjustment.

Like the aforementioned brain surgeon, you and Nigel have found yourselves transported into a new job, management, which requires you to interact with—oh my—*people*, not compilers. And if you thought today's Java compilers are buggy and unpredictable, just *wait* until you have your first prima donna programmer problem. Managing teams of humans makes C++ templates look positively *trivial*.

There *are* techniques to managing successful software projects. The state of the art has evolved beyond nails and tap-dancing shoes. We've got hammers and screwdrivers and double-bevel sliding compound miter saws. The goal of this book is to introduce you to as many of the techniques as I could think of, at every level, from the team lead estimating schedules to the software CEO developing competitive strategy. You'll learn:

- How to hire and motivate the best people—the single most critical factor in a successful software project
- How to make estimates and schedules that work, and why you need them
- How to design software features and write specifications that are actually useful, not just "write-once-read-never" binders used for building cubicle extensions
- How to avoid common pitfalls of software development, and why programmers are always wrong when they insist on "throwing it out and starting over"
- How to organize and motivate teams, and why programmers need offices with doors that close
- When to write your own code from scratch even if there's an almost good enough version you can download from the Net
- Why it always seems like software projects stall after the first couple of months

- What it means to have a software strategy, and why BeOS was doomed from day one
- And a whole lot more

It's highly subjective. I have been forced, in the interest of brevity, to leave out the words "in my opinion" from the beginning of each sentence because, as it turns out, every single sentence in the book is my opinion. And it's not complete, but it's probably a good start.

~

Ah, So, You've Seen My Website . . .

Much of this book's content first appeared as a series of articles on my website, *Joel on Software* (www.joelonsoftware.com), where I've been writing up my thoughts for the last couple of years. The book you hold in your hands is, I hope, a heck of a lot more *cohesive* than the website, where by *cohesive* I mean "can read in the bathtub without fear of electrocution."

We've organized the book for you in three major sections. The first section is all about developing software in the small: everything you should do in your own team to make software that won't hurt people. The second section contains a collection of articles about managing programmers and programming teams. The third section is a little bit more random, but mostly focuses on the big strategy of creating a sustainable software development business. You'll learn why bloatware always wins the day, you'll learn why Ben & Jerry's is not like Amazon, and I'll try to make a case that software development methodologies are usually a sign of scantily competent workforces.

There's more stuff here, too, but you might as well just dive in and start reading it.

part one

Bits and Bytes: The Practice of Programming

one

CHOOSING A LANGUAGE

Sunday, May 5, 2002

Why do developers choose one programming language over another for a given task?

Sometimes I choose raw C when I need blazing speed.

When I want something that will run on Windows with as small a distribution as possible, I often choose C++ with MFC statically linked.

When we need a GUI that will run on Mac, Windows, and Linux, a common choice is Java. Although the GUI will not be perfect, it will work.

For rapid GUI development and really smooth UIs, I like Visual Basic, but I know that I'm going to have to pay the price in the size of the distributable and the fact that I'll be locked into Windows.

For a command-line tool that must run on any UNIX machine and doesn't need to be fast, Perl is a good choice.

If you have to run inside a web browser, JavaScript is the really the only choice. In a SQL stored procedure, you usually get to choose between one vendor's proprietary SQL derivative or go home.

~

What's the Point?

But I hardly ever choose a language based on syntax. Yeah, I prefer the {}; languages (C/C++/C#/Java). And I have lots of opinions about what makes a "good" syntax. But I wouldn't accept a 20MB runtime just to get semicolons.

Which makes me wonder a bit about .NET's cross-language strategy. The idea is, choose any language you want, there are zillions, and they all work the same way.

VB.NET and C#.NET are virtually identical except for tiny syntactic differences. And other languages that want to be part of the .NET world need to support at least a core set of features and types, or they won't be able to Play Well With Others. But how do I develop a UNIX command-line utility in .NET? How do I develop a tiny Windows EXE in less than 16K in .NET?

It seems like .NET gives us a "choice" of languages precisely where we couldn't care less about it—in the syntax.

two

BACK TO BASICS

I spend a lot of time on my website talking about exciting "big picture" stuff like .NET versus Java, XML strategy, Lock-In, competitive strategy, software design, architecture, and so forth. All this stuff is a layer cake, in a way. At the top layer, you've got software strategy. Below that, we think about architectures like .NET, and below that, individual products: software development products like Java or platforms like Windows.

Go lower on the cake, please. DLLs? Objects? Functions? No! Lower! At some point you're thinking about lines of code written in programming languages.

Still not low enough. Today I want to think about CPUs. A little bit of silicon moving bytes around. Pretend you are a beginning programmer. Tear away all that knowledge you've built up about programming, software, management, and get back to the lowest level Von Neumann fundamental stuff. Wipe J2EE out of your mind for a moment. Think *bytes*.

Why are we doing this? I think that some of the biggest mistakes people make—even at the highest architectural levels—come from having a weak or broken understanding of a few simple things at the very lowest levels. You've built a marvelous palace, but the foundation is a mess. Instead of a nice cement slab, you've got rubble down there. So the palace looks nice, but occasionally the bathtub slides across the bathroom floor and you have no idea what's going on.

So today, take a deep breath. Walk with me, please, through a little exercise which will be conducted using the C programming language.

the first part of strcat has to scan through the destination string every time, looking for that dang null terminator again and again, this function is much slower than it needs to be and doesn't scale well at all. Lots of code you use every day has this problem. Many file systems are implemented in a way that it's a bad idea to put too many files in one directory, because performance starts to drop off dramatically when you get thousands of items in one directory. Try opening an overstuffed Windows recycle bin to see this in action—it takes hours to show up, which is clearly not linear in the number of files it contains. There must be a Shlemiel the Painter's Algorithm in there somewhere. Whenever something seems like it should have linear performance but it seems to have n-squared performance, look for hidden Shlemiels. They are often hidden by your libraries. Looking at a column of strcats or a strcat in a loop doesn't exactly shout out "n-squared," but that is what's happening.

How do we fix this? A few smart C programmers implemented their own mystrcat as follows:

```
char* mystrcat( char* dest, char* src )
{
    while (*dest) dest++;
    while (*dest++ = *src++);
    return --dest;
}
```

What have we done here? At very little extra cost we're returning a pointer to the *end* of the new, longer string. That way, the code that calls this function can decide to append further without rescanning the string:

```
char bigString[1000];    /* I never know how much to allocate... */
char *p = bigString;
bigString[0] = '\0';
p = mystrcat(p,"John, ");
p = mystrcat(p,"Paul, ");
p = mystrcat(p,"George, ");
p = mystrcat(p,"Joel ");
```

This is, of course, linear in performance, not n-squared, so it doesn't suffer from degradation when you have a lot of stuff to concatenate.

The designers of Pascal were aware of this problem and "fixed" it by storing a byte count in the first byte of the string. These are called *Pascal strings*. They can contain zeros and are not null terminated. Because the largest number you can fit in a byte is 255, Pascal strings are limited to 255 bytes in length, but because they are not null terminated, they occupy the same amount of memory as ASCIZ strings. The great thing about Pascal strings is that you never have to have a loop just to figure out the length of your string. Finding the length of a string in Pascal is one assembly instruction instead of a whole loop. It is monumentally faster.

The old Macintosh operating system used Pascal strings everywhere. Many C programmers on other platforms used Pascal strings for speed. Excel uses Pascal strings internally, which is why strings in many places in Excel are limited to 255 bytes, and it's also one reason Excel is blazingly fast.

For a long time, if you wanted to put a Pascal string literal in your C code, you had to write

```
char* str = "\006Hello!";
```

Yep, you had to count the bytes by hand, yourself, and hardcode it into the first byte of your string. Lazy programmers would do this, and have slow programs:

```
char* str = "*Hello!";
str[0] = strlen(str) - 1;
```

Notice in this case you've got a string that is null terminated (the compiler did that) as well as a Pascal string. I used to call these *fucked strings* because it's easier than calling them *null-terminated Pascal strings*, but this is a G-rated channel, so *you* will have use the longer name.

I elided an important issue earlier. Remember this line of code?

```
char bigString[1000];    /* I never know how much to allocate... */
```

Since we're looking at the bits today, I shouldn't have ignored this. I should have done this correctly: figured out how many bytes I needed and allocated the right amount of memory.

Shouldn't I have?

Because otherwise, you see, a clever hacker will read my code and notice that I'm only allocating 1000 bytes and *hoping* it will be enough, and they'll find some clever way to trick me into strcatting an 1100-byte string into my 1000 bytes of memory, thus overwriting the stack frame and changing the return address so that when this function returns, it executes some code that the hacker himself wrote. This is what they're talking about when they say that a particular program has a *buffer overflow* susceptibility. It was the number one cause of hacks and worms in the olden days before Microsoft Outlook made hacking easy enough for teenagers to do.

OK, so all those programmers are just lame-asses. They should have figured out how much memory to allocate.

But really, C does *not* make this easy on you. Let's go back to my Beatles example:

```
char bigString[1000];    /* I never know how much to allocate... */
char *p = bigString;
bigString[0] = '\0';
p = mystrcat(p,"John, ");
p = mystrcat(p,"Paul, ");
p = mystrcat(p,"George, ");
p = mystrcat(p,"Joel ");
```

How much *should* we allocate? Let's try doing this The Right Way.

```
char* bigString;
int i = 0;
i = strlen("John, ")
    + strlen("Paul, ")
    + strlen("George, ")
    + strlen("Joel ");
bigString = (char*) malloc (i + 1);
/* remember space for null terminator! */
...
```

My eyes glazeth over. You're probably about ready to change the channel already. I don't blame you, but bear with me because it gets really interesting.

We have to scan through all the strings once just figuring out how big they are, then we scan through them again concatenating. At least if you use Pascal strings the strlen operation is fast. Maybe we can write a version of strcat that reallocates memory for us.

That opens *another* whole can of worms: memory allocators. Do you know how malloc works? The nature of malloc is that it has a long linked list of available blocks of memory called the *free chain*. When you call malloc, it walks the linked list looking for a block of memory that is big enough for your request. Then it cuts that block into two blocks—one the size you asked for, the other with the extra bytes—and gives you the block you asked for, and puts the leftover block (if any) back into the linked list. When you call free, it adds the block you freed onto the free chain. Eventually, the free chain gets chopped up into little pieces, and you ask for a big piece, and there are no big pieces available in the size you want. So malloc calls a timeout and starts rummaging around the free chain, sorting things out, and merging adjacent small free blocks into larger blocks. This takes three days. The end result of all this mess is that the performance characteristic of malloc is that it's never very fast (it always walks the free chain), and sometimes, unpredictably, it's shockingly slow while it cleans up. (This is, incidentally, the same performance characteristic of garbage-collected systems, surprise surprise, so all the claims people make about how garbage collection imposes a performance penalty are not entirely true, since typical malloc implementations had the same kind of performance penalty, albeit milder.)

Smart programmers minimize the potential disruption of malloc by always allocating blocks of memory that are powers of 2 in size. You know, 4 bytes, 8 bytes, 16 bytes, 18446744073709551616 bytes, etc. For reasons that should be intuitive to anyone who plays with Lego, this minimizes the amount of weird fragmentation that goes on in the free chain. Although it may seem like this wastes space, it is also easy to see how it never wastes more than 50 percent of the space. So your program uses no more than twice as much memory as it needs to, which is not that big a deal.

Suppose you wrote a smart strcat function that reallocates the destination buffer automatically. Should it always reallocate it to the exact size needed? My teacher and mentor Stan Eisenstat[4] suggests that when you call realloc, you should always double the size of memory that was previously allocated. That means that you never have to call realloc more than $lg(n)$ times, which has decent performance characteristics even for huge strings, and you never waste more than 50 percent of your memory.

Anyway. Life just gets messier and messier down here in byte-land. Aren't you glad you don't have to write in C anymore? We have all these great languages like Perl and Java and VB and XSLT that never make you think of anything like this; they just deal with it, somehow. But occasionally, the plumbing infrastructure sticks up in the middle of the living room, and we have to think about whether to use a String class or a StringBuilder class, or some such distinction, because the compiler is still not smart enough to understand everything about what we're trying to accomplish and is trying to help us *not* write inadvertent Shlemiel-the-Painter algorithms.

This essay was provoked after I wrote an off-the-cuff comment on my weblog stating that you can't implement the SQL statement SELECT author FROM books fast when your data is stored in XML.[5] Just in case everybody didn't understand what I was talking about, and now that we've been rolling around in the CPU all day, this assertion might make more sense.

How does a relational database implement SELECT author FROM books? In a relational database, every row in a table (e.g., the books table) is exactly the same length in bytes, and every field is always at a fixed offset from the beginning of the row. So, for example, if each record in the books table is 100 bytes long, and the author field is at offset 23, then authors are stored at bytes 23, 123, 223, 323, etc. What is the code to move to the next record in the result of this query? Basically, it's this:

```
pointer += 100;
```

---

4. See www.cs.yale.edu/people/faculty/eisenstat.html.

5. See www.joelonsoftware.com/articles/fog0000000296.html.

One CPU instruction. Faaaaaaaaaast.

Now let's look at the books table in XML.

```
<?xml blah blah>
<books>
  <book>
    <title>UI Design for Programmers</title>
    <author>Joel Spolsky</author>
  </book>
  <book>
    <title>The Chop Suey Club</title>
    <author>Bruce Weber</author>
  </book>
</books>
```

Quick question. What is the code to move to the next record? Uh...

At this point a good programmer would say, well, let's parse the XML into a tree in memory so that we can operate on it reasonably quickly. The amount of work that has to be done here by the CPU to SELECT author FROM books will bore you absolutely to tears. As every compiler writer knows, lexing and parsing are the slowest part of compiling. Suffice it to say that it involves a lot of string stuff, which we discovered is slow, and a lot of memory allocation stuff, which we discovered is slow, as we lex, parse, and build an abstract syntax tree in memory. That assumes that you *have* enough memory to load the whole thing at once. With relational databases, the performance of moving from record to record is fixed and is, in fact, *one CPU instruction*. That's very much by design. And thanks to memory mapped files, you have to load only those pages of disk that you are actually going to use. With XML, if you preparse, the performance of moving from record to record is fixed, but there's a huge startup time, and if you don't preparse, the performance of moving from record to record varies based on the length of the record before it and is still hundreds of CPU instructions long.

What this means to me is that you can't use XML if you need performance and have lots of data. If you have a little bit of data, or if what you're doing doesn't have to be fast, XML is a fine format. And if you really want the best of both worlds, you have to come up with a way to store metadata next to your XML, something like Pascal strings' byte count, which give you hints about where things are in the file so that you don't have to parse and scan for them. But of course then you can't use text editors to edit the file because that messes up the metadata, so it's not really XML anymore.

For those three gracious members of my audience who are still with me at this point, I hope you've learned something or rethought something. I hope that thinking about boring first-year computer-science stuff like how strcat and malloc actually work has given you new tools to think about the latest top-level strategic and architectural decisions that you make in dealing with technologies like XML. For homework, think about why Transmeta chips will always feel sluggish. Or why the original HTML spec for TABLES was so badly designed that large tables on web pages can't be shown quickly to people with modems. Or about why COM is so dang fast but not when you're crossing process boundaries. Or about why the NT guys put the display driver into kernelspace instead of userspace.

These are all things that require you to think about bytes, and they affect the big top-level decisions we make in all kinds of architecture and strategy. This is why my view of teaching is that first-year CS students need to start at the basics, using C and building their way up from the CPU. I am actually physically disgusted that so many computer science programs think that Java is a good introductory language, because it's "easy" and you don't get confused with all that boring string/malloc stuff, but you can learn cool OOP stuff which will make your big programs ever so modular. This is a pedagogical disaster waiting to happen. Generations of graduates are descending on us and creating Shlemiel the Painter algorithms right and left, and they don't even realize it, because they fundamentally have no idea that strings are, at a very deep level, difficult, even if you can't quite see that in your Perl script. If you want to teach somebody something well, you have to start at the very lowest level. It's like *Karate Kid*. Wax on, wax off. Wax on, wax off. Do that for three weeks. Then knocking the other kid's head off is easy.

```
 emacs@localhost.localdomain                          _ □ ×

  File  Edit  Options  Buffers  Tools  C  Help

   ◇  ▨  ×  ▢  ▨  ↩  ✂  ▨  ▨  ▧  ▨  ▨  ?

  int main()
  {
    char bigString[1000];    /* I never know how much to allocate... */
    char *p = bigString;
    bigString[0] = '\0';
    p = mystrcat(p, "John, ");
    p = mystrcat(p, "Paul, ");
    p = mystrcat(p, "George, ");
    p = mystrcat(p, "Joel ");

    printf("%s", bigString);

    return 0;
  }

 -u:**   a.c            (C Abbrev)--L14--All------------------------------
```

The neat thing about The Joel Test is that it's easy to get a quick "yes" or "no" to each question. You don't have to figure out lines-of-code-per-day or average-bugs-per-inflection-point. Give your team 1 point for each "yes" answer. The bummer about The Joel Test is that you *really shouldn't* use it to make sure that your nuclear power plant software is safe.

A score of 12 is perfect, 11 is tolerable, but score 10 or lower and you've got serious problems. The truth is that most software organizations are running with a score of 2 or 3, and they need *serious* help, because companies like Microsoft run at 12 full-time.

Of course, these are not the only factors that determine success or failure: In particular, if you have a great software team working on a product that nobody wants, well, people aren't going to want it. And it's possible to imagine a team of "gunslingers" that doesn't do any of this stuff that still manages to produce incredible software that changes the world. But, all else being equal, if you get these 12 things right, you'll have a disciplined team that can consistently deliver.

~

1. Do you use source control?

I've used commercial source control packages, and I've used CVS,[2] which is free, and let me tell you, CVS is *fine*. But if you don't have source control, you're going to stress out trying to get programmers to work together. Programmers have no way to know what other people did. Mistakes can't be rolled back easily. The other neat thing about source control systems is that the source code itself is checked out on every programmer's hard drive—I've never heard of a project using source control that lost a lot of code.

---

2. See www.cvshome.org/.

~

2. Can you make a build in one step?

By this I mean: How many steps does it take to make a shipping build from the latest source snapshot? On good teams, there's a single script you can run that does a full checkout from scratch; rebuilds every line of code; makes the EXEs, in all their various versions, languages, and #ifdef combinations; creates the installation package; and creates the final media—CD-ROM layout, download website, whatever.

If the process takes any more than one step, it is prone to errors. And when you get closer to shipping, you want to have a very fast cycle of fixing the "last" bug, making the final EXEs, etc. If it takes 20 steps to compile the code, run the installation builder, etc., you're going to go crazy and you're going to make silly mistakes.

For this very reason, the last company I worked at switched from Wise to InstallShield: we *required* that the installation process be able to run, from a script, automatically, overnight, using the NT scheduler, and Wise couldn't run from the scheduler overnight, so we threw it out. (The kind folks at Wise assure me that their latest version does support nightly builds.)

~

3. Do you make daily builds?

When you're using source control, sometimes one programmer accidentally checks in something that breaks the build. For example, they've added a new source file, and everything compiles fine on their machine, but they forgot to add the source file to the code repository. So they lock their machine and go home, oblivious and happy. But nobody else can work, so they have to go home too, unhappy.

Breaking the build is so bad (and so common) that it helps to make daily builds to ensure that no breakage goes unnoticed. On large teams, one good way to ensure that breakages are fixed right away is to do the daily build every afternoon at, say, lunchtime. Everyone does as many check-ins as possible before lunch. When they come back, the build is done. If it worked, great! Everybody checks out the latest version of the source and goes on working. If the build failed, you fix it, but everybody can keep on working with the pre-build, unbroken version of the source.

On the Excel team we had a rule that whoever broke the build was responsible, as their "punishment," for babysitting the builds until someone else broke it. This was a good incentive not to break the build, and a good way to rotate everyone through the build process so that everyone learned how it worked.

Read more about daily builds in my article "Daily Builds Are Your Friend."[3]

~

4. Do you have a bug database?

I don't care what you say. If you are developing code—even on a team of one—without an organized database listing all known bugs in the code, you are going to ship low-quality code. Lots of programmers think they can hold the bug list in their heads. Nonsense. I can't remember more than two or three bugs at a time, and the next morning, or in the rush of shipping, they are forgotten. You absolutely have to keep track of bugs formally.

Bug databases can be complicated or simple. A minimal useful bug database must include the following data for every bug:

- complete steps to reproduce the bug
- expected behavior
- observed (buggy) behavior
- who it's assigned to
- whether it has been fixed or not

---

3. See Chapter 10.

If the complexity of bug tracking software is the only thing stopping you from tracking your bugs, just make a simple five-column table with these crucial fields and *start using it.*

For more on bug tracking, read Painless Bug Tracking.[4]

~

5. Do you fix bugs before writing new code?

The very first version of Microsoft Word for Windows was considered a "death march" project. It took forever. It kept slipping. The whole team was working ridiculous hours, the project was delayed again, and again, and again, and the stress was incredible. When the dang thing finally shipped, years late, Microsoft sent the whole team off to Cancun for a vacation, then sat down for some serious soul-searching.

What they realized was that the project managers had been so insistent on keeping to the schedule that programmers simply rushed through the coding process, writing extremely bad code, because the bug-fixing phase was not a part of the formal schedule. There was no attempt to keep the bug count down. Quite the opposite. The story goes that one programmer, who had to write the code to calculate the height of a line of text, simply wrote "return 12;" and waited for the bug report to come in about how his function is not always correct. The schedule was merely a checklist of features waiting to be turned into bugs. In the postmortem, this was referred to as *infinite defects methodology.*

To correct the problem, Microsoft universally adopted something called a *zero defects methodology.* Many of the programmers in the company giggled, since it sounded like management thought they could reduce the bug count by executive fiat. Actually, zero defects meant that at any given time, the highest priority is to eliminate bugs *before* writing any new code. Here's why.

---

4. See www.joelonsoftware.com/articles/fog0000000029.html.

At the design stage, when you discover problems, you can fix them easily by editing a few lines of text. Once the code is written, the cost of fixing problems is dramatically higher, both emotionally (people hate to throw away code) and in terms of time, so there's resistance to actually fixing the problems. Software that wasn't built from a spec usually winds up badly designed and the schedule gets out of control. This seems to have been the problem at Netscape, where the first four versions grew into such a mess that management stupidly decided to throw out the code and start over.[6] And then they made this mistake all over again with Mozilla, creating a monster that spun out of control and took *several years* to get to alpha stage.

My pet theory is that this problem can be fixed by teaching programmers to be less reluctant writers by sending them off to take an intensive course in writing.[7] Another solution is to hire smart program managers who produce the written spec. In either case, you should enforce the simple rule "no code without spec."

You can learn all about writing specs by reading Chapters 5 through 8.

~

8. Do programmers have quiet working conditions?

There are extensively documented productivity gains provided by giving knowledge workers space, quiet, and privacy. The classic software management book *Peopleware* documents these productivity benefits extensively.[8]

---

6. See Chapter 24.

7. For example, the course *Daily Themes* at Yale University (see www.yale.edu/engl450b/) is famous for requiring students to write an essay every day.

8. Tom DeMarco and Timothy Lister, *Peopleware: Productive Projects and Teams, Second Edition* (Dorset House Publishing, 1999).

Here's how it works. We all know that knowledge workers work best by getting into "flow," also known as being "in the zone," where they are fully concentrated on their work and fully tuned out of their environment. They lose track of time and produce great stuff through absolute concentration. This is when they get all of their productive work done. Writers, programmers, scientists, and even basketball players will tell you about being in the zone.

The trouble is, getting into "the zone" is not easy. When you try to measure it, it looks like it takes an average of 15 minutes to start working at maximum productivity. Sometimes, if you're tired or have already done a lot of creative work that day, you just can't get into the zone and you spend the rest of your work day fiddling around, reading the Web and playing Tetris.

The other trouble is that it's so easy to get knocked *out* of the zone. Noise, phone calls, going out for lunch, having to drive five minutes to Starbucks for coffee, and interruptions by coworkers—*especially* interruptions by coworkers—all knock you out of the zone. If a coworker asks you a question, causing a one-minute interruption, but this knocks you out of the zone badly enough that it takes you half an hour to get productive again, your overall productivity is in serious trouble. If you're in a noisy bullpen environment like the type that caffeinated dotcoms love to create, with marketing guys screaming on the phone next to programmers, your productivity will plunge as knowledge workers get interrupted time after time and never get into the zone.

With programmers, it's especially hard. Productivity depends on being able to juggle a lot of little details in short-term memory all at once. Any kind of interruption can cause these details to come crashing down. When you resume work, you can't remember any of the details (like local variable names you were using, or where you were up to in implementing that search algorithm) and you have to keep looking these things up, which slows you down a lot until you get back up to speed.

Here's the simple algebra. Let's say (as the evidence seems to suggest) that if we interrupt a programmer, even for a minute, we're really blowing away 15 minutes of productivity. For this example, let's put two programmers, Jeff and Mutt, in open cubicles next to each other in a standard Dilbert veal-fattening farm. Mutt can't remember the name of the Unicode version of the strcpy function. He could look it up, which takes 30 seconds, or he could ask Jeff, which takes 15 seconds. Since he's sitting right next to Jeff, he asks Jeff. Jeff gets distracted and loses 15 minutes of productivity (to save Mutt 15 seconds).

Now let's move them into separate offices with walls and doors. Now when Mutt can't remember the name of that function, he could look it up, which still takes 30 seconds, or he could ask Jeff, which now takes 45 seconds and involves standing up (not an easy task given the average physical fitness of programmers!). So he looks it up. So now Mutt loses 30 seconds of productivity, but we save 15 minutes for Jeff. Ahhh!

〜

9. Do you use the best tools money can buy?

Writing code in a compiled language is one of the last things that still can't be done instantly on a garden-variety home computer. If your compilation process takes more than a few seconds, getting the latest and greatest computer is going to save you time. If compiling takes even 15 seconds, programmers will get bored while the compiler runs and switch over to reading *The Onion*,[9] which will suck them in and kill hours of productivity.

Debugging GUI code with a single-monitor system is painful if not impossible. If you're writing GUI code, two monitors will make things much easier.

Most programmers eventually have to manipulate bitmaps for icons or toolbars, and most programmers don't have a good bitmap editor available. Trying to use Microsoft Paint to manipulate bitmaps is a joke, but that's what most programmers have to do.

At my last job,[10] the system administrator kept sending me automated spam complaining that I was using more than—get this—220 megabytes

---

9. See http://www.theonion.com.
10. See Chapter 32.

of hard drive space on the server. I pointed out that given the price of hard drives these days, the cost of this space was significantly less than the cost of the *toilet paper* I used. Spending even ten minutes cleaning up my directory would be a fabulous waste of productivity.

Top-notch development teams don't torture their programmers. Even minor frustrations caused by using underpowered tools add up, making programmers grumpy and unhappy. And a grumpy programmer is an unproductive programmer.

To add to all this, programmers are easily bribed by giving them the coolest, latest stuff. This is a far cheaper way to get them to work for you than actually paying competitive salaries!

~

10. Do you have testers?

If your team doesn't have dedicated testers, at least one for every two or three programmers, you are either shipping buggy products, or you're wasting money by having $100/hour programmers do work that can be done by $30/hour testers. Skimping on testers is such an outrageous false economy that I'm simply blown away that more people don't recognize it. Chapter 22 has more on this.

~

11. Do new candidates write code during their interview?

Would you hire a magician without asking them to show you some magic tricks? Of course not. Would you hire a caterer for your wedding without tasting their food? I doubt it. (Unless it's Aunt Marge, and she would hate you for*ever* if you didn't let her make her "famous" chopped liver cake.)

Yet, every day, programmers are hired on the basis of an impressive résumé or because the interviewer enjoyed chatting with them. Or they

2 and 3. Hmm. I've also heard from a lot of developers, fed up with disorganized "gunslinger" software development practices, who turned down new jobs at companies that seemed to be pathologically low scorers on The Joel Test. And I've heard great results from team managers who used The Joel Test as a step-by-step team improvement process, working their way up.

In the meantime, it looks like a lot of development organizations have gone far, far beyond The Joel Test and into the throes of advanced bureaucratic arteriosclerosis. You can tell when this happens because people spend more time preparing for meetings than developing software. It's possible to get a perfect 12 on The Joel Test and then screw up life with so much politics and overhead that nothing gets done. Don't tell them I said this, but since the early 1990s when I worked at Microsoft, all evidence is that that company has more or less ground to a halt due to its immense size, internal politics, and bureaucratic profligacy. Need proof? The Tablet PC—something only a Microsoft middle manager could love—seems to have been designed so that Program Managers in Redmond, Washington, can spend an entire day in meetings without getting too far behind on their daily email load. It's not just a Microsoft phenomenon. If you find yourself spending too much time installing and configuring gigantic software methodology systems, or software called "Visual Something Something Enterprise Architect," or going back and forth reeducating your team between Extreme Programming and UML until their heads spin when you should be developing a software product, even if you're doing real well on The Joel Test, you may be in trouble.

four

THE ABSOLUTE MINIMUM EVERY SOFTWARE DEVELOPER ABSOLUTELY, POSITIVELY MUST KNOW ABOUT UNICODE AND CHARACTER SETS (NO EXCUSES!)

Wednesday, October 8, 2003

Ever wonder about that mysterious Content-Type tag? You know, the one you're supposed to put in HTML and you never quite know what it should be?

Did you ever get an email from your friends in Bulgaria with the subject line "???? ?????? ??? ????"?

I've been dismayed to discover just how many software developers aren't really completely up to speed on the mysterious world of character sets, encodings, Unicode, all that stuff. A couple of years ago, a beta tester for FogBUGZ[1] was wondering whether it could handle incoming email in Japanese. Japanese? They have email in Japanese? I had no idea. When I looked closely at the commercial ActiveX control we were using to parse MIME email messages, we discovered it was doing exactly the wrong thing with character sets, so we actually had to write heroic code to undo the wrong conversion it had done and redo it correctly. When I looked into another commercial library, it, too, had a completely broken character code implementation. I corresponded with the developer of that package and he sort of thought they "couldn't do anything about it." Like many programmers, he just wished it would all blow over somehow.

---

1. Our bug tracking product; see www.fogcreek.com/FogBUGZ.

But it won't. When I discovered that the popular web development tool PHP has almost complete ignorance of character encoding issues,[2] blithely using 8 bits for characters, making it darn near impossible to develop good international web applications, I thought, *enough is enough*.

So I have an announcement to make: If you are a programmer working in the twenty-first century and you don't know the basics of characters, character sets, encodings, and Unicode, and I *catch* you, I'm going to punish you by making you peel onions for six months in a submarine. I swear I will.

And one more thing:

IT'S NOT THAT HARD.

In this article I'll fill you in on exactly what *every working programmer* should know. All that stuff about "plain text = ASCII = characters are 8 bits" is not only wrong, it's hopelessly wrong, and if you're still programming that way, you're not much better than a medical doctor who doesn't believe in germs. Please do not write another line of code until you finish reading this article.

Before I get started, I should warn you that if you are one of those rare people who knows about internationalization, you will find my entire discussion a little bit oversimplified. I'm really just trying to set a minimum bar here so that everyone can understand what's going on and can write code that has a *hope* of working with text in any language other than the subset of English that doesn't include words with accents. And I should warn you that character handling is only a tiny portion of what it takes to create software that works internationally, but I can only write about one thing at a time, so today it's character sets.

∿

A Historical Perspective

The easiest way to understand this stuff is to go chronologically. You probably think I'm going to talk about very old character sets like EBCDIC here. Well, I won't. EBCDIC is not relevant to your life. We don't have to go that far back in time.

---

2. See ca3.php.net/manual/en/language.types.string.php.

Back in the semi-olden days, when UNIX was being invented and K&R were writing *The C Programming Language*,[3] everything was very simple. EBCDIC was on its way out. The only characters that mattered were good old unaccented English letters, and we had a code for them called ASCII, which was able to represent every character using a number between 32 and 127.[4] Space was 32, the letter A was 65, etc. This could conveniently be stored in 7 bits. Most computers in those days were using 8-bit bytes, so not only could you store every possible ASCII character, but you had a whole bit to spare, which, if you were wicked, you could use for your own devious purposes: the dim bulbs at WordStar actually turned on the high bit to indicate the last letter in a word, condemning WordStar to English text only. Codes below 32 were called *unprintable* and were used for cussing. Just kidding. They were used for control characters, like 7 which made your computer beep and 12 which caused the current page of paper to go flying out of the printer and a new one to be fed in.

	0	1	2	3	4	5	6	7	8	9	A	B	C	D	E	F
0	NUL	SOH	STX	ETX	EOT	ENQ	ACK	BEL	BS	HT	LF	VT	FF	CR	SO	SI
1	DLE	DC1	DC2	DC3	DC4	NAK	SYN	ETB	CAN	EM	SUB	ESC	FS	GS	RS	US
2	space	!	"	#	$	%	&	'	(	)	*	+	,	-	.	/
3	0	1	2	3	4	5	6	7	8	9	:	;	<	=	>	?
4	@	A	B	C	D	E	F	G	H	I	J	K	L	M	N	O
5	P	Q	R	S	T	U	V	W	X	Y	Z	[	\	]	^	_
6	`	a	b	c	d	e	f	g	h	i	j	k	l	m	n	o
7	p	q	r	s	t	u	v	w	x	y	z	{	|	}	~	DEL

And all was good, assuming you were an English speaker.

Because bytes have room for up to 8 bits, lots of people got to thinking, "gosh, we can use the codes 128–255 for our own purposes." The trouble was, *lots* of people had this idea at the same time, and they had their own ideas of what should go where in the space from 128 to 255. The IBM-PC had something that came to be known as the OEM character set, which provided some accented characters for European

---

3. Brian Kernighan and Dennis Ritchie, *The C Programming Language* (Prentice Hall, 1978).

4. For more information on ASCII characters, see www.robelle.com/library/smugbook/ascii.html.

languages and a bunch of line-drawing characters—horizontal bars, vertical bars, horizontal bars with little dingle-dangles dangling off the right side, etc.—and you could use these line-drawing characters to make spiffy boxes and lines on the screen, which you can still see running on the 8088 computer at your dry cleaner's. In fact, as soon as people started buying PCs outside of America, all kinds of different OEM character sets were dreamed up, which all used the top 128 characters for their own purposes. For example, on some PCs the character code 130 would display as é, but on computers sold in Israel it was the Hebrew letter Gimel (ג), so when Americans would send their résumés to Israel they would arrive as rגsumגs. In many cases, such as Russian, there were lots of different ideas of what to do with the upper 128 characters, so you couldn't even reliably interchange Russian documents.

Eventually, this OEM free-for-all got codified in the ANSI standard. In the ANSI standard, everybody agreed on what to do below 128, which was pretty much the same as ASCII, but there were lots of different ways to handle the characters from 128 and up, depending on where you lived. These different systems were called *code pages*.[5] So for example in Israel DOS used a code page called 862, while Greek users used 737. They were the same below 128 but different from 128 up, where all

---

5. For more information on code pages, see www.i18nguy.com/unicode/
codepages.html#msftdos.

the funny letters resided. The national versions of MS-DOS had dozens of these code pages, handling everything from English to Icelandic, and they even had a few "multilingual" code pages that could do Esperanto and Galician *on the same computer! Wow!* But getting, say, Hebrew and Greek on the same computer was a complete impossibility unless you wrote your own custom program that displayed everything using bitmapped graphics, because Hebrew and Greek required different code pages with different interpretations of the high numbers.

Meanwhile, in Asia, even more crazy things were going on to take into account the fact that Asian alphabets have thousands of letters, which were never going to fit into 8 bits. This was usually solved by the messy system called DBCS, the "double byte character set," in which *some* letters were stored in 1 byte and others took 2 bytes. It was easy to move forward in a string, but dang near impossible to move backward. Programmers were encouraged not to use s++ and s-- to move backward and forward, but instead to call functions such as Windows' AnsiNext and AnsiPrev, which knew how to deal with the whole mess.

But still, most people just pretended that a byte was a character and a character was 8 bits and as long as you never moved a string from one computer to another, or spoke more than one language, it would sort of always work. But of course, as soon as the Internet happened, it became quite commonplace to move strings from one computer to another, and the whole mess came tumbling down. Luckily, Unicode had been invented.

~

Unicode

Unicode was a brave effort to create a single character set that included every reasonable writing system on the planet, and some make-believe ones like Klingon, too. Some people are under the misconception that Unicode is simply a 16-bit code where each character takes 16 bits and therefore there are 65,536 possible characters. This is not, actually, correct. It is the single most common myth about Unicode, so if you thought that, don't feel bad.

other byte.[7] Phew. Not every Unicode string in the wild has a byte order mark at the beginning.

For a while it seemed like that might be good enough, but programmers were complaining. "Look at all those zeros!" they said, since they were Americans and they were looking at English text which rarely used code points above U+00FF. Also, they were liberal hippies in California who wanted to *conserve (sneer)*. If they were Texans, they wouldn't have minded guzzling twice the number of bytes. But those Californian wimps couldn't bear the idea of *doubling* the amount of storage it took for strings, and anyway, there were already all these doggone documents out there using various ANSI and DBCS character sets and who's going to convert them all? *Moi?* For this reason alone, most people decided to ignore Unicode for several years, and in the meantime things got worse.

Thus was invented the brilliant concept of UTF-8.[8] UTF-8 was another system for storing your string of Unicode code points, those magic U+ numbers, in memory using 8-bit bytes.[9] In UTF-8, every code point from 0 through 127 is stored *in a single byte*. Only code points 128 and above are stored using 2, 3, in fact, up to 6 bytes.

Hex Min	Hex Max	Byte Sequence in Binary
00000000	0000007F	0vvvvvvv
00000080	000007FF	110vvvvv 10vvvvvv
00000800	0000FFFF	1110vvvv 10vvvvvv 10vvvvvv
00010000	001FFFFF	11110vvv 10vvvvvv 10vvvvvv 10vvvvvv
00200000	03FFFFFF	111110vv 10vvvvvv 10vvvvvv 10vvvvvv 10vvvvvv

This has the neat side effect that English text looks *exactly the same in UTF-8 as it did in ASCII,* so Americans don't even notice anything wrong. Only the rest of the world has to jump through hoops. Specifically, Hello, which was U+0048 U+0065 U+006C U+006C

---

7. For more information on byte order marks, see msdn.microsoft.com/library/default.asp?url=/library/en-us/intl/unicode_42jv.asp.

8. See www.cl.cam.ac.uk/~mgk25/ucs/utf-8-history.txt.

9. For more information on UTF-8, see www.utf-8.com/.

U+006F, will be stored as 48 65 6C 6C 6F, which (behold!) is the same as it was stored in ASCII, and ANSI, and every OEM character set on the planet. Now, if you are so bold as to use accented letters or Greek letters or Klingon letters, you'll have to use several bytes to store a single code point, but the Americans will never notice. (UTF-8 also has this nice property: Ignorant old string-processing code that wants to use a single 0 byte as the null-terminator will not truncate strings.)

So far I've told you *three* ways of encoding Unicode. The traditional store-it-in-two-byte methods are called UCS-2 (because it has two bytes) or UTF-16 (because it has 16 bits), and you still have to figure out if it's high-endian UCS-2 or low-endian UCS-2. And there's the popular new UTF-8 standard, which has the nice property of also working respectably if you have the happy coincidence of English text and brain-dead programs that are completely unaware that there is anything other than ASCII.[10]

There are actually a bunch of other ways of encoding Unicode. There's something called UTF-7, which is a lot like UTF-8 but guarantees that the high bit will always be zero, so that if you have to pass Unicode through some kind of draconian police-state email system that thinks 7 bits are *quite enough, thank you,* it can still squeeze through unscathed. There's UCS-4, which stores each code point in 4 bytes, which has the nice property that every single code point can be stored in the same number of bytes, but, golly, even the Texans wouldn't be so bold as to waste *that* much memory.

And in fact now that you're thinking of things in terms of platonic ideal letters which are represented by Unicode code points, those Unicode code points can be encoded in any old-school encoding scheme, too! For example, you could encode the Unicode string for Hello (U+0048 U+0065 U+006C U+006C U+006F) in ASCII, or the old OEM Greek Encoding, or the Hebrew ANSI Encoding, or any of several hundred encodings that have been invented so far, *with one catch*: Some of the letters might not show up! If there's no equivalent for the Unicode code point you're trying to represent in the encoding you're trying to represent it in, you usually get a little question mark: ? Or, if you're *really* good, a box.

---

10. See www.zvon.org/tmRFC/RFC2279/Output/chapter2.html.

There are hundreds of traditional encodings which can only store *some* code points correctly and change all the other code points into question marks. Some popular encodings of English text are Windows-1252 (the Windows 9x standard for Western European languages) and ISO-8859-1, aka Latin-1 (also useful for any Western European language).[11] But try to store Russian or Hebrew letters in these encodings and you get a bunch of question marks. UTF 7, 8, 16, and 32 all have the nice property of being able to store *any* code point correctly.

~

The Single Most Important Fact About Encodings

If you completely forget everything I just explained, please remember one extremely important fact. *It does not make sense to have a string without knowing what encoding it uses.* You can no longer stick your head in the sand and pretend that "plain" text is ASCII.

There Ain't No Such Thing As Plain Text

If you have a string, in memory, in a file, or in an email message, you have to know what encoding it is in or you cannot interpret it or display it to users correctly.

Almost every stupid "my website looks like gibberish" or "she can't read my emails when I use accents" problem comes down to one naive programmer who didn't understand the simple fact that if you don't tell me whether a particular string is encoded using UTF-8 or ASCII or ISO 8859-1 (Latin 1) or Windows 1252 (Western European), I simply cannot display it correctly or even figure out where it ends. There are over a hundred encodings and above code point 127, all bets are off.

---

11. For an overview of the ISO 8859-1 character set, see www.htmlhelp.com/reference/charset/.

How do we preserve this information about what encoding a string uses? Well, there are standard ways to do this. For an email message, you are expected to have a string in the header of the form

```
Content-Type: text/plain; charset="UTF-8"
```

For a web page, the original idea was that the web server would return a similar Content-Type http header along with the web page itself—not in the HTML itself, but as one of the response headers that are sent before the HTML page.

This causes problems. Suppose you have a big web server with lots of sites and hundreds of pages contributed by lots of people in lots of different languages and all using whatever encoding their copy of Microsoft FrontPage saw fit to generate. The web server itself wouldn't really *know* what encoding each file was written in, so it couldn't send the Content-Type header.

It would be convenient if you could put the Content-Type of the HTML file right in the HTML file itself, using some kind of special tag. Of course this drove purists crazy; how can you *read* the HTML file until you know what encoding it's in?! Luckily, almost every encoding in common use does the same thing with characters between 32 and 127, so you can always get this far on the HTML page without starting to use funny letters:

```
<html>
<head>
<meta http-equiv="Content-Type" content="text/html; charset=utf-8">
```

But that meta tag really has to be the very first thing in the <head> section, because as soon as the web browser sees this tag, it's going to stop parsing the page and start over after reinterpreting the whole page using the encoding you specified.

What do web browsers do if they don't find any Content-Type in either the http headers or the meta tag? Internet Explorer actually does something quite interesting: It tries to guess, based on the frequency

five

PAINLESS FUNCTIONAL SPECIFICATIONS
PART 1: WHY BOTHER?

Monday, October 2, 2000

When The Joel Test[1] first appeared, one of the biggest sore points readers reported had to do with writing specs. As I've said before, specs are like flossing: Everybody knows they should be writing them, but nobody does.

Why won't people write specs? People claim that it's because they're saving time by skipping the spec-writing phase. They act as if spec writing was a luxury reserved for NASA space shuttle engineers, or people who work for giant, established insurance companies. Balderdash. First of all, failing to write a spec is the *single biggest unnecessary risk* you take in a software project. It's as stupid as setting off to cross the Mojave desert with just the clothes on your back, hoping to "wing it." Programmers and software engineers who dive into code without writing a spec tend to think they're cool gunslingers, shooting from the hip. They're not. They are terribly unproductive. They write bad code and produce shoddy software, and they threaten their projects by taking giant risks which are completely uncalled for.

I believe that on any nontrivial project (more than about one week of coding or more than one programmer), if you don't have a spec, you will *always* spend more time and create lower-quality code. Here's why.

The most important function of a spec is to *design the program*. Even if you are working on code all by yourself, and you write a spec solely for

---

1. See Chapter 3.

your own benefit, the act of writing the spec—describing how the program works in minute detail—will force you to actually *design* the program.

Let's visit two imaginary programmers at two companies. Speedy, at Hasty Bananas Software, never writes specs. "Specs? We don't need no stinkin' specs!" At the same time, Mr. Rogers, over at The Well-Tempered Software Company, refuses to write code until the spec is completely nailed down. These are only two of my many imaginary friends.

Speedy and Mr. Rogers have one thing in common: Both are in charge of backward compatibility for version 2.0 of their respective products.

Speedy decides that the best way to provide backward compatibility is to write a converter that simply converts 1.0 version files into 2.0 version files. She starts banging that out. Type, type, type. Clickety clickety clack. Hard drives spin. Dust flies. After about two weeks, she has a reasonable converter. But Speedy's customers are unhappy. Speedy's code will force them to upgrade everyone in the company at once to the new version. Speedy's biggest customer, Nanner Splits Unlimited, refuses to buy the new software. Nanner Splits needs to know that version 2.0 will still be able to work on version 1.0 files *without* converting them. Speedy decides to write a *backward* converter and then hook it into the "save" function. It's a bit of a mess, because when you use a version 2.0 feature, it *seems* to work, until you go to save the file in 1.0 format. Only then are you told that the feature you used half an hour ago doesn't work in the old file format. So the backward converter took another two weeks to write, and it don't work so nice. Elapsed time, four weeks.

Now, Mr. Rogers over at Well-Tempered Software Company (colloquially, "WellTemperSoft") is one of those nerdy organized types who *refuses* to write code until he's got a spec. He spends about 20 minutes designing the backward compatibility feature the same way Speedy did, and comes up with a spec that basically says:

> When opening a file created with an older version of the product, the file is converted to the new format.

The spec is shown to the customer, who says "wait a minute! We don't want to switch everyone at once!" So Mr. Rogers thinks some more and amends the spec to say:

> When opening a file created with an older version of the product, the file is converted to the new format in memory. When saving this file, the user is given the option to convert it back.

Another 20 minutes have elapsed.

Mr. Rogers' boss, an object nut, looks at this and thinks something might be amiss. He suggests a different architecture.

> The code will be factored to use two interfaces: V1 and V2. V1 contains all the version one features, and V2, which inherits from V1, adds all the new features. Now V1::Save can handle the backward compatibility while V2::Save can be used to save all the new stuff. If you've opened a V1 file and try to use V2 functionality, the program can warn you right away, and you will have to either convert the file or give up the new functionality.

20 more minutes.

Mr. Rogers is grumpy. This refactoring will take three weeks, instead of the two weeks he originally estimated! But it does solve *all* the customer problems, in an elegant way, so he goes off and does it.

Total elapsed time for Mr. Rogers: three weeks and one hour. Elapsed time for Speedy: four weeks. But Speedy's code is not as good.

The moral of the story is that with a contrived example, you can prove anything. Oops. No, that's not what I meant to say. The moral of the story is that when you design your product in a human language, it takes only a few minutes to try thinking about several possibilities, revising, and improving your design. Nobody feels bad just deleting a paragraph in a word processor. But when you design your product in a programming language, it takes *weeks* to do iterative designs. What's worse, a programmer who's just spent two weeks writing some code is *ship when we're good and ready.* But for almost any kind of real business, you just have to know how long things are going to take, because developing a product costs *money.* You wouldn't buy a pair of *jeans* without knowing what the price is, so how can a responsible business decide whether to build a product without knowing how long it will take and, therefore, how much it will cost? For more on scheduling, read Chapter 9.

A terribly common error is having a debate over how something should be designed, and then *never resolving the debate.* Brian Valentine, the lead developer on Windows 2000, was famous for his motto "Decisions in 10 minutes or less, or the next one is free."[4]

In too many programming organizations, every time there's a design debate, nobody ever manages to make a *decision,* usually for political reasons. So the programmers only work on uncontroversial stuff. As time goes on, all the hard decisions are pushed to the end. *These projects are the most likely to fail.* If you are starting a new company around a new technology and you notice that your company is constitutionally incapable of making decisions, you might as well close down now and return the money to the investors, because you ain't never gonna ship nothing.

Writing a spec is a great way to nail down all those irritating design decisions, large and small, that get covered up if you don't have a spec. Even small decisions can get nailed down with a spec. For example, if you're building a website with membership, you might all agree that if the user forgets their password, you'll mail it to them. Great. But that's not enough to write the code. To write the code, you need to know the actual *words* in that email. At most companies, programmers aren't trusted with words that a user might actually see (and for good reason, much of the time). So a marketing person or a PR person or some other English major is likely to be required to come up with the precise wording of the message. "Dear Shlub, here's the password you forgot. Try not to be so careless in the future." When you force yourself to write a *good, complete* spec (and I'll talk a lot more about that soon), you notice all these things and you either fix them or at least you mark them with a big red flag.

---

4. Microsoft press release, "Valentine and His Team of 4,200 Complete the Largest Software Project in History," Microsoft.com, February 16, 2000. See www.microsoft.com/presspass/features/2000/02-16brianv.asp.

OK. We're on the same page now. Specs are motherhood and apple pie. I suspect that most people understand this, and my rants, while amusing, aren't teaching you anything new. So why *don't* people write specs? It's not to save time, because it *doesn't*, and I think most coders recognize this. (In most organizations, the only "specs" that exist are staccato, one-page text documents that a programmer banged out in Notepad *after* writing the code and *after* explaining that damn feature to the three-hundredth person.)

I think it's because so many people don't like to write. Staring at a blank screen is horribly frustrating. Personally, I overcame my fear of writing by taking a class in college that required a three- to five-page essay once a week. Writing is a muscle. The more you write, the more you'll be able to write. If you need to write specs and you can't, start a journal, create a weblog, take a creative writing class, or just write a nice letter to every relative and college roommate you've blown off for the last four years. Anything that involves putting words down on paper will improve your spec writing skills. If you're a software development manager and the people who are supposed to be writing specs aren't, send them off for one of those two-week creative writing classes in the mountains.

If you've never worked in a company that does functional specifications, you may never have seen one. In the next chapter, I'll show you a short, sample spec for you to check out, and we'll talk about what a good spec needs to have.

six

PAINLESS FUNCTIONAL SPECIFICATIONS
PART 2: WHAT'S A SPEC?

TUESDAY, OCTOBER 3, 2000

I've been writing about *functional specifications*, not *technical* specifications. People get these mixed up. I don't know if there's any standard terminology, but here's what *I* mean when I use these terms:

A *functional specification* describes how a product will work entirely from the user's perspective. It doesn't care how the thing is implemented. It talks about features. It specifies screens, menus, dialogs, and so on.

A *technical specification* describes the internal implementation of the program. It talks about data structures, relational database models, choice of programming languages and tools, algorithms, etc.

When you design a product, inside and out, the most important thing is to nail down the user experience. What are the screens, how do they work, what do they do. Later, you worry about how to get from here to there. There's no use arguing about what programming language to use before you've decided what your product is going to *do*. In this series, I'm only talking about *functional specifications*.

Following is a short sample spec to give you an idea of what a good functional specification looks like.

Nongoals

This version will *not* support the following features:

- multiple time zones for one member (All members are assumed to be in the same time zone.)
- changing passwords
- appointments

WhatTimeIsIt.com Flowchart

We'll have time later to go into mind-numbing detail, but for now, let's look at a quick flowchart of the service so you get the big picture. This flowchart is not complete, but it does give you the right idea for the "storyboard" of using WhatTimeIsIt.com:

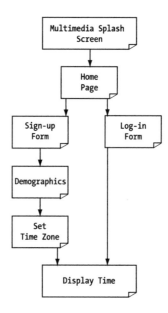

Screen-by-Screen Specification

WhatTimeIsIt.com consists of quite a few different screens. Most screens will follow a standard format, with a look and feel to be designed in the future by a graphic designer. This document is more concerned with the functionality and the interaction design, not the exact look and layout.

All screens are created in HTML. (The single exception is the Splash Screen, which is created using Macromedia Shockwave).

Each screen in WhatTimeIsIt.com is known by a canonical name which will always appear, in this document, in bold text, so you know we're referring to a screen by name, for example, **Home Page.**

Splash Screen

An annoying, gratuitous Shockwave animation that plays stupid music and drives everyone crazy. **Splash Screen** will be commissioned by a high-paid graphics animation *boutique* in a loft in Soho from people who bring their dogs to work, wear found objects safety-pinned to their ears, and go to Starbucks four times *before lunch.*

After the animation has played for about 10 seconds, a link that says "SKIP THIS" will fade into view in the bottom right corner. To avoid people seeing this and clicking on it, SKIP THIS will be so far down and to the right that most people won't see it. It should be at least 800 pixels from the left border of the animation and 600 pixels from the top.

Clicking on SKIP THIS goes to **Home Page.** When the animation is complete, it will redirect the browser to **Home Page** automatically.

Open Issue   If Marketing allows, we should deposit a cookie on the user's computer if he or she clicks SKIP THIS, which will cause the animation to always be skipped in the future. Frequent visitors should not have to see the animation more than once. I talked to Jim in Marketing about this and he's going to take part in convening a committee of Sales, Marketing, and PR to discuss.

Home Page

Displayed when the Shockwave animation is complete, the **Home Page** serves three purposes:

1. Allow people to learn about the service and consider whether they want to sign up

2. Allow members who have already signed up to log on

3. Allow people who want to sign up to create an account

The **Home Page** looks like this:

WhatTimeIsIt._com_

Welcome to WhatTimeIsIt._com_, the service that tells you _exactly_ what time it is!

(Your results may vary. We are not responsible for delays in transmission or on your computer which could cause the _actual_ time to be a bit later than the time displayed. This service is provided _as-is_ and is merely for entertainment purposes, not for accurate time-keeping. Do not stick WhatTimeIsIt._com_ in your ear or use it to clean your ear.)

WhatTimeIsIt._com_ is easy and fun. If you're not a member, sign up today and start finding out what time it is!

Already a member? Click here to log on!

Not a member yet? Don't worry - membership is _free_! Yes, that's right, FREE! Just click here to sign up, and within _minutes_ you'll be able to find out what time it is!

Privacy Notice | About Us | Jobs | Contact Us
About **WhatTimeIsIt.**_com_

On this, and on *all screens*, clicking on the WhatTimeIsIt.com logo in the top-left corner goes back to **Home Page.**

> **Technical Note**   Because of the high similarity between the various screens, some system of *include*s should be used on the server so that if the name of the service changes, or if we can't purchase the domain name we want, we'll be able to change all the screens in one place. I suggest Vignette Story Server. Sure, it's overkill. Sure, it costs $200,000. But it's a heck of a lot easier than using server-side includes!

Clicking on the link that says "click here to log on" goes to **Log In Form.** Clicking on the link that says "click here to sign up" goes to **Sign Up Form.** The other five links display pages with static text to be provided by management, which are beyond the scope of this specification. They will not have to change very often.

Log In Form

The **Log In Form** is used by current members to log into their accounts in order to find out the current time. It looks like this:

WhatTimeIsIt. *com*

Please enter your email address:

Enter your password:

Not a member yet? Don't worry – membership is *free*! Yes, that's right, FREE! Just click here to sign up, and within *minutes* you'll be able to find out what time it is!

Log In

Privacy Notice | About Us | Jobs | Contact Us
About **WhatTimeIsIt.** *com*

Forgot your password? Just enter your email address and we'll email it to you.

The right side of the screen behaves the same way as described previously under **Home Page**.

The email box allows for up to 60 characters to be typed. The password box allows for up to 12 characters to be typed. To disguise characters and prevent hacking, as the user types in the password box, asterisks (*) will appear instead of the characters that they typed.

Technical Note   This is accomplished using <INPUT TYPE=PASSWORD>

When the user clicks *Log In*, the following checks are performed on the server:

1. If the email address was provided, but it could not be a real email address because it is not formatted correctly (e.g., there is no @ sign or it contains characters that are not permitted in email addresses by RFC-822), the server returns another page that looks just like **Log In Form**, only this time, a red error message is inserted above the address box, saying "The email address you provided is not valid. Please double check it." Although this text is in red, the text "Please enter your email address" still appears in black. The incorrect email address that the user originally typed will now be pre-populated in the edit box.

2. If the email address was provided, but it does not correspond to a registered member, the server returns another page that looks just like **Log In Form,** only this time, a red error message is inserted above the address box, saying "The email address you provided is not a member. Please double check it. To become a member, click on the link on the

right side of the screen." Although this text is in red, the text "Please enter your email address" still appears in black. The incorrect email address that the user originally typed will now be pre-populated in the edit box. [Question to developers. Can we use JavaScript in this case so that if the user then clicks on the link to become a member, we automatically pre-populate the email address on the sign up form?]

3. If the email address was provided, and it does correspond to a registered member, but no password was typed at all, we send an email to that address containing the password. The subject of the email is: Your WhatTimeIsIt.com membership. The email is in *plain text*. The exact wording of this email is still being debated hotly by the board of directors and will be provided sometime before shipping. [Developers: for now I suggest using a nasty word. That will light a fire under Chucks' seat.]

4. If the email address was provided, and it does correspond to a registered member, and a password was provided, but the password is incorrect, the server returns another page that looks just like **Log In Form**, only this time, a red error message is inserted above the password box, saying "The password you provided is not valid. Please double check it. Remember, passwords are *case-sensitive*." If the password typed does not contain any lowercase alphabetic characters, we add this text to the message: "Perhaps you've accidentally turned on CAPS LOCK?" Whenever the password is incorrect, the **Log In Form** comes back with the password box *clear*.

5. If the email address and password are OK, jump straight to **Display Time**.

Open Issue   Need to decide about JavaScript in case #2.

Open Issue   Need wording for password email from CEO.

Here are some of the things I put in every spec.

A disclaimer. Pure self-defense. If you put a paragraph saying something like "This spec is not complete," people won't come into your office to bite your head off. As time goes on, when the spec starts to be complete, you can change it to say "this spec is complete, to the best of my knowledge, but if I forgot something, please tell me." Which reminds me, every spec needs:

An author. One author. Some companies think that the spec should be written by a *team*. If you've ever tried group writing, you know that there is no worse torture. Leave the group writing to the management consulting firms with armies of newly minted Harvard-educated graduates who need to do a ton of busywork so that they can justify their huge fees. Your specs should be owned and written by *one person*. If you have a big product, split it up into areas and give each area to a different person to spec separately. Other companies think that it's egotistic or not "good teamwork" for a person to "take credit" for a spec by putting their name on it. *Nonsense.* People should take *responsibility* and *ownership* of the things that they specify. If something's wrong with the spec, there should be a designated spec owner, with their name printed right there on the spec, who is responsible for fixing it.

Scenarios. When you're designing a product, you need to have some real live scenarios in mind for how people are going to use it. Otherwise, you end up designing a product that doesn't correspond to any real-world usage (like the :CueCat).[1] Pick your product's audiences and imagine a fictitious, totally imaginary but totally *stereotypical* user from each audience who uses the product in a totally typical way. Chapter 9 of my UI design book[2] talks about creating fictional users and scenarios.

---

1. See www.joelonsoftware.com/articles/fog0000000037.html.

2. Joel Spolsky, *User Interface Design for Programmers* (Apress, 2001). See
    www.joelonsoftware.com/uibook/chapters/fog0000000065.html.

This is where you put them. The more vivid and realistic the scenario, the better job you will do designing a product for your real or imagined users, which is why I tend to put in lots of made-up details.

Nongoals. When you're building a product with a team, everybody tends to have their favorite real or imagined pet features that they just can't live without. If you do them all, it will take infinite time and cost too much money. You have to start culling features right away, and the best way to do this is with a "nongoals" section of the spec. Things we are just *not going to do*. A nongoal might be a feature you won't have ("no telepathic user interface!") or it might be something more general ("We don't care about performance in this release. The product can be slow, as long as it works. If we have time in version 2, we'll optimize the slow bits.") These nongoals are likely to cause some debate, but it's important to get it out in the open as soon as possible. "Not gonna do it!"

An overview. This is like the table of contents for your spec. It might be a simple flowchart, or it might be an extensive architectural discussion. Everybody will read this to get the big picture, then the details will make more sense.

Details, details, details. Finally you go into the details. Most people will skim this until they need to know a particular detail. When you're designing a web-type service, a good way to do this is to give every possible screen a canonical name, and provide a chapter describing each one in utter and mind-numbing detail.

Details are the most important thing in a functional spec. You'll notice in the sample spec how I go into outrageous detail talking about all the error cases for the login page. What if the email address isn't valid? What if the password is wrong? All of these cases correspond to real code that's going to be written, but, more importantly, these cases correspond to *decisions* that somebody is going to have to make. Somebody has to decide what the policy is going to be for a forgotten password. If you don't decide, you can't write the code. The spec needs to document the decision.

Open issues. It's OK for the first version of the spec to leave open issues. When I write a first draft, I always have lots of open issues, but I flag them (using a special style so I can search for them) and, if appropriate, discuss the alternatives. By the time the programmers start work, all of these need to be stomped out. (You might think it's OK to just let the programmers start on all the easy stuff, and you'll solve the open

programmer would be responsible for writing all the code, but he or she would rely on a team of junior programmers as "code slaves." Instead of worrying about debugging every function, the master programmer would basically just prototype each function, creating the bare outline, and then throw it to one of the junior programmers to implement. (Of course, Simonyi would be the Master Master Programmer.) The term "Master Programmer" was a bit too medieval, so Microsoft went with "Program Manager."

Theoretically, this was supposed to solve the Mythical Man-Month problem, because nobody has to talk to anyone else—every junior programmer only talks to the one program manager, and so communication grows at $O(n)$ instead of $O(n^2)$.

Well, Simonyi may know Hungarian Notation,[2] but he doesn't know *Peopleware*.[3] Nobody wants to be a code slave. The system didn't work at all. Eventually, Microsoft discovered that despite the alleged Mythical Man-Month, you can still add smart people to a team and get increased output, although at decreasing marginal values. The Excel team had 50 programmers when I was there, and it was marginally more productive than a team of 25 would have been—but not *twice* as productive.

The idea of master/slave programming was discredited, but Microsoft still had these people called program managers bouncing around. A smart man named Jabe Blumenthal basically reinvented the position of program manager. Henceforth, the program manager would own the *design* and the *spec* for products.

Since then, program managers at Microsoft gather requirements, figure out what the code is supposed to do, and *write the specs*. There are usually about five programmers for every program manager; these programmers are responsible for implementing in code what the program manager has implemented in the form of a spec. A program manager also needs to coordinate marketing, documentation, testing, localization, and all the other annoying details that programmers shouldn't spend time on. Finally, program managers at Microsoft are supposed to

2. Charles Simonyi, "Hungarian Notation," Microsoft.com, n.d. See msdn.microsoft.com/library/default.asp?url=/library/en-us/dnvsgen/html/hunganotat.asp.

3. Tom DeMarco and Timothy Lister, *Peopleware: Productive Projects and Teams, 2nd Edition* (Dorset House, 1999).

have the "big picture" of the company in mind, while programmers are free to concentrate on getting their bits of code exactly right.

Program managers are invaluable. If you've ever complained about how programmers are more concerned with technical elegance than with marketability, you need a program manager. If you've ever complained about how people who can write good code never do a good job of writing good English, you need a program manager. If you've ever complained about how your product seems to drift without any clear direction, you need a program manager.

~

How Do You Hire a Program Manager?

Most companies don't even have the concept of program manager. I think that's too bad. In my time, the groups at Microsoft with strong program managers had very successful products: Excel, Windows 95, and Access come to mind. But other groups (such as MSN 1.0 and Windows NT 1.0) were run by developers who generally ignored the program managers (who weren't very good anyway, and probably deserved to be ignored), and their products were not as successful.

Here are three things to avoid:

1. **Don't promote a coder to be a program manager.** The skills for being a good program manager (writing clear English, diplomacy, market awareness, user empathy, and good UI design) are very rarely the skills for being a good coder. Sure, some people can do both, but they are rare. Rewarding good coders by promoting them to a *different position*, one that involves writing English, not C++, is a classic case of the Peter Principle: People tend to be promoted to their level of incompetence.[4]

---

4. Laurence Peter with Raymond Hull, *The Peter Principle* (Buccaneer Books, 1996).

2. **Don't let the marketing people be program managers.** No offense, but I think my readers will agree that good marketing people rarely have a good enough grasp of the technology issues to design products.

   Basically, program management is a separate career path. All program managers need to be very technical, but they don't have to be good coders. Program managers study UI, meet customers, and *write specs*. They need to get along with a wide variety of people—from "moron" customers, to irritating hermit programmers who come to work in Star Trek uniforms, to pompous sales guys in $2000 suits. In some ways, program managers are the glue of software teams. Charisma is crucial.

3. **Don't have coders *report to* the program manager.** This is a subtle mistake. As a program manager at Microsoft, I designed the Visual Basic (VBA) strategy for Excel and completely speced out, to the smallest detail, how VBA should be implemented in Excel. My spec ran to about 500 pages. At the height of development for Excel 5.0, I estimated that every morning, 250 people came to work and basically worked off of that huge spec I wrote. I had no idea who all these people were, but there were about a dozen people on the Visual Basic team alone just *writing documentation* for this thing (not to mention the team writing documentation from the Excel side, or the full-time person who was responsible for hyperlinks in the help file). The weird thing was that I was at the bottom of the reporting tree. That's right. *Nobody* reported to me. If I wanted people to do something, I had to convince them that it was the right thing to do. When Ben Waldman, the lead developer, didn't want to do something I had speced out, he just didn't do it. When the testers complained that something I had speced was impossible to test completely, I had to simplify it. *If any of these people had reported to me, the product wouldn't have been as good.* Some of them would have thought that it's inappropriate to second-guess a superior. Other times, I would have just put my foot down and *ordered* them to do it my way, out of conceit or nearsightedness. As it was, I had no choice but to build consensus. This form of decision making was the best way to get *the right thing* done.

eight

PAINLESS FUNCTIONAL SPECIFICATIONS
PART 4: TIPS

Sunday, October 15, 2000

OK, we've talked about why you need a spec, what a spec has in it, and who should write them. In this fourth and final part of the series, I'll share some of my advice for writing good specs.

The biggest complaint you'll hear from teams that *do* write specs is that nobody reads them. When nobody reads specs, the people who write them tend to get a little bit cynical. It's like the old Dilbert cartoon in which engineers use stacks of 4-inch thick specs to build extensions to their cubicles. At your typical big, bureaucratic company, everybody spends months and months writing boring specs. Once the spec is done, it goes up on the shelf, never to be taken down again, and the product is implemented from scratch without any regard to what the spec said, because nobody read the spec, because it was *so dang mind-numbing*. The very process of writing the spec might have been a good exercise, because it forced everyone, at least, to think over the issues. But the fact that the spec was shelved (unread and unloved) when it was completed makes people feel like it was all a bunch of work for naught.

Also, if your spec never gets read, you get a lot of arguments when the finished product is delivered. Somebody (management, marketing, or a customer) says: "wait a minute! You promised me that there would be a clam steamer! Where's the clam steamer?" And the programmers say, "no, actually, if you look on the spec on chapter 3, subchapter 4, paragraph 2.3.0.1, you'll see it says quite explicitly 'no clam steamer.'" But

~

Rule 2: Writing a Spec Is Like Writing Code for a Brain to Execute

Here's why I think that programmers have trouble writing good specs.

When you write *code*, your primary audience is *the compiler*. Yeah, I know, people have to read code, too, but it's generally very hard for them.[3] For most programmers it's hard enough to get the code into a state where the compiler reads it and correctly interprets it; worrying about making human-readable code is a luxury. Whether you write

```
void print_count( FILE* a, char  *  b, int c ){
    fprintf(a, "there are %d %s\n", c, b);}
main(){ int n; n =
10; print_count(stdout, "employees", n) /* code
deliberately obfuscated */ }
```

or

```
printf("there are 10 employees\n");
```

you get the same output. Which is why, if you think about it, you tend to get programmers who write things like

Assume a function AddressOf(*x*) which is defined as the mapping from a user *x*, to the RFC-822 compliant email address of that user, an ANSI string. Let us assume user A and user B, where A wants to send an email to user B. So user A initiates a new message using any (but not all) of the techniques defined elsewhere, and types AddressOf(B) in the To: editbox.

---

3. See Chapter 24.

This could also have been speced as

> Miss Piggy wants to go to lunch, so she starts a new email and types Kermit's address in the "To:" box.
>
> **Technical Note:** The address must be a standard Internet address (RFC-822 compliant).

They both "mean" the same thing, *theoretically*, except that the first example is impossible to understand unless you carefully decode it, and the second example is easy to understand. Programmers often try to write specs which look like dense academic papers. They think that a "correct" spec needs to be "technically" correct, and then they are off the hook.

The mistake is that when you write a spec, in addition to being correct, it has to be *understandable*, which, in programming terms, means that it needs to be written so that the human brain can "compile" it. One of the big differences between computers and human brains is that computers are willing to sit there patiently while you define the terms that you want to use later. But humans won't understand what you're talking about unless you motivate it first. Humans don't want to have to *decode* something, they just want to read it in order and understand it. For humans, you have to provide the big picture and *then* fill in the details. With computer programs, you start at the top and work your way to the bottom, with full details throughout. A computer doesn't care if your variable names are meaningful. A human brain understands things much better if you can paint a vivid picture in their mind by telling a story, even if it's just a fragment of a story, because our brains have evolved to understand stories.

If you show a chessboard, in the middle of a real game of chess, to an experienced chess player for even a second or two, they will instantly be able to memorize the position of every piece. But if you move around a couple of pieces in nonsensical ways that couldn't happen in normal play (for example, put some pawns on the first row, or put both black bishops on black squares), it becomes much, much harder for them to memorize the board. This is different from the way computers think. A computer program that could memorize a chess board could memorize both possible and impossible layouts with equal ease. The way the human brain works is *not* random access; pathways tend to be strengthened in our brains and some things are just easier to understand than other things because they are more common.

So, when you're writing a spec, try to imagine the person you are addressing it to, and try to imagine what you're asking them to understand at every step. Sentence by sentence, ask yourself if the person reading this sentence will *understand it* at a deep level, in the context of what you've already told them. If some members of your target audience don't know what RFC-822 is, you either have to define it, or, at the very least, bury the mention of RFC-822 in a technical note, so that the executive-types who read the spec won't give up and stop reading the first time they see a lot of technical jargon.

~

Rule 3: Write as Simply as Possible

Don't use stilted, formal language because you think it's unprofessional to write in simple sentences. Use the simplest language you can.

People use words like "utilize" because they think that "use" looks unprofessional. (There's that word "unprofessional" again. Any time somebody tells you that you shouldn't do something because it's "unprofessional," you know that they've run out of *real* arguments.) In fact, I think that many people think that clear writing means that something is wrong.

Break things down to short sentences. If you're having trouble writing a sentence clearly, break it into two or three shorter sentences.

Avoid walls of text: entire pages with just text. People get scared and don't read them. When was the last time you noticed a popular magazine or newspaper with entire pages of text? Magazines will go so far as to take a quote from the article and print it, in the middle of the page, in a giant font, just to avoid the appearance of a full page of text. Use numbered or bulleted lists, pictures, charts, tables, and lots of white space so that the reading "looks" fluffier.

in a giant font, just to avoid the appearance of a full page of text. Use numbered or bulleted lists, pictures, charts, tables, and lots of white space so that the reading "looks" fluffier.

> **❝ ❝Magazines will go so far as to take a quote from the article and print it, in the middle of the page, in a giant font, just to avoid the appearance of a full page of text. ❞ ❞**

Nothing improves a spec more than lots and lots of screenshots A picture can be worth a thousand words. Anyone who writes specs for Windows software should invest in a copy of Visual Basic and learn to

Nothing improves a spec more than lots and lots of screenshots. A picture can be worth a thousand words. Anyone who writes specs for Windows software should invest in a copy of Visual Basic and learn to use it *at least* well enough to create mockups of the screens. (For the Mac, use REAL Basic; for web pages, use FrontPage or Dreamweaver.) Then capture these screenshots (Ctrl+PrtSc) and paste them into your spec.

~

Rule 4: Review and Reread Several Times

Um, well, I was originally planning to have a lengthy exegesis of this rule here, but this rule is just too simple and obvious. Review and reread your spec several times, OK? When you find a sentence that isn't *super* easy to understand, rewrite it.

I've saved so much time by not explaining Rule 4 that I'm going to add another rule.

all their code and starting over: the same mistake that doomed Ashton-Tate, Lotus, and Apple's MacOS to the recycle bins of software history. Netscape has seen its browser share go from about 80 percent to about 20 percent during this time, and all the while it could do nothing to address competitive concerns, because its key software product was disassembled in 1000 pieces on the floor and was in no shape to drive anywhere. That single bad decision, more than anything else, was the nuclear bomb Netscape blew itself up with. (Jamie Zawinski's world-famous tantrum[1] has the details; I'll talk more about this in Chapter 24.)

So, *you have to make a schedule*. This is something almost no programmer wants to do. In my experience, the vast majority just try to get away with not making a schedule at all. Of the few that make a schedule, most are only doing it because their boss made them do it, halfheartedly, and nobody actually *believes* the schedule except for upper management, which simultaneously believes that "no software project is ever on time" and in the existence of UFOs.

So why doesn't anybody make a schedule? Two key reasons. One, it's a real pain. Two, nobody believes that it's worth anything. Why go to all the trouble working on a schedule if it's not going to be right? There is a perception that schedules are consistently wrong, and only get worse as time goes on, so why suffer for naught?

Here's a simple, painless way to make schedules that are actually correct.

~

1. Use Microsoft Excel.

Don't use anything fancy like Microsoft Project. The trouble with Microsoft Project is that it assumes that you want to spend a lot of time worrying about dependencies. A dependency is when you have two tasks, one of which must be completed before the next one can begin.

---

1.   See www.jwz.org/gruntle/nomo.html.

I've found that with software, the dependencies are so obvious that it's just not worth the effort to formally keep track of them.

Another problem with Project is that it assumes that you're going to want to be able to press a little button and "rebalance" the schedule. Inevitably, this means that it's going to rearrange things and reassign things to different people. For software, this just doesn't make sense. Programmers are not interchangeable. It takes seven times longer for John to fix Rita's bug than for Rita to fix Rita's bug. And if you try to put your UI programmer on a WinSock problem, she'll stall and waste a week getting up to speed on WinSock programming. The bottom line is that Project is designed for building office buildings, not software.

~

2. Keep it simple.

The standard format I use for schedules is so simple you can memorize it. You start with just seven columns:

	1	2	3	4	5	6	7
1	Feature	Task	Priority	Orig Est	Curr Est	Elapsed	Remain
2	Spell Checker	Add Menu Item	1	12	8	8	0
3	Spell Checker	Main Dialog	1	8	12	8	4
4	Spell Checker	Dictionary	2	4	4	4	0
5	Grammar Checker	Add Menu Item	1	16	16	0	16
6							
7							
8							

Schedule.xls — Sheet1 / Sheet2 / Sheet3

If you have several developers, you can either keep a separate sheet for each developer, or you can make a column with the name of the developer working on each task.

~

3. Each feature should consist of several tasks.

A feature is something like adding a spell checker to your program. Adding a spell checker consists of quite a few discrete tasks that the programmer has to do. The most important part of making a schedule is making this list of tasks. Thus the cardinal rule:

~

4. Only the programmer who is going to write the code can schedule it.

A ny system where management writes a schedule and hands it off to programmers is doomed to fail. Only the programmer who is going to do the work can figure out what steps they will need to take to implement that feature. And only the programmer can estimate how long each one will take.

~

5. Pick very fine-grained tasks.

T his is the most important part to making your schedule work. Your tasks should be measured in *hours*, not days. (When I see a schedule measured in days, or even weeks, I know it's not real.) You might think that a schedule with fine-grained tasks is merely more *precise*. Wrong! Very wrong! When you start with a schedule with rough tasks and then break it down into smaller tasks, you will find that you get a *different result*, not just a more precise one. It is a *completely different number*. Why does this happen?

When you have to pick fine-grained tasks, you force yourself to actually figure out what steps you are going to have to take. Write subroutine *foo*. Create dialog such and such. Read the wawa file. These steps are easy to estimate, because you've written subroutines, created dialogs, and read wawa files before.

If you are sloppy, and pick big "chunky" tasks ("implement grammar correction"), then you *haven't really thought about what you are going to do*. And when you haven't thought about what you're going to do, you just can't know how long it will take.

As a rule of thumb, each task should be from 2 to 16 hours. If you have a 40-hour (one week) task on your schedule, you're not breaking it down enough.

Here's another reason to pick fine-grained tasks: it forces you to *design* the damn feature. If you have a hand-wavy feature called "Internet Integration" and you schedule three weeks for it, you are *doomed*, buddy. If you have to figure out what subroutines you're going to write, you are forced to *pin down* the feature. By being forced to plan ahead at this level, you eliminate a lot of the instability in a software project.

⌒

6. Keep track of the original and current estimate.

When you first add a task to the schedule, estimate how long it's going to take in hours and put that in both the Orig[inal] Est[imate] and Curr[ent] Est[imate] columns. As time goes on, if a task is taking longer (or shorter) than you thought, you can update the Curr Est column as much as you need. This is the best way to learn from your mistakes and teach yourself how to estimate tasks well. Most programmers have no idea how to guess how long things will take. That's OK. As long as you are continuously learning and continuously updating the schedule as you learn, the schedule will work. (You may have to cut features or slip, but the schedule will still be working correctly, in the sense that it will constantly be telling you when you have to cut features or slip). I've found that most programmers become very good schedulers with about one year of experience.

When the task is done, the Curr Est and Elapsed fields will be the same, and the Remain field will recalc to 0.

~

7. Update the elapsed column every day.

You do not really have to watch your stopwatch while you code. Right before you go home, or go to sleep under the desk if you're one of *those* geeks, pretend you've worked for eight hours (ha!), figure out which tasks you've worked on, and sprinkle about eight hours in the elapsed column accordingly. The remaining time field is then calculated automatically by Excel.

At the same time, update the Curr Est column for those tasks to reflect the new reality. *Updating your schedule daily should only take about two minutes.* That's why this is the Painless Schedule Method— it's quick and easy.

~

8. Put in line items for vacations, holidays, etc.

If your schedule is going to take about a year, each programmer will probably take 10 to 15 days of vacation. You should have a feature in your schedule called vacations, one for holidays, and anything else that consumes people's time. The idea is that the ship date can be calculated by adding up the remaining time column and dividing by 40—that's how many weeks of work are left, including everything.

~

9. Put debugging time into the schedule!

Debugging is the hardest to estimate. Think back to the last project you worked on. Chances are, debugging took from 100 to 200 percent of the time it took to write the code in the first place. This has to be a line item in the schedule, and it will probably be the largest line item.

Here's how it works. Let's say a developer is working on wawa. The Orig Est was 16 hours, but so far it has taken 20 hours and it looks like it needs another 10 hours of work. So the developer enters 30 under Curr Est and 20 under Elapsed.

At the end of the milestone, all these "slips" have probably added up to quite a bit. Theoretically, to accommodate these slips, we have to cut features in order to ship on time. Luckily, the first feature we can cut is this great big feature called Buffer which has lots o' hours already allocated for it.

In principle, developers debug code as they write it. A programmer should never, ever work on new code if they could instead be fixing bugs. The bug count must stay as low as possible at all times, for two reasons:

1. It's easier to fix bugs the same day you wrote the code. It can be very hard and time-consuming to fix bugs a month later when you've forgotten exactly how the code works.

2. Fixing bugs is like doing science. It is impossible to estimate when you will make the discovery and solve the bug. If there are only one or two outstanding bugs at any given time, it's easy to estimate when the product will ship, because there's not much un-estimable science in your future. On the other hand, if there are hundreds or thousands of outstanding bugs, it is impossible to predict when they will all be fixed.

You might be able to get 20 percent more raw code out of people by begging everybody to work super hard, no matter how tired they get. Boom, debugging time *doubles*. An idiotic move that backfires in a splendidly karmic way.

But you can never get $3n$ from n, ever, and if you think you can, please email me the stock ticker of your company so I can short it.

~

13. A schedule is like wood blocks.

If you have a bunch of wood blocks, and you can't fit them into a box, you have two choices: get a bigger box, or remove some blocks. If you thought you could ship in six months, but you have 12 months on the schedule, you will have to delay shipping or find some features to delete. You just can't shrink the blocks, and if you pretend you can, then you are merely depriving yourself of a useful opportunity to actually *see into the future* by lying to yourself about what you see there.

And you know, the other great byproduct of keeping schedules like this is that you *are* forced to delete features. Why is this good? Suppose you have two features: one which is really useful and will make your product really great (example: tables in Netscape 2.0), and another one which is really easy and which the programmers would love to code (example: the BLINK tag), but which serves no useful or marketing purpose.

If you don't make a schedule, the programmers will do the easy/fun feature first. Then they'll run out of time, and you will have no choice but to slip the schedule to do the useful/important feature.

If you do make a schedule, even before you start working, you'll realize that you have to cut something, so you'll cut the easy/fun feature and just do the useful/important feature. By forcing yourself to choose some features to cut, you wind up making a more powerful, better product with a better mix of good features that ships sooner.

I remember working on Excel 5. Our original feature list was huge and would have gone *way* over schedule. Oh my! we thought. Those are *all* super important features! How can we live without a macro editing wizard?

As it turns out, we had no choice, and we cut what we thought was "to the bone" to make the schedule. Everybody felt unhappy about the cuts. To assuage our feelings, we simply told ourselves that we weren't *cutting* the features, we were simply *deferring them* to Excel 6, since they were less important.

As Excel 5 was nearing completion, I started working on the Excel 6 spec with a colleague, Eric Michelman. We sat down to go through the list of "Excel 6" features that had been cut from the Excel 5 schedule. We were absolutely *shocked* to see that the list of cut features was the shoddiest list of features you could imagine. Not *one* of those features was worth doing. I don't think a single one of them was ever done, even in the next three releases. The process of culling features to fit a schedule was the best thing we could have done. If we hadn't done this, Excel 5 would have taken twice as long and included 50 percent useless crap features. (I have absolutely no doubt that this is exactly what's happening to Netscape 5/Mozilla: They have no schedule, they have no definitive feature list, nobody was willing to cut any features, and they just never shipped. When they do ship, they'll have lots of poxy features like IRC clients that they just shouldn't have been spending time on.)

Things You Should Know About Excel

One of the reasons that Excel is such a great product for working on software schedules is that the only thing most Excel programmers use Excel for is maintaining their software schedules! (Not many of them are running business what-if scenarios—these are programmers, here!)

Shared Lists: Using the File | Shared Lists command (Tools | Share Workbook in later versions) allows everyone to open the file at the same time and edit things at the same time. Since your whole team should be updating the schedule constantly, this really helps.

AutoFilter: This is a great way to filter the schedule so that, for example, you only see all of the features that are assigned to you. Combined with Auto Sort, you can see all of the features assigned to you in order of priority, which is effectively your "to do" list. Cooooool!

Pivot Tables: This is a great way to see summaries and crosstabulations. For example, you can make a chart showing the remaining hours for each developer for each priority. Pivot Tables are like sliced bread and chocolate milkshakes. You gotta learn how to use them because they make Excel a million times more powerful.

The WORKDAY Function: A part of Excel's Analysis Toolpak, the WORKDAY function is all you need to get calendar dates out of a painless schedule.

ten

DAILY BUILDS ARE YOUR FRIEND

In 1982, my family took delivery of the very first IBM-PC in Israel. We actually went down to the warehouse and waited while our PC was delivered from the port. Somehow, I convinced my dad to get the fully decked-out version, with *two* floppy disks, 128K memory, and both a dot-matrix printer (for fast drafts) and a Brother Letter-Quality Daisy Wheel printer, which sounds exactly like a machine gun when it is operating, only louder. I think we got almost every accessory available: PC-DOS 1.0, the $75 technical reference manual with a complete source code listing of the BIOS, Macro Assembler, and the stunning IBM Monochrome display with a full 80 columns and...lowercase letters! The whole thing cost about $10,000 including Israel's then-ridiculous import taxes. Extravagant!

Now, "everybody" knew that BASIC was a children's language that requires you to write spaghetti code and turns your brain into Camembert cheese. So we shelled out $600 for IBM Pascal, which came on three floppy diskettes. The compiler's first pass was on the first diskette, the second pass was on the second diskette, and the linker was on the third diskette. I wrote a simple "hello, world" program and compiled it. Total time elapsed: 8 minutes.

Hmm. That's a long time. I wrote a batch file to automate the process and shaved it down to 7 1/2 minutes. Better. But when I tried to write long programs like my stunning version of Othello which *always* beat me, I spent most of the time waiting for compiles. "Yep," a professional programmer told me, "we used to keep a sit-up board in the office and do sit-ups while we were doing compiles. After a few months of programming I had killer abs."

Here are some of the many benefits of daily builds:

1. When a bug is fixed, testers get the new version quickly and can retest to see if the bug was really fixed.

2. Developers can feel more secure that a change they made isn't going to break any of the 1024 versions of the system that get produced, without actually *having* an OS/2 box on their desk to test on.

3. Developers who check in their changes right before the scheduled daily build know that they aren't going to hose everybody else by checking in something which "breaks the build"—that is, something that causes *nobody* to be able to compile. This is the equivalent of the Blue Screen of Death for an entire programming team, and happens a lot when a programmer forgets to add a new file they created to the repository. The build runs fine on *their* machines, but when anyone else checks out, they get linker errors and are stopped cold from doing any work.

4. Outside groups like marketing, beta customer sites, and so forth who need to use the immature product can pick a build that is known to be fairly stable and keep using it for a while.

5. By maintaining an archive of all daily builds, when you discover a really strange, new bug and you have no idea what's causing it, you can use binary search on the historical archive to pinpoint when the bug first appeared in the code. Combined with good source control, you can probably track down which check-in caused the problem.

6. When a tester reports a problem that the programmer thinks is fixed, the tester can say which build they saw the problem in. Then the programmer looks at when he checked in the fix and figure out whether it's *really* fixed.

Here's how to do them. You need a daily build server, which will probably be the fastest computer you can get your hands on. Write a script that checks out a complete copy of the current source code from the repository (you *are* using source control, aren't you?) and then build, from scratch, every version of the code that you ship. If you have an installer or setup program, build that too. Everything you ship to customers should be produced by the daily build process. Put each build in its own directory, coded by date. Run your script at a fixed time every day.

Here are some tips for daily builds:

- It's crucial that *everything* it takes to make a final build is done by the daily build script, from checking out the code up to and including putting the bits up on a web server in the right place for the public to download (although during the development process, this will be a test server, of course). That's the only way to ensure that there is *nothing* about the build process that is only "documented" in one person's head. You never get into a situation where you can't release a product because only Shaniqua knows how to create the installer, and she was hit by a bus. On the Juno team, the only thing you needed to know to create a full build from scratch was where the build server was, and how to double-click on its Daily Build icon.

- There is nothing worse for your sanity than when you are trying to ship the code, and there's *one tiny bug*, so you fix that one tiny bug right on the daily build server and ship it. As a golden rule, you should only ship code that has been produced by a full, clean daily build that started from a complete checkout.

- Set your compilers to maximum warning level (-W4 in Microsoft's world; -Wall in gcc land) and set them to stop if they encounter even the smallest warning.

- If a daily build is broken, you run the risk of stopping the whole team. Stop everything and keep rebuilding until it's fixed. Some days, you may have multiple daily builds.

- Your daily build script should report failures, via email, to the whole development team. It's not too hard to grep the logs for "error" or "warning" and include that in the email, too. The script can also append status reports to an HTML page visible to everyone so programmers and testers can quickly determine which builds were successful.

- One rule we followed on the Microsoft Excel team, to great effect, was that whoever broke the build became responsible for babysitting builds until somebody else broke it. In addition to serving as a clever incentive to keep the build working, it rotated almost everybody through the job of buildmaster so everybody learned about how builds are produced.

- If your team works in one time zone, a good time to do builds is at lunchtime. That way, everybody checks in their latest code right before lunch, the build runs while they're eating, and when they get back, if the build is broken, everybody is around to fix it. As soon as the build is working, everybody can check out the latest version without fear that they will be hosed by a broken build.

- If your team is working in two time zones, schedule the daily build so that the people in one time zone don't hose the people in the other time zone. On the Juno team, the New York people would check things in at 7 p.m. New York time and go home. If they broke the build, the Hyderabad, India, team would get into work (at about 8 p.m. New York Time) and be completely stuck for a whole day. We started doing two daily builds, about an hour before each team went home, and completely solved that problem.

Here are some other sources for further reading on this topic:

- Some discussion on tools for daily builds is online at discuss.fogcreek.com/joelonsoftware/default.asp?cmd= show&ixPost=862.

- Making daily builds is important enough that it's 1 of the 12 steps to better code in Chapter 3.

- There's a lot of interesting stuff about the builds made (weekly) by the Windows NT team in G. Pascal Zachary's book *Showstopper*.[2]

- Steve McConnell writes about daily builds on his website at www.construx.com/stevemcc/bp04.htm.

---

2. G. Pascal Zachary, *Showstopper! The Breakneck Race to Create Windows NT and the Next Generation at Microsoft* (The Free Press, 1994).

eleven

HARD-ASSED BUG FIXIN'

Tuesday, July 31, 2001

Software quality, or the lack thereof, is something everybody loves to gripe about. Now that I have my own company, I finally decided to do something about it. Over the last two weeks, we stopped everything at Fog Creek to ship a new incremental version of FogBUGZ with the goal of eliminating all known bugs (there were about 30).

As a software developer, fixing bugs is a good thing. Right? Isn't it always a good thing?

No!

Fixing bugs is only important when the value of having the bug fixed exceeds the cost of fixing it.

These things are hard, but not impossible, to measure. Let me give you an example. Suppose you operate a peanut-butter-and-jelly sandwich factory. Your factory produces 100,000 sandwiches a day. Recently, because of the introduction of some new flavors (garlic peanut butter with spicy habanero jam), demand for your product has gone through the roof. The factory is operating full-out at 100,000 sandwiches, but the demand is probably closer to 200,000. You just can't make any more. And each sandwich earns you a profit of 15 cents. So you're losing $15,000 a day in potential earnings because you don't have enough capacity.

Building a new factory would cost way too much. You don't have the capital, and you're afraid that spicy/garlicky sandwiches are just a fad which will pass, anyway. But you're still losing that $15,000 a day.

It's a good thing you hired Jason. Jason is a 14-year-old programmer who hacked into the computers that run the factory, and believes that he has come up with a way to speed up the assembly line by a factor of two.

~

2. Make sure you get economic feedback.

Y ou may not be able to figure out *exactly* how much it's worth to fix each bug, but there's something you *can* do: charge the "cost" of tech support back to the business unit. In the early 1990s, Microsoft began a financial reorganization under which each product unit was charged for the full cost of all tech support calls. So the product units started insisting that PSS (Microsoft's tech support) provide lists of Top Ten Bugs regularly. When the development team concentrated on those, product support costs plummeted.

This is a bit in contradiction with the new trend of letting the tech support department pay for its own operation, something that most large companies do. At Juno, tech support was expected to break even by charging people for tech support. By moving the economic burden of bugs onto the users themselves, you lose what limited ability you might have had to detect the damage they were causing. (Instead, you get irate users who resent having to pay for *your* bug, who tell their friends, and you can't even measure how much that costs you. To be fair to Juno, the product itself was free, so stop yer bitchin'.)

One way of resolving the two is *not* to charge the user when the support call was caused by a bug in your own product. Microsoft does this, and it's quite nice, and I've never paid for a call to Microsoft! Instead, charge the $245 or whatever one developer incident costs these days back to the product unit. That blows away their profit completely for the product they sold you (several times over), and creates exactly the right economic incentives. Which reminds me of one reason DOS games were a *terrible* business ... to get them to look good and run fast, you usually needed strange video drivers, and a single tech support call about the video drivers would blow away the profit you could make from *20* copies of your product, assuming Egghead and Ingram and that ad on MTV hadn't already guzzled away *all* your earnings.

~

3. Figure out what it's worth to you to fix them all.

At Fog Creek Software, well, we're a tiny company (except in our own minds), and the development team just takes the tech support calls. The cost was running about one hour per day, which, based on our consulting rates, is somewhere around $75,000 a year. We were pretty confident that we could get that down to 15 minutes a day by fixing all known bugs.

Using very sloppy numbers here, that means that the net present value of the savings would be about $150,000. That justifies 62 days of work; if you can do it in less than 62 person-days, it's worth doing.

Using the handy estimation feature built into FogBUGZ, we calculated that it would take 20 person-days (two people two weeks) to fix everything—that's $48,000 "spent" for a return of $150,000, which is a great return on investment *just on the basis of the tech support savings*. (Observe that you could substitute the cost of programmers' salaries and overhead instead of our consulting rate and get the same 3:1 result, since it cancels out.)

I haven't even begun to count the value from having a better product, but I can start doing that, too. We had 55 crashes on the demo server during the month of July with the old code, representing 17 distinct users. You have to imagine that at least *one* of those people decided not to buy FogBUGZ because they thought it was buggy when they ran the demo (although I don't have real statistics for that). In any case the lost sales were probably costing us somewhere between $7,000 and $100,000 in present value. (If you were serious enough, it wouldn't be too hard to get a real number.)

Next question. Can you charge more for a less buggy product? That would add a whole bunch of value to debugging. I suspect that at the extremes, bug count does affect price, but I am hard-pressed to think of an example from the world of packaged software where this has been the case.

~

Please Don't Beat Me Up!

Inevitably, people read essays like this and come to silly conclusions, like, Joel doesn't think you should fix bugs. In fact, I think that for most of the kinds of bugs that most people fix, there's a clear return on investment. But there may be an even higher monetary value to doing something *other* than fixing every last bug. If you have to decide between fixing the bug for OS/2 guy and adding a new feature that will sell 20,000 copies of your software to General Electric, well, sorry, OS/2 guy. And if you're dumb enough to think that it's *still* more important to fix OS/2 than to add the GE feature, maybe your competitors won't be and you'll be out of business.

With all that said, I'm optimistic at heart, and I believe that there is a lot of hidden value to producing very high quality products that is not very easy to capture. Your employees will be prouder. Fewer of your customers will send you back your CD in the mail after microwaving it and chopping it to bits with an ax. So I tend to err on the side of quality (indeed, we fixed *every known bug* in FogBUGZ, not just the big bang ones) and take pride in that, and feel confident, by the complete elimination of errors from the demo server, that we have a rock-solid product.

twelve

FIVE WORLDS

My first full-time job was in an industrial bread bakery. There were two huge rooms: one where the bread was baked, and one where it was put in boxes. In the first room, everybody dealt with dough problems all day. Dough got stuck in the machines, on your hands, in your hair, on your shoes, and everybody carried a little paint scraper to clean up dough jams. In the second room, everybody dealt with crumb problems all day. Crumbs got stuck in the machines, in your hair, and everybody carried around little brushes. I thought about how every job has its bugbear—its own private source of perpetual irritation—and gave thanks that I didn't have a job in a razor blade factory.

With programming, we have bugbears, too, and the bugbears in the first room are different from the bugbears in the second room, but for some reason you could read just about every book on software development that's ever been written without even knowing about the rooms, let alone the bugbear-variation.

I've spent most of my post-bread career creating commercial software intended to be used by millions of people. The first time I read that Extreme Programming thinks it's a requirement to have "the customer" on the team, I thought, *the* customer? Hmm. Working on the email client for Juno, a major national ISP, we had *millions* of customers, including an awful lot of sweet old grandmas who don't get much coverage in the team-building literature.

I would do consulting gigs for corporate developers and blather on about how "when I was at Microsoft, blah blah blah . . ." they would look arrows are usually decided poorly on such projects. As a result, geo-graphically dispersed teams have done far better at cloning existing software where little or no design is required. But most open source software still needs to run in the wild and is therefore shrinkwrap.

Web Based

Software like Hotmail, eBay, or even a content site still needs to be easy to use and must run on many browsers. Most users will have "the monopoly browser," but the noisiest users for some odd reason all seem to use Precambrian browsers that couldn't display standards-compliant HTML correctly if Jeffrey Zeldman himself was *built into* the program, so all-in-all you spend a lot of time searching Google for things like "Netscape 4.72 CSS font bug." Although the developers have the luxury of (at least) some control over the "deployment" environment—the computers in the data center—they have to deal with a wide variety of web browsers and a large number of users, so I consider this basically a variation of shrinkwrap.

Consultingware

This variant of shrinkwrap requires so much customization and installa-tion that you need an army of consultants to install it, at outrageous cost. CRM and CMS packages often fall in this category. One starts to suspect that the software itself doesn't actually *do* anything; it is just an excuse to get an army of consultants in the door billing at $300 an hour. Although consultingware is disguised as shrinkwrap, the high cost of an implementation means this is really more like *internal* software.

∼

2. Internal

Internal software only has to work in one situation on one company's computers. This makes it a lot easier to develop. You can make lots of assumptions about the environment under which it will run. You can require a particular version of Internet Explorer, or Microsoft Office, or

Windows NT 4.0 service pack *six*. If you need a graph, let Excel build it for you; everybody in our department has Excel. (But try that with shrinkwrap and you eliminate half of your potential customers.)

Corporate developers hate to admit this, but with internal software, usability is a lower priority, because a limited number of people need to use the software, and they don't have any choice in the matter, and they will just have to deal with it. And a lot of times the software can be a lot buggier than what you could get away with in the shrinkwrap world. Speed of development is more important. Because the value of the development effort is spread over only one company, the amount of development resources that can be justified is significantly lower. Microsoft can afford to spend $200,000,000 developing an operating system that's only worth about $98 to the average person. But when Chattanooga Railroad LLP develops a proprietary choochoo trading platform, that investment must make sense for a single company. To get a reasonable ROI, internal developers can't spend as much as someone would on shrinkwrap. In fact, one key difference between internal and shrinkwrap software is that for internal software, after a certain point, spending any more money to make it more solid or easier to use has sharply diminishing returns; with shrinkwrap, that last 1 percent of stability or ease of use can be a key competitive advantage. So sadly, lots of internal software sucks pretty badly even while accomplishing what it needs to accomplish perfectly. This can be depressing for young, enthusiastic developers who need to be persuaded to stop when the software is "good enough."

$\sim$

3. Embedded

This software has the unique property that it goes in a piece of hardware and in almost every case can never be updated. (Even if it can *technically* be updated, it won't be. Trust me. Nobody downloads EPROM flash upgrades for their microwave ovens.) This is a whole different world, here. The quality requirements are very high, because there are no second chances. You may be dealing with a CPU that runs dramatically more slowly than the typical desktop processor, so developers may have to spend a lot of time optimizing and hand-tuning. Fast code is more important than elegant code. The input and output devices available to you may be limited. The GPS system in the car I rented last week had such pathetic I/O that the usability was dismal. Have you ever tried to input an address on a device without a keyboard? Or followed directions on a map that didn't seem much bigger than a Casio watch? But I digress.

~

4. Games

Games are unique for two reasons. First, the economics of game development are hit-oriented. Some games are hits, many more games are failures, and if you want to make money on game software, you recognize this and make sure that you have a portfolio of games so that the blockbuster hit makes up for the losses on the failures. This is more like movies than software.

The bigger issue with the development of games is that there's only one version. Once people have played to the end of *Duke Nukem 3D* and killed the big boss, they are not going to upgrade to *Duke Nukem 3.1D* just to get some bug fixes and new weapons. It's too boring. So games have the same quality requirements as embedded software and an incredible financial imperative to get it right the first time, whereas shrinkwrap developers, squinting at their DLLs, at least have the luxury of knowing that if 1.0 sucks and nobody buys it, they can make 2.0 better, and people might.

~

5. Throwaway

The fifth world, included for completeness, is throwaway code. This is code that you create temporarily solely for the purpose of obtaining something else, and you never need to use the code again once you obtain that thing. For example, you might write a little shell script that massages an input file that you got into the format you need it for some other purpose, and this is a onetime operation. Throwaway code has no bugbears whatsoever, although some law of business states that throwaway code rapidly becomes internal code which some MBA will spot and say "we can spin off a whole business out of this" and *ta da!* another consultingware company offering brittle "enterprise solutions" is born.

~

Know Your World

OK, we live in different worlds. Big deal. Why does all this matter? Here's an important thing to know. Whenever you read one of those books about programming methodologies written by a full-time software development guru/consultant, chances are they are talking about internal, corporate software development. Not shrinkwrapped software, not embedded software, and certainly not games. Why? Because corporations are the people who hire these gurus. They're paying the bill. (Trust me, id Software is *not* about to hire Ed Yourdon to talk about structured analysis.)

Lately, I've been learning a lot about Extreme Programming (XP). For many types of projects, XP and other agile methods would be a breath of fresh air from the stilted, boring, dysfunctional "processes" in many a programming shop, and there's no question that techniques such as test-driven development are fantastic if you can use them. But therein lies the catch: *if you can use them.* There are a bunch of holes in XP, which may or may not be a problem for your situation. For example, nobody has really been able to get test-driven development to work for GUI development. I've built an entire web application server using test-driven development, and it worked fabulously, because an application server doesn't do much more than transform strings. But I've never been able to get automated testing of *any* sort to work on my GUIs. At best you can do subcutaneous automated testing, which doesn't help when you have to implement drag-n-drop.

XP also assumes that refactoring is easy, especially if you have tests to ensure that nothing breaks. That's true for monolithic projects, especially in-house projects that don't interact with anything else. But I *can't* change the schema of my company's product FogBUGZ willy-nilly, because so many of our customers have already written code to it, and if I broke their code, they would never upgrade, and then I couldn't pay programmers, and the whole house of cards comes a-tumblin' down. Careful analysis and design can't be skipped when you need to play well with others. So I've been trying to discover how to adopt the best of agile methodologies to the shrinkwrap world while recognizing where it just doesn't fit.

Most things in software development are the same no matter what kind of project you're working on, but not everything. When somebody tells you about methodology, think about how it applies to the work *you're* doing. Think about where the person is coming from. In any case, we should all be able to learn something from each other. *Each world has its own bugbears.* If you're a corporate developer using server-based Java, stop pretending that the reason you don't live in DLL Hell is because Java is inherently a better programming language. You don't live in DLL Hell *because your program only runs on one box.* If you're a game developer, stop whining about how slow interpreted bytecode is. *It's not for you.* It's for the internal developers who only have four accounts receivable people "banging" on their software. Respect and understand each other's dough/breadcrumb problems and help make Usenet more civilized!

thirteen

PAPER PROTOTYPING

FRIDAY, MAY 16, 2003

Years ago, the Excel team was trying to figure out if it would be a good idea to allow users to drag and drop cells using the mouse. They had a couple of interns "whip up a prototype" suitable for usability testing, using the cutting-edge Visual Basic 1.0. Building the prototype took all summer, because it had to duplicate so much of Excel's real functionality or you couldn't do a real usability test.

The conclusion of usability testing? Yes, it was a good feature! The programmer in charge spent *maybe* a week and completely implemented the drag-and-drop feature. The joke is, of course, that the whole *point* of creating a prototype is to "save time."

A year later, another top-secret Microsoft team built a complete prototype for a new user interface using the cutting-edge product Asymetrix Toolbook[1] (good lord, it's hard to believe that thing is still around, but it is). This prototype took something like a year to build. The product? Microsoft Bob,[2] the PCjr of the software world. Another wasted prototype.

I've basically given up on software prototypes. If the prototype can do everything the product can do, it might as well *be* the product, and if it can't, it's not much use. Luckily, there's a much better idea: paper prototypes, which neatly solve this problem and the iceberg problem[3] in one fell swoop.

---

1. See www.asymetrix.com/en/toolbook/index.asp.
2. See toastytech.com/guis/bob2.html.
3. See Chapter 25.

A paper prototype is simple: it's just a piece of paper where you've drawn—in pencil—a mock-up of the user interface. The messier the better. You show it to a few people and ask them how they'd accomplish a given task. There's no risk of getting bogged down in discussions of fonts and colors, since there are no fonts and colors—just pencil scratches. And since you obviously didn't put much effort into anything, people don't self-censor their opinions because they're afraid of hurting your feelings.

Paper prototypes are dramatically cheaper than anything you can do with software tools, and you can even do real usability tests; you just stand behind the sheet of paper with a good eraser, a pencil, and scissors. As your usability subject tells you what they do ("click there!") you can swap things around on the fly. Need to test a wizard? All you have to do is make a sheet of paper for each page of the wizard and prepare some index cards with possible error messages.

For more about paper prototyping, read Carolyn Snyder's book[4] on the subject. It is an essential reference for anyone designing user interfaces, and it's well written to boot.

---

4. Carolyn Snyder, *Paper Prototyping: The Fast and Easy Way to Design and Refine User Interfaces* (Morgan Kaufmann, 2003).

fourteen

DON'T LET ARCHITECTURE ASTRONAUTS SCARE YOU

SATURDAY, APRIL 21, 2001

When great thinkers think about problems, they start to see patterns. They look at the problem of people sending each other word-processor files, and then they look at the problem of people sending each other spreadsheets, and they realize that there's a general pattern: sending files. That's one level of abstraction already. Then they go up one more level: People *send* files, but web browsers also *"send"* requests for web pages. And when you think about it, calling a method on an object is like sending a message to an object! It's the same thing again! Those are all *sending* operations, so our clever thinker invents a new, higher, broader abstraction called *messaging*, but now it's getting *really* vague and nobody really knows what they're talking about any more. Blah.

When you go too far up, abstraction-wise, you run out of oxygen. Sometimes, smart thinkers just don't know when to stop, and they create these absurd, all-encompassing, high-level pictures of the universe that are all good and fine, but don't actually mean anything at all.

These are the people I call Architecture Astronauts. It's very hard to get them to write code or design programs, because they won't stop thinking about architecture. They're astronauts because they are so high above the oxygen level, I don't know *how* they're breathing. They tend to work for really big companies that can afford to have lots of unproductive people with really advanced degrees that don't contribute to the bottom line.

A recent example illustrates this. Your typical Architecture Astronaut will take a fact like "Napster is a peer-to-peer service for downloading music" and ignore everything but the architecture, thinking it's interesting or a new virtual machine? These things might be good architectures, and they will certainly benefit the developers that use them, but they are *not*, I repeat, *not*, a good substitute for the messiah riding his white ass into Jerusalem, or world peace. No, Microsoft, computers are *not* suddenly going to start reading our minds and doing what we want automatically just because everyone in the world has to have a Passport account. No, Sun, we're *not* going to be able to analyze our corporate sales data "as simply as putting a DVD into your home theater system."

Remember that the architecture people are solving problems that they think they can solve, not problems that are *useful* to solve. SOAP + WSDL may be the Hot New Thing, but it doesn't really let you do anything you couldn't do before using other technologies—if you had a reason to. All that Distributed Services Nirvana the Architecture Astronauts are blathering about was promised to us in the past, if we used DCOM, or JavaBeans, or OSF DCE, or CORBA.

It's nice that we can use XML now for the format on the wire. Whoopee. But that's about as interesting to me as learning that my supermarket uses trucks to get things from the warehouse. Yawn. *Mangos*, that's interesting. Tell me something new that I can do that I couldn't do before, O Astronauts, or stay up there in space and don't waste any more of my time.

fifteen

FIRE AND MOTION

SUNDAY, JANUARY 6, 2002

Sometimes I just can't get anything done.

Sure, I come into the office, putter around, check my email every ten seconds, read the web, even do a few brainless tasks like paying the American Express bill. But getting back into the flow of writing code just doesn't happen.

These bouts of unproductiveness usually last for a day or two. But there have been times in my career as a developer when I went for weeks at a time without being able to get anything done. As they say, I'm not in flow. I'm not in the zone. I'm not anywhere.

Everybody has mood swings; for some people they are mild, for others they can be more pronounced or even dysfunctional. And the unproductive periods do seem to correlate somewhat with gloomier moods.

It makes me think of those researchers who say that basically, people *can't* control what they eat, so any attempt to diet is bound to be short term and they will always yoyo back to their natural weight. Maybe as a software developer I really can't control when I'm productive, and I just have to take the slow times with the fast times and hope that they average out to enough lines of code to make me employable.

What drives me crazy is that ever since my first job, I've realized that as a developer, I usually average about two or three hours a day of productive coding. When I had a summer internship at Microsoft, a fellow intern told me he was actually only going into work from 12 to 5 every day. Five hours, minus lunch, and his team *loved* him because he still managed to get a lot more done than average. I've found the same thing to be true. I feel a little bit guilty when I see how hard everybody else seems to be working, and

I get about two or three quality hours in a day, and still I've always been one of the most productive members of the team. That's probably why when *Peopleware*[1] and Extreme Programming insist on eliminating overtime and working strictly 40-hour weeks, they do so secure in the knowledge that this won't reduce a team's output.

But it's not the days when I "only" get two hours of work done that worry me. It's the days when I can't do *anything*.

I've thought about this a lot. I tried to remember the time when I got the most work done in my career. It was probably when Microsoft moved me into a beautiful, plush new office with large picture windows overlooking a pretty stone courtyard full of cherry trees in bloom. Everything was clicking. For months I worked nonstop grinding out the detailed specification for Excel Basic—a monumental ream of paper going into incredible detail covering a gigantic object model and programming environment. I literally never stopped. When I had to go to Boston for MacWorld, I took a laptop with me and documented the Window class sitting on a pleasant terrace at HBS.

Once you get into flow, it's not too hard to keep going. Many of my days go like this: 1) get into work, 2) check email, read the Web, etc., 3) decide that I might as well have lunch before getting to work, 4) get back from lunch, 5) check email, read the web, etc., 6) finally decide that I've got to get started, 7) check email, read the Web, etc., 8) decide again that I *really* have to get started, 9) launch the damn editor and, 10) write code nonstop until I don't realize that it's already 7:30 p.m.

Somewhere between step 8 and step 9 there seems to be a bug, because I can't always make it across that chasm. For me, just getting started is the *only* hard thing. An object at rest tends to remain at rest. There's something incredible heavy in my brain that is extremely hard to get up to speed, but once it's rolling at full speed, it takes no effort to keep it going. Like a bicycle decked out for a cross-country, self-supported bike trip:[2] When you first start riding a bike with all that gear, it's hard to believe how much work it takes to get rolling, but once you are rolling, it feels just as easy as riding a bike without any gear.

---

1. Tom Demarco and Timothy Lister, *Peopleware: Productive Projects and Teams, Second Edition* (Dorset House, 1999).
2. See joel.spolsky.com/biketrip/.

Maybe this is the key to productivity: *just getting started*. Maybe when pair programming works, it works because when you schedule a pair programming session with your buddy, you force each other to get started.

When I was an Israeli paratrooper, a general stopped by to give us a little speech about strategy. In infantry battles, he told us, there is only one strategy: Fire and Motion. You move toward the enemy while firing your weapon. The firing forces him to keep his head down so he can't fire at you. (That's what the soldiers mean when they shout "cover me." It means, "fire at our enemy so he has to duck and can't fire at me while I run across this street, here." It works.) The motion allows you to conquer territory and get closer to your enemy, where your shots are much more likely to hit their target. If you're not moving, the enemy gets to decide what happens, which is not a good thing. If you're not firing, the enemy will fire at you, pinning you down.

I remembered this for a long time. I noticed how almost every kind of military strategy, from air force dogfights to large-scale naval maneuvers, is based on the idea of Fire and Motion. It took me another 15 years to realize that the principle of Fire and Motion is how you get things done in life. You have to move forward a little bit, every day. It doesn't matter if your code is lame and buggy and nobody wants it. If you are moving forward, writing code and fixing bugs constantly, time is on your side. Watch out when your competition fires at you. Do they just want to force you to keep busy reacting to their volleys, so you can't move forward?

Think of the history of data access strategies to come out of Microsoft. ODBC, RDO, DAO, ADO, OLEDB, now ADO.NET—All New! Are these technological imperatives? The result of an incompetent design group that needs to reinvent data access every goddamn year? (That's probably it, actually.) But the end result is just cover fire. The competition has no choice but to spend all their time porting and keeping up, time that they can't spend writing new features. Look closely at the software landscape. The companies that do well are the ones who rely least on big companies and don't have to spend all their cycles catching up and reimplementing and fixing bugs that crop up only on Windows XP. The companies who stumble are the ones who spend too much time reading tea leaves to figure out the future direction of

Microsoft. People get worried about .NET and decide to rewrite their whole architecture for .NET because they think they have to. Microsoft is shooting at you, and it's just cover fire so that they can move forward and you can't, because this is how the game is played, Bubby. Are you going to support HailStorm?[3] SOAP?[4] RDF?[5] Are you supporting it because your customers need it, or because someone is firing at you and you feel like you have to respond? The sales teams of the big companies understand cover fire. They go into their customers and say, "OK, you don't have to buy from us. Buy from the best vendor. But make sure that you get a product that supports (XML / SOAP / CDE / J2EE), because otherwise you'll be Locked In The Trunk."[6] Then when the little companies try to sell into that account, all they hear is obedient CTOs parroting "Do you have J2EE?" And they have to waste all their time building in J2EE even if it doesn't really make any sales, and gives them no opportunity to distinguish themselves. It's a checkbox feature—you do it because you need the checkbox saying you have it, but nobody will use it or needs it. And it's cover fire.

Fire and Motion, for small companies like mine, means two things. You have to have time on your side,[7] and you have to move forward every day. Sooner or later you will win. All I managed to do yesterday is improve the color scheme in FogBUGZ just a little bit. That's OK. It's getting better all the time. Every day, our software is better and better, and we have more and more customers and that's all that matters. Until we're a company the size of Oracle, we don't have to think about grand strategies. We just have to come in every morning and somehow, launch the editor.

3. See wmf.editthispage.com/discuss/msgReader$3194?mode=topic.

4. See radiodiscuss.userland.com/soap.

5. See www.w3.org/RDF/.

6. Dave Winer, "The Micro Channel Architecture," DaveNet, July 6, 2001. See davenet.userland.com/2001/07/06/theMicroChannelArchitecture.

7. See Chapter 36.

sixteen

CRAFTSMANSHIP

MONDAY, DECEMBER 1, 2003

Making software is not a manufacturing process. In the 1980s everyone was running around terrified that Japanese software companies were setting up "software factories" that could churn out high-quality code on an assembly line. It didn't make any sense then and it doesn't make sense now. Shoving a lot of programmers into a room and lining them up in neat rows did not really help get the bug counts down.

If writing code is not assembly line style production, what is it? Some have proposed the label *craftsmanship*. That's not quite right, either, because I don't care what you say: That dialog box in Windows that asks you how you want your help file indexed does not in any way, shape, or form resemble what any normal English speaker would refer to as "craftsmanship."

Writing code is not *production*. It's not always craftsmanship (though it can be). It's *design*. Design is that nebulous area where you can add value faster than you add cost. The *New York Times Magazine* has been raving about the iPod[1] and how Apple is one of the few companies that knows how to use good design to add value.

---

1. Rob Walker, "The Guts of a New Machine," *The New York Times*, November 30, 2003, late edition—final, section 6, page 78, column 1.

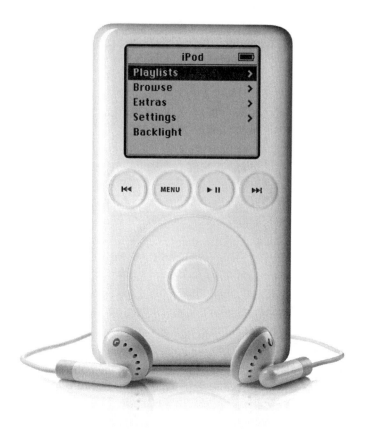

Courtesy Apple Computer, Inc.
For more info: http://www.apple.com/pr/photos/ipod/03ipod.html

But I've talked enough about design; I want to talk about craftsmanship for a minute: what it is and how you recognize it.

I'd like to tell you about at a piece of code I've been rewriting for CityDesk 3.0: the file import code. (Advertisement: CityDesk is my company's easy-to-use content management product.)

The spec seems about as simple as any snippet of code can be. The user chooses a file using a standard dialog box, and the program copies that file into the CityDesk database.

This turned out to be a great example of one of those places where "the last 1 percent of the code takes 90 percent of the time." The first draft of the code looked like this:

1. Open the file.

2. Read it all into a big byte array.

3. Store the byte array in a record.

Worked great. For reasonable-sized existing files, it was practically instantaneous. It had a few little bugs, which I worked through one at a time.

The big bug surfaced when I stress-tested it by dragging a 120MB file into CityDesk. Now, it is not common by any means for people to post 120MB files on their websites. In fact, it's quite rare. But it's not impossible, either. The code worked, but took almost a minute and provided no visual feedback—the app just froze and appeared to be completely locked up. This is obviously not ideal.

From a UI perspective, what I really wanted was for long operations to bring up a progress bar of some sort, along with a Cancel button. In the ideal world, you would be able to continue doing other operations with CityDesk while the file copy proceeded in the background. There were three obvious ways to do this:

1. From a single thread, polling frequently for input events

2. By launching a second thread and synchronizing it carefully

3. By launching a second process and synchronizing it less carefully

My experience with #1 is that it never quite works. It is too hard to ensure that all the code throughout your application can be run safely while a file copy operation is in progress. And Eric S. Raymond has convinced me that threads are usually not as good a solution as separate processes;[2] indeed, years of experience have shown me that programming with multiple threads creates much additional complexity and

---

2. See www.faqs.org/docs/artu/ch07s03.html#id2923889.

introduces whole new categories of dangerously frightful heisenbugs.[3] #3 seemed like a good solution, especially since our underlying database is multi-user and doesn't mind lots of processes banging on it at the same time. So that's what I'm planning to do when I get back from Thanksgiving vacation.

Notice, though, the big picture. We've gone from read the file/save it in the database to something significantly more complicated: launch a child process, tell *it* to read the file and save it in the database, add a progress bar and cancel button to the child process, and then some kind of mechanism so the child can notify the parent when the file has arrived so it can be displayed. There will also be some work passing command-line arguments to the child process, and making sure the window focus behaves in an expected manner, and handling the case of the user shutting down their system while a file copy is in progress. I would guesstimate that when all is said and done, I'll have ten times as much code to handle large files gracefully, code that maybe 1 percent of our users will ever see.

And of course, a certain type of programmer will argue that my new child-process architecture is inferior to the original. It's "bloated" (because of all the extra lines of code). It has more potential for bugs, because of all the extra lines of code. It's overkill. It's somehow emblematic of why Windows is an inferior operating system, they will say. "What's all this about progress indicators?" they sneer. Just hit Ctrl+Z and then "ls -l" repeatedly and watch to see if the file size is growing!

The moral of the story is that sometimes fixing a 1 percent defect takes 500 percent effort. This is not unique to software, no sirree, now that I'm managing all these construction projects I can tell you that. Last week, finally, our contractor finally put the finishing touches on the new Fog Creek offices.[4] This consisted of installing shiny blue acrylic on the front doors, surrounded by aluminum trim with a screw every 20cm. If you look closely at the picture, the aluminum trim goes all the way around each door. Where the doors meet, there are two pieces of vertical trim right next to each other. It's hard to tell from the picture, but the screws in the middle strips are *almost* but not *exactly* lined up. They are,

---

3. For more information on heisenbugs, see c2.com/cgi/like?HeisenBug.

4. See www.joelonsoftware.com/articles/BionicOffice.html.

maybe, 2mm off. The carpenter working on this measured carefully, but he was installing the trim while the doors were on the ground, not mounted in place, and when the doors were mounted—oops—it became clear that the screws were not exactly lined up.

This is probably not that uncommon; there are lots of screws in our office that don't line up perfectly. The problem is that fixing this once the holes are drilled would be ridiculously expensive. Since the correct placement for the screws is only a couple of millimeters away, you can't just drill new holes in the door; you'd probably have to replace the whole door. It's just not worth it. Another case where fixing a 1 percent defect takes 500 percent effort, and it explains why so many artifacts in our world are 99 percent good, not 100 percent good. Our architect never stops raving about some really, really expensive house in Arizona where every screw lined up.

It comes down to an attribute of software that most people think of as *craftsmanship*. When software is built by a true craftsman, all the screws line up. When you do something rare, the application behaves

~

Searching

Most of the academic work on searching is positively *obsessed* with problems like "what happens if you search for 'car,' and the document you want says 'automobile.'"

Indeed there is an awful lot of academic research into concepts like *stemming,* in which the word you searched for is de-conjugated, so that searching for "searching" also finds documents containing the word "searched" or "sought."

So when the big Internet search engines like Altavista first came out, they bragged about how they found zillions of results. An Altavista search for Joel on Software yields 1,033,555 pages. This is, of course, useless. The known Internet contains maybe a billion pages. By reducing the search from one billion to one million pages, Altavista has done absolutely nothing for me.

The *real* problem in searching is how to *sort the results.* In defense of the computer scientists, this is something nobody even *noticed* until they starting indexing gigantic corpora the size of the Internet.

But somebody noticed. Larry Page and Sergey Brin over at Google realized that ranking the pages in the right order was more important than grabbing every possible page. Their PageRank algorithm[1] is a great way to sort the zillions of results so that the one you want is probably in the top ten. Indeed, search for Joel on Software on Google and you'll see that it comes up first. On Altavista, it's not even on the first five pages, after which I gave up looking for it.

---

1. See www.google.com/technology/index.html.

~

Antialiased Text

Antialiasing was invented way back in 1972 at the Architecture Machine Group of MIT, which was later incorporated into the famous Media Lab. The idea is that if you have a color display that is low resolution, you might as well use shades of gray to create the "illusion" of resolution. Here's how that looks:

Aa Aa

Notice that the normal text on the left is nice and sharp, while the antialiased text on the right appears to be blurred on the edges. If you squint or step back a little bit, the normal text has weird "steps" due to the limited resolution of a computer display. But the antialiased text looks smoother and more pleasant.

So this is why everybody got excited about antialiasing. It's everywhere, now. Microsoft Windows even includes a checkbox to turn it on for all text in the system.

The problem? If you try to read a paragraph of antialiased text, it just looks blurry. There's nothing I can do about it, it's the truth. Compare these two paragraphs:

Antialiasing was invented way back in 1972 at the Architecture Machine Group of MIT, which was later incorporated into the famous Media Lab.

Antialiasing was invented way back in 1972 at the Architecture Machine Group of MIT, which was later incorporated into the famous Media Lab.

The paragraph on the left is not antialiased; the one on the right was antialiased using Corel PHOTO-PAINT. Frankly, antialiased text just looks *bad*.

Somebody finally noticed this: the Microsoft Typography group.[2] They created several excellent fonts like Georgia and Verdana which are "designed for easy screen readability." Basically, instead of creating a high-resolution font and then trying to hammer it into the pixel grid, they finally accepted the pixel grid as a "given" and designed a font that fits neatly into it. Somebody *didn't* notice this: the Microsoft Reader group, which is using a form of antialiasing they call "ClearType" designed for color LCD screens, which, I'm sorry, still looks blurry, even on a color LCD screen.[3]

Before I get lots of irate responses for the graphics professionals among my readers, I should mention that antialiasing is still a great technique for two things: headlines and logos, where the overall appearance is more important than the sustained readability; and pictures. Antialiasing is a great way to scale photographic images to smaller sizes.

~

Network Transparency

Ever since the first networks, the "holy grail" of networking computing has been to provide a programming interface in which you can access remote resources *the same way* as you access local resources. The network becomes "transparent."

One example of network transparency is the famous RPC (remote procedure call),[4] a system designed so that you can call procedures (subroutines) running on another computer on the network exactly as if they were running on the local computer. An awful lot of energy went into this. Another example, built on top of RPC, is Microsoft's Distributed

---

2. For more information on Microsoft typography, see www.microsoft.com/truetype/default.asp.

3. "First ClearType screens posted," Microsoft.com, January 26, 2000. See www.microsoft.com/ typography/links/News.asp?NID=1135. Since I wrote this, ClearType has become a standard feature in Microsoft Windows XP, and it's greatly improved.

4. For more information on RPC, see searchwebservices.techtarget.com/sDefinition/ 0,,sid26_gci214272,00.html.

COM (DCOM),[5] in which you can access objects running on another computer as if they were on the current computer.

Sounds logical, right?

Wrong.

There are three very major differences between accessing resources on another machine and accessing resources on the local machine:

1. Availability

2. Latency

3. Reliability

When you access another machine, there's a good chance that machine will not be available, or the network won't be available. And the speed of the network means that it's likely that the request will take a while: you might be running over a modem at 28.8kbps. Or the other machine might crash, or the network connection might go away while you are talking to the other machine (when the cat trips over the phone cord).

Any reliable software that uses the network absolutely must take this into account. Using programming interfaces that hide all this stuff from you is a great way to make a lousy software program.

A quick example: suppose I've got some software that needs to copy a file from one computer to another. On the Windows platform, the old "transparent" way to do this is to call the usual CopyFile method, using UNC names for the files such as \\SERVER\SHARE\Filename.

If all is well with the network, this works nicely. But if the file is a megabyte long, and the network is being accessed over a modem, all kinds of things go wrong. The entire application freezes while a megabyte file is transferred. There is no way to make a progress indicator, because when CopyFile was invented, it was assumed that it would always be "fast." There is no way to resume the transfer if the phone connection is lost.

5. For more information on DCOM, see www.microsoft.com/com/tech/dcom.asp.

Realistically, if you want to transfer a file over a network, it's better to use an API like FtpOpenFile and its related functions. No, it's not the same as copying a file locally, and it's harder to use, but this function was built with the knowledge that network programming is different than local programming, and it provides hooks to make a progress indicator, to fail gracefully if the network is unavailable or becomes unavailable, and to operate asynchronously.

Conclusion: The next time someone tries to sell you a programming product that lets you access network resources the same way as you access local resources, run full speed in the opposite direction.

eighteen

BICULTURALISM

Sunday, December 14, 2003

By now, Windows and UNIX are functionally more similar than different. They both support the same major programming metaphors, from command lines to GUIs to web servers; they are organized around virtually the same panoply of system resources, from nearly identical file systems to memory to sockets and processes and threads. There's not much about the core set of services provided by each operating system to limit the kinds of applications you can create.

What's left is cultural differences. Yes, we all eat food, but over there, they eat raw fish with rice using wood sticks, while over here, we eat slabs of ground cow on bread with our hands. A cultural difference doesn't mean that American stomachs can't digest sushi, or that Japanese stomachs can't digest Big Macs, and it doesn't mean that there aren't lots of Americans who eat sushi or Japanese who eat burgers, but it does mean that Americans getting off the plane for the first time in Tokyo are confronted with an overwhelming feeling that this place is *strange*, dammit, and no amount of philosophizing about how *underneath we're all the same, we all love and work and sing and die* will overcome the fact that Americans and Japanese can never *really* get comfortable with each others' toilet arrangements.

What are the cultural differences between UNIX and Windows programmers? There are many details and subtleties, but for the most part it comes down to one thing: UNIX culture values code which is useful to other programmers, while Windows culture values code which is useful to nonprogrammers.

and that are mostly designed to be flexible and powerful. Unfortunately, since programmers do not have access to the source code for those components, they can be used only in ways that were precisely foreseen and allowed for by the component developers at Microsoft, which doesn't always work out. And sometimes there are bugs, usually the fault of the person calling the API, which are difficult or impossible to debug without the source code. The UNIX cultural value of visible source code makes it an easier environment to develop for.[7] Any Windows developer will tell you about the time he spent four days tracking down a bug because, say, he thought that the memory size returned by LocalSize would be the same as the memory size he originally requested with LocalAlloc, or some similar bug he could have fixed in ten minutes if he could see the source code of the library. To illustrate this, Raymond invents an amusing story that will ring true to anyone who has ever used a library in binary form.[8]

So you get these religious arguments. UNIX is better because you can debug into libraries. Windows is better because Aunt Marge gets some confirmation that her email was actually sent. Actually, one is not *better* than another; they simply have different values. In UNIX, making things better for other programmers is a core value, and in Windows, making things better for Aunt Marge is a core value.

Let's look at another cultural difference. Raymond says, "Classic UNIX documentation is written to be telegraphic but complete.... The style assumes an active reader, one who is able to deduce obvious unsaid consequences of what is said, and who has the self-confidence to trust those deductions. Read every word carefully, because you will seldom be told anything twice." Oy vey, I thought, he's actually *teaching young programmers to write more impossible* man *pages*.

For end users, you'll never get away with this. Raymond may call it "oversimplifying condescension," but the Windows culture understands that end users don't like reading,[9] and if they concede to read your documentation, they will only read the minimum amount, and so you have to explain things repeatedly... indeed the hallmark of a good Windows

7. Raymond, *The Art of UNIX Programming*, p. 379.

8. Ibid., p. 376.

9. Joel Spolsky, *User Interface Design for Programmers* (Apress, 2001). See www.joelonsoftware.com/uibook/chapters/fog0000000062.html.

help file is that any single topic can be read by itself by an average reader without assuming knowledge of any other help topic.

How did we get different core values? This is another reason Raymond's book is so good: He goes deeply into the history and evolution of UNIX and brings new programmers up to speed with all the accumulated history of the culture back to 1969. When UNIX was created and when it formed its cultural values, there *were no end users.* Computers were expensive, CPU time was expensive, and learning about computers meant learning how to program. It's no wonder that the culture that emerged valued things that are useful to other programmers. By contrast, Windows was created with one goal only: to sell as many copies as conceivable at a profit. Scrillions of copies. "A computer on every desktop and in every home" was the explicit goal of the team that created Windows, set its agenda, and determined its core values. Ease of use for nonprogrammers was the only way to get on every desk and in every home and thus usability *über alles* became the cultural norm. Programmers, as an audience, were an extreme afterthought.

The cultural schism is so sharp that UNIX has never really made any inroads on the desktop. Aunt Marge can't really use UNIX, and repeated efforts to make a pretty front end for UNIX that Aunt Marge *can* use have failed, entirely because these efforts were done by programmers who were steeped in the UNIX culture. For example, UNIX has a value of separating policy from mechanism[10] which, historically, came from the designers of X.[11] This directly led to a schism in user interfaces; nobody has ever quite been able to agree on all the details of how the desktop UI should work, *and they think this is OK,* because their culture values this diversity, but for Aunt Marge it is very much *not* OK to have to use a different UI to cut and paste in one program than she uses in another. So here we are, 20 years after UNIX developers started trying to paint a good UI on their systems, and we're still at the point where the CEO of the biggest Linux vendor is telling people that home users should just use Windows.[12] I have heard economists claim that Silicon Valley could never be re-created in, say, France, because the French

---

10. Raymond, *The Art of UNIX Programming*, p. 16–17.

11. See www.x.org/.

12. Munir Kotadia, "Red Hat recommends Windows for consumers," ZDNet UK, November 4, 2003. See news.zdnet.co.uk/software/linuxunix/0,39020390,39117575,00.htm.

culture puts such a high penalty on failure that entrepreneurs are not willing to risk it. Maybe the same thing is true of Linux: It may never be a desktop operating system because the culture values things which prevent it. OS X is the proof: Apple finally created UNIX for Aunt Marge, but only because the engineers and managers at Apple were firmly of the end-user culture (which I've been imperialistically calling "the Windows Culture," even though historically it originated at Apple). They rejected the UNIX culture's fundamental norm of programmer-centricity. They even renamed core directories—heretical!—to use common English words like "applications" and "library" instead of "bin" and "lib."

Raymond does attempt to compare and contrast UNIX to other operating systems, and this is really the weakest part of an otherwise excellent book, because he really doesn't know what he's talking about. Whenever he opens his mouth about Windows, he tends to show that his knowledge of Windows programming comes mostly from reading newspapers, not from actual Windows programming. That's OK; he's not a Windows programmer; we'll forgive that. As is typical from someone with a deep knowledge of one culture, he knows what his culture values but doesn't quite notice the distinction between parts of his culture that are universal (killing old ladies, programs that crash: *always bad*) and parts of the culture that apply only when you're programming for programmers (eating raw fish, command-line arguments: *depends on audience*).

There are too many monocultural programmers who, like the typical American kid who never left St. Paul, Minnesota, can't quite tell the difference between a cultural value and a core human value. I've encountered too many UNIX programmers who sneer at Windows programming, thinking that Windows is heathen and stupid. Raymond all too frequently falls into the trap of disparaging the values of other cultures without considering where they came from. It's rather rare to find such bigotry among Windows programmers, who are, on the whole, solution-oriented and nonideological. At the very least, Windows programmers will concede the faults of their culture and say pragmatically, "Look, if you want to sell a word processor to a lot of people, it has to run on their computers, and if that means we use the Evil Registry instead of elegant ~/.rc files to store our settings, so be it." The very fact that the UNIX world is so full of self-righteous cultural superiority, "advocacy," and Slashdot-karma-whoring sectarianism while the

Windows world is more practical ("yeah, whatever, I just need to make a living here") stems from a culture that feels itself under siege, unable to break out of the server closet and hobbyist market and onto the mainstream desktop. This haughtiness-from-a-position-of-weakness is the biggest flaw of *The Art of UNIX Programming*, but it's not really a big flaw: On the whole, the book is so full of incredibly interesting insight into so many aspects of programming that I'm willing to hold my nose during the rare smelly ideological rants because there's so much to learn about universal ideals from the rest of the book. Indeed, I would recommend this book to developers of any culture in any platform with any goals, because so many of the values that it trumpets are universal. When Raymond points out that the CSV format is inferior to the /etc/passwd format, he's trying to score points for UNIX against Windows,[13] but you know what? He's right. /etc/passwd *is* easier to parse than CSV, and if you read his book, you'll know why, and you'll be a better programmer.

13. Raymond, *The Art of UNIX Programming*, p. 109.

off of their own important work to give you a useful crash report unless you make it completely automatic.

Now that I have my own company, I've made sure that nearly all of our code reports errors back to the development team automatically. Even software that we write for internal use only notifies the development team if a crash occurs. I'm going to share methods and lessons about collecting crash reports from the field that I've learned over the years.

~

Collecting Data

OK, so your code crashed. In almost every programming environment, there's some way to recover from the crash at a central location (see the sidebars for some examples). At this point, instead of letting the program die, we display our automated crash reporting dialog box, which is short and to the point:

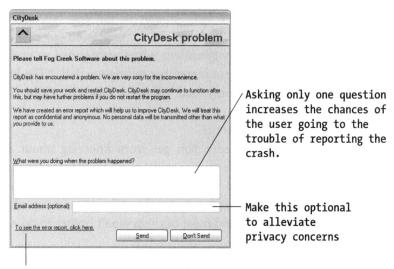

Asking only one question increases the chances of the user going to the trouble of reporting the crash.

Make this optional to alleviate privacy concerns

To ensure privacy and anonymity, provide a way for the user to see exactly what is being transmitted.

One thing I've learned over the years is that the more questions you ask people, the less likely they are to answer. So we ask only the bare minimum number of questions that we think will help us diagnose the problem. Almost any other important information can probably be obtained automatically; for example, what version of operating system they are using, how much RAM they have, etc.

It's important to emphasize the anonymity and privacy of this crash submittal. People working on confidential data may not be willing to submit a crash report if they suspect we're about to upload all their sensitive work, so we provide a link that users can click on to see exactly what we're going to transmit. To avoid even the appearance of impropriety, be careful to tell people about any automatically gathered information that you're transmitting, too.

The next question is, what data should we collect automatically that will help our developers find the crash? There is a temptation to grab *everything*—every bit of system information you can find: the versions of every DLL and COM control on the user's system, even a complete core dump.

After several years working as a developer and never quite knowing what I'm supposed to do with core dumps, I have discovered that collecting this data is not, actually, necessary. We've found that knowing the exact line of code where the code crashed is enough information to fix almost any crash. For those rare cases where this isn't enough information, you can contact one of the users who experienced the crash via email and ask for any additional information that might help.

The benefit of gathering so little information is that the crash reporting process is very fast, making users less impatient. Just checking the version numbers of all the DLLs and COM controls can take quite a while, especially when you factor in the upload time over modems, and this effort very rarely provides useful information. Even if you discover that a certain crash happens with only a certain version of one of Microsoft's system DLLs, what are you going to do about it? You still have to fix the code to work around the crash.

Data We Collect Automatically

- The exact version of our product

- The OS version and the version of Internet Explorer (So many parts of Windows are actually provided by Internet Explorer and its components that this is important even for GUI applications.)

- The file and line number in the code where the crash occurred

- The error message, as a string

- A unique numeric code for this type of error

- The user's description of what they were doing

- The user's email address

When the user provides their email address, developers can hit the Reply button in the database to send them an email message on the spot if they need additional information. The database automatically keeps a copy of all the correspondence related to this bug, incoming and outgoing, in the bug report itself.

~

Phoning Home

Thanks to the pervasiveness of the Internet, there's almost always one best way to send the information home: over the Web. By sending a standard HTTP request, you will get your bug report past almost any kind of firewall customers may have in place. Virtually every programming environment now has built-in libraries to send an HTTP request and get the response back. For example, on Windows, there are built-in functions in the WININET library that use Internet Explorer's network transport code to send an HTTP request and get the response. The best thing about these functions is that even if the user has configured his web browser to go through a proxy server, which is common inside firewalls, the WININET calls will automatically go through the proxy server, with no additional work on your part.

Our server returns a very short XML file that indicates that the report was received, and includes a message that is displayed to the user. If your application is web based, there's something even easier you can do: display a web page containing a form that submits data to your server.

For certain types of applications, instead of sending the crash report right away, you may want to try writing it out to a file or the registry, and then sending it the next time the user launches the program. I call this technique *delayed transmission*. Although this will delay the report a bit, it has the advantage that if the crash was severe enough that the application is too messed up to transmit a bug report, you'll still get the report.

All crash reports arrive at Fog Creek via a single URL on our public-facing server. Our bug tracking database receives bug reports via this unique URL. In fact, that URL is the only public access to our database; everything else is locked out, so people can submit bugs, but they can't get into the database. Here's what a bug report looks like in FogBUGZ:

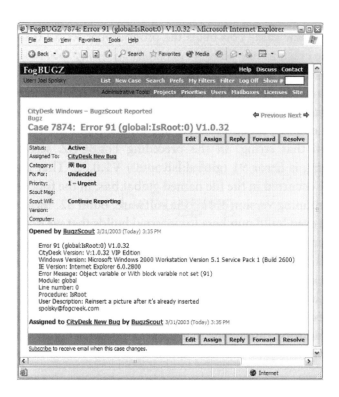

months ago; they just won't remember enough details. But I've found that if the same crash has happened several times, inevitably one of the users has given me enough clues about what they were doing that I can repro the bug in the lab. Indeed, it's very rare to know that a given line of code has crashed without having a good idea for what the problem might be, even if it's hard to figure out the repro case. Once, I literally worked my way backward through the code doing arithmetic and using applied logic to figure out repro steps. Hmm, if this is crashing, then this value must be negative. If it's negative, then this IF statement must have been true. And so on, until I figured out what combination of values led to the crash and realized what must have caused them.

~

Triage

As soon as you build an automatic crash-reporting system, no matter how rock solid it is, you're going to get a pretty steady stream of crash reports. So good triage skills—deciding which bugs are most important to fix, and ignoring the others—are more important than usual.

When I investigate the reports we receive, I usually discover various signs of bugs that we're probably never going to fix. For example:

- The user's computer is failing or has faulty RAM.
- The user is experimenting by manually editing our files.
- The user is running an old operating system like Windows 95 that is in the advanced stages of crashing.
- The user is running our program under severe low-memory conditions, possibly with a full disk and full memory.

And sometimes, you just can't figure out what caused the crash, especially with crashes that only happened *once*. In fact, my policy is that I won't even *look* at a crash that only happened once. We've got bigger fish to fry. If it's not reproducible in the field, it's not likely to be reproducible in the lab.

~

Is This for You?

So, now that you've seen what's involved, is crash reporting for you? The answer, to some extent, depends on your user base.

If you're developing corporate software for in-house use, you're probably not going to get as much value out of automatic crash reporting. Corporate software is usually written to solve a particular problem, at great expense relative to off-the-shelf software. Once the problem is solved, it's not worth spending any more money on that particular project. If the code crashes once a week, it can be annoying, but there may be no business justification to spend several thousand dollars having a developer fix it. It might be *nice*, but it would not be *profitable*. Idealistic software developers on in-house projects are often disappointed to discover that as soon as their code is "good enough," their managers tell them to stop working on it. It has solved the business problem, even if the quality could be better, and any marginal work has zero return on investment. Still, many corporate software developers are forced to work literally without any QA or testing staff, and automatic crash detection may be the only way to get any kind of bug reports at all.

On the other hand, if you're developing shrinkwrapped or consumer software, quality is, quite literally, a competitive advantage. And your software will be running in a hostile environment. Consumer PCs are a *mess*. No two are the same. They've all got slightly different hardware and software configurations. PC companies ship these things with every imaginable piece of junkware preinstalled. And a lot of consumers gleefully download and install every shiny new object they can get their hands on, including those oh-so-clever utilities that actually inject themselves into the process spaces of other running applications. And most home users don't know enough about computers to keep their systems operating well. In such a hostile environment, automatic crash reporting is the only way to get to the level of quality that the market demands. Building a robust system to handle crashes from the field, report them, classify them, and track them will delight your customers and pay for itself many times over in the quality of code that you ship.

~

Handling Crashes

Handling Crashes in Visual Basic Code

Because a typical Visual Basic 6.0 event-driven program has so many entry points (one for each event that you handle), the only way to catch crashes that occur *anywhere* in the code is to add error handling to *every* function. Here's what *all* our functions look like:

```
Private Sub cmd_Click()
On Error GoTo ERROR_cmd_Click

    ... the actual code for the function ...
    Exit Sub

ERROR_cmd_Click:
    HandleError "moduleName", "cmd_Click"
End Sub
```

Adding this code can be a pain; luckily there's a utility you can get called ErrorAssist (http://www.errorassist.com), which will add error-trapping code to all your functions automatically. In every case, we just call a global function called HandleError, which displays our custom crash dialog.

Handling Crashes in Windows API Code

The Win32 API contains a concept called *structured exception handling*. When a crash occurs, Windows searches for the current *unhandled exception handler* function and calls it. If there is no unhandled exception function, it will display the usual user-aggressive "This program has performed an illegal operation" dialog.

To install your own unhandled exception function, you have to do two things. First, implement your own function of the form

```
LONG UnhandledExceptionFilter(
  STRUCT _EXCEPTION_POINTERS *ExceptionInfo
);
```

Then call the SetUnhandledExceptionFilter function, passing in a pointer to your UnhandledExceptionFilter function.

Another way to accomplish the same thing from C++ code is to surround the main entry point with a __try/__catch clause. Notice the two underlines, which cause the compiler to handle structured exceptions that come from low-level failures like dereferencing null pointers, not the garden-variety C++ exceptions you throw yourself and handle with try and catch.

Search for *Using Structured Exception Handling* in the Windows Platform SDK or MSDN for more details.

Handling Crashes in ASP Applications

Microsoft's Internet Services Manager lets you set up a custom error-handling page, either HTML or ASP, which is processed for any scripting errors that aren't handled with On Error statements. In particular, when an ASP application crashes or has an unhandled error of any sort, the page is redirected to the error handler for "500;100" errors. In all our applications, we have an ASP page set up to catch 500;100 errors.

That page contains the following key bit of VBScript code:

```
Set objASPError = Server.GetLastError
```

Now you'll have an object called objASPError, which contains lots of useful data about the crash that just occurred, including the file and the line number.

Sample code for handling ASP errors comes preinstalled on every computer with IIS: look in the \windows\help\iishelp\common directory for a file called 500-100.asp. This simply displays the details of the ASP error to the end user. Using the 500-100.asp file as a starting point, you can create your own customized message page containing a form with hidden elements containing the crash data. The form should have an action attribute that submits all the error information to another web page.

twenty

THE GUERILLA GUIDE
TO INTERVIEWING

Pop quiz.

A motley gang of anarchists, free-love advocates, and banana-rights agitators have hijacked *The Love Boat* out of Puerto Vallarta and are threatening to sink it in seven days with all 616 passengers and 327 crew members unless their demands are met. The demand? A million dollars in small unmarked bills, and a GPL implementation of WATFIV, the esteemed Waterloo Fortran IV compiler. (It's surprising how few things the free-love people can find to agree on with the banana-rights people.)

As chief programmer of the Festival Cruise programming staff, you've got to decide if you can deliver a Fortran compiler from scratch in seven days. You've got a staff of two programmers to help you.

Can you do it?

"Well, I suppose, it depends," you say. One of the benefits of writing this book is that I get to put words into your mouth and you can't do a darn thing about it.

On what?

"Um, will my team be able to use UML-generating tools?"

Does that really matter? Three programmers, seven days, Waterloo Fortran IV. Are UML tools going to make or break it?

"I guess not."

OK, so, what does it depend on?

something. The trick is to tell the difference between the superstars and the maybes, because the secret is that you don't want to hire any of the maybes. Ever.

At the end of the interview, you must be prepared to make a sharp decision about the candidate. There are only two possible outcomes to this decision: *Hire* or *No Hire*. There is no other possible answer. *Never* say, "Hire, but not for my team." This is rude and implies that the candidate is not smart enough to work with you, but maybe he's smart enough for those losers over in that other team. If you find yourself tempted to say "Hire, but not in my team," simply translate that mechanically to "No Hire," and you'll be OK. Even if you have a candidate who would be brilliant at doing your particular task, but wouldn't be very good in another team, that's a *No Hire*. In software, things change so often and so rapidly that you need people who can succeed at just about any programming task that you throw at them. If for some reason you find an idiot savant who is really, really, really good at SQL but completely incapable of ever learning any other topic, *No Hire*. You'll solve some short-term pain in exchange for a lot of long-term pain.

Never say "Maybe, I can't tell." If you can't tell, that means *No Hire*. It's really easier than you'd think. Can't tell? Just say no! If you are on the fence, that means *No Hire*. Never say, "Well, Hire, I guess, but I'm a little bit concerned about..."; that's a *No Hire* as well. Mechanically translate all the waffling to "no," and you'll be all right.

Why am I so hardnosed about this? It's because it is much, *much* better to reject a good candidate than to accept a bad candidate. A bad candidate will cost a lot of money and effort and waste other people's time fixing all their bugs. Firing someone you hired by mistake can take months and be nightmarishly difficult, especially if they decide to be litigious about it. In some situations it may be completely impossible to fire anyone. Bad employees demoralize the good employees. And they might be bad programmers but really *nice people* or maybe they *really need this job*, so you can't bear to fire them, or you can't fire them without pissing everybody off, or whatever. It's just a bad scene.

On the other hand, if you reject a good candidate, I mean, I *guess* in some existential sense an injustice has been done, but, hey, if they're so smart, don't worry, they'll get *lots* of good job offers. Don't be afraid that you're going to reject too many people and you won't be able to find anyone to hire. During the interview, it's not your problem. Of course, it's important to seek out good candidates. But once you're actually interviewing someone, pretend that you've got 900 more people lined up outside the door. Don't lower your standards no matter how hard it seems to find those great candidates.

OK, I didn't tell you the most important part—how do you know whether to hire someone?

In principle, it's simple. You're looking for people who are

1. Smart

2. Get things done

That's it. That's all you're looking for. Memorize that. Recite it to yourself before you go to bed every night. You don't have enough time to figure out much more in a short interview, so don't waste time trying to figure out whether the candidate might be pleasant to be stuck in an airport with, or whether they really know ATL and COM programming or if they're just faking it.

People who are *Smart* but don't *Get Things Done* often have PhDs and work in big companies where nobody listens to them because they are completely impractical. They would rather mull over something academic about a problem rather than ship on time. These kind of people can be identified because they love to point out the theoretical similarity between two widely divergent concepts. For example, they will say, "Spreadsheets are really just a special case of programming language," and then go off for a week and write a thrilling, brilliant whitepaper about the theoretical computational linguistic attributes of a spreadsheet as a programming language. Smart, but not useful. The other way to identify these people is that they have a tendency to show up at your office, coffee mug in hand, and try to start a long conversation about the relative merits of Java introspection vs. COM type libraries *on the day you are trying to ship a beta.*

People who *Get Things Done* but are not *Smart* will do stupid things, seemingly without thinking about them, and somebody else will have to come clean up their mess later. This makes them net *liabilities* to the company because not only do they fail to contribute, but they also soak up good people's time. They are the kind of people who copy big chunks of code around rather than writing a subroutine, because it gets the job done, just not in the smartest way.

How do you detect *smart* in an interview? The first good sign is that you don't have to explain things over and over again. The conversation just flows. Often, the candidate says something that shows real insight, or brains, or mental acuity. So an important part of the interview is creating a situation where someone can show you how smart they are. The worst kind of interviewer is the blowhard. That's the kind who blabs the whole time and barely leaves the candidate time to say, "yes, that's *so* true, I *couldn't agree with you more.*" Blowhards hire everyone; they think that the candidate must be smart because "he thinks so much like me!"

The second worst kind of interviewer is the Quiz Show Interviewer. This is the kind of person who thinks that smart means "knows a lot of facts." They just ask a bunch of trivia questions about programming and give points for correct answers. Just for fun, here is the worst interview question on Earth: "What's the difference between varchar and varchar2 in Oracle 8i?" This is a terrible question. There is no possible, imaginable correlation between people who know that particular piece of trivia and people who you want to hire. Who cares what the difference is? You can find out online in about 15 seconds! Remember, smart does *not* mean "knows the answer to trivia questions." Anyway, software teams want to hire people with *aptitude*, not a particular skill set. Any skill set that people can bring to the job will be technologically obsolete in a couple of years, anyway, so it's better to hire people who are going to be able to learn any new technology rather than people who happen to know how to make JDBC talk to a MySQL database *right this minute.*

But in general, the way to learn the most about a person is to let them do the talking. Give them open-ended questions and problems.

So, what do you ask?

∽

What to Ask

My personal list of interview questions originates from my first job at Microsoft. There are actually hundreds of famous Microsoft interview questions. Everybody has a set of questions that they really like. You, too, will develop a particular set of questions and a personal interviewing style that helps you make the Hire/No Hire decision. Here are some techniques I have used that have been successful.

Before the interview, I read over the candidate's résumé and jot down an interview plan on a scrap of paper. That's just a list of questions I want to ask. Here's a typical plan for interviewing a programmer:

1. Introduction

2. Question about recent project candidate worked on

3. Impossible Question

4. Programming Question

5. Are you satisfied?

6. Do you have any questions?

I am very, very careful to avoid anything that might give me some preconceived notions about the candidate. If you think someone is smart before they even walk into the room, just because they have a PhD from MIT, then nothing they can say in one hour is going to overcome your initial prejudice. If you think they are a bozo because they went to community college, nothing they can say will overcome that initial impression. An interview is like a very, very delicate scale—it's very hard to judge someone based on a one-hour interview, and it may seem like a very close call. But if you know a little bit about the candidate beforehand, it's like a big weight on one side of the scale, and the interview is useless. Once, right before an interview, a recruiter came into my office. "You're going to *love* this guy," she said. *Boy* did this make me mad. What I should have said was, "Well, if you're so sure I'm going to love him, why don't you just hire him instead of wasting my time going through this interview." But I was young and naive, so I interviewed him. When he said not-so-smart things, I thought to myself, "gee, must be the exception that proves the rule." I looked at everything he said through rose-colored glasses. I wound up saying *Hire* even though he was a crappy candidate. You know what? Everybody else who interviewed him said *No Hire*. So, don't listen to recruiters, don't ask around about the person before you interview them, and never, ever talk to the other interviewers about the candidate until you've both made your decisions independently. That's the scientific method.

Smart candidates will realize that you are not quizzing them on their knowledge, and they will enthusiastically leap into trying to figure out some back-of-the-envelope answer. "Well, let's see, the population of L.A. is about 7 million; each person in L.A. has about 2.5 cars..." Of course it's OK if they are radically wrong. The important thing is that they leapt into the question enthusiastically. They may try to figure out the capacity of a gas station. "Gee, it takes 4 minutes to tank up, gas stations have about 10 pumps and are open about 18 hours a day..." They may try to figure it out by area. Sometimes they will surprise you with their creativity or ask for a Los Angeles *Yellow Pages*. All good signs.

Not-so-smart candidates will get flustered and upset. They will just stare at you like you landed from Mars. You have to coach them. "Well, if you were building a new city the size of Los Angeles, how many gas stations would you put in it?" You can give them little hints. "How long does it take to fill up a tank of gas?" Still, with not-smart candidates, you will have to drag them along while they sit there stupidly and wait for you to rescue them. These people are not problem solvers, and you don't want them working for you.

4. Programming Question

For this part of the interview, which should take up most of the time, I ask candidates to write a small function in C (or whatever language they are comfortable with). Here are some typical problems I would ask:

1. Reverse a string in place

2. Reverse a linked list

3. Count all the bits that are on in a byte

4. Binary search

5. Find the longest run in a string

6. atoi

7. itoa (great, because they have to use a stack or strrev)

Don't give them any problems that take more than about ten lines of code; you won't have time for that.

Let's look at a couple of these in detail. 1). Reverse a string in place. Every candidate I've ever interviewed in my life has done this wrong the first time. Without exception, they try to allocate another buffer and reverse the string into that buffer. The trouble is, who allocates the buffer? Who frees the buffer? In giving this question to dozens of candidates, I found out an interesting fact: Most people who think that they know C really do not understand memory or pointers. They just don't get it. It's amazing that these people are working as programmers, but they are. With this question, here are some ways to judge the candidate:

Is their function fast? Look at how many times they call strlen. I've seen $O(n^2)$ algorithms for strrev when it should be $O(n)$, because they are calling strlen again and again in a loop.

Do they use pointer arithmetic? This is a good sign. Many "C programmers" just don't know how to make pointer arithmetic work. Now, ordinarily, I wouldn't reject a candidate just because he lacked a particular skill. However, I've come to realize that understanding pointers in C is not a skill, it's an aptitude. In first-year computer science classes, there are always about 200 kids at the beginning of the semester, all of whom wrote complex adventure games in BASIC for their PCs when they were four years old. They are having a good ol' time learning Pascal in college, until one day their professor introduces pointers, and suddenly, *they don't get it*. They just don't understand anything any more. Ninety percent of the class goes off and becomes Political Science majors, then they tell their friends that there weren't enough good-looking members of the appropriate sex in their CompSci classes, that's why they switched. *For some reason most people seem to be born without the part of the brain that understands pointers.* Pointers require a complex form of doubly indirected thinking that some people just can't do, and it's pretty crucial to good programming. A lot of the "script jocks" who started programming by copying JavaScript snippets into their web pages and went on to learn Visual Basic never learned about pointers, and they can never quite produce code of the quality you need.

Let's look at problem 3, Count the bits in a byte. You're not looking to see if they learned the bitwise operators in C, because that's something you can look up. Feel free to help them with those. The interesting thing is to watch them write a subroutine that counts all the bits in a byte, then ask them to make it faster. Really smart candidates will create a lookup table (after all, it's only got 256 entries) that they only have to create once. With good candidates, you can have a really interesting conversation about the different space/speed tradeoffs. Press them further: Tell them you don't want to spend any time building the lookup table during initialization. Brilliant candidates might even suggest a caching scheme where bits are counted the first time they are used, and then stored in a lookup table so they don't have to be counted if they are used again. Really, really brilliant candidates will try to devise a way to compute the table using some kind of a shortcut taking advantage of the patterns that occur. The general idea is that they can refine the code, optimize it, and come up with ideas for improving it.

Reassure candidates that you understand that it's hard to write code without an editor, and you will forgive them if their paper gets really messy. Also you understand that it's hard to write bug-free code without a compiler, and you will take that into account.

Some signs of a good programmer: They tend to have some kind of a variable naming convention, even a primitive one. Good programmers tend to use really short variable names for loop indices. If they name their loop index CurrentPagePositionLoopCounter, it is a sure sign that they have not written a lot of code in their life. In C, look for good habits like putting the constant on the left-hand side of the "==" (e.g., if (0==x) instead of if (x==0)), which prevents accidentally using a "=" resulting in an assignment instead of a test. Some programmers think this is awkward and think that the compiler should catch those errors for you, so I'm not saying you should always use 0==x, but if you see it, it's probably a good sign. Good programmers instinctively know what the invariant should be in a while loop. They know without thinking that to iterate through an array in C, it's always while (index < length), not <=. In C++, they make their destructors virtual.

Good programmers plan before they write code, especially when pointers are involved. For example, if you ask them to reverse a linked list, good candidates will always make a little drawing on the side and draw all the pointers and where they go. They have to. It is humanly impossible to write code to reverse a linked list without drawing little boxes with arrows between them. Bad programmers will start writing code right away.

5. Are You Satisfied?

Inevitably, you will see a bug in their function. So we come to the next question from my interview plan: Are you satisfied with that code? You may want to ask, "OK, so where's the bug?" The quintessential Open-Ended Question From Hell. All programmers make mistakes, and there's nothing wrong with that; they just have to be able to find them. With the string functions, most college kids forget to null-terminate the new string. With almost any function, they are likely to have off-by-one errors. They will forget semicolons sometimes. Their function won't work correctly on 0 length strings, or it will GPF if malloc fails, and so on. Very, very rarely, you will find a candidate who doesn't have any bugs the first time. In this case, this question is even more fun. When you say, "There's a bug in that code," they will review their code carefully, and then you get to see if they can be diplomatic yet firm in asserting that the code is perfect.

6. Do You Have Any Questions?

As the last step in an interview, ask the candidate if they have any questions. Remember, even though you're interviewing them, the good candidates have lots of choices about where to work, and they're using this day to figure out if they want to work for you.

Some interviewees try to judge if the candidate asks "intelligent" questions. Personally, I don't care what questions they ask; by this point I've already made my decision. The trouble is, candidates have to see about five or six people in one day, and it's hard for them to ask five or six people different, brilliant questions, so if they don't have any questions, fine.

I always leave about five minutes at the end of the interview to sell the candidate on the company and the job. This is actually important *even if your decision is No Hire.* If you've been lucky enough to find a really good candidate, you want to do everything you can at this point to make sure that they want to come work for you. But even if they are a bad candidate, you want them to like your company and go away with a positive impression.

Ah, I just remembered that I promised to give you some more examples of really bad questions to avoid.

Treating your rocket-scientist employees as if they were still in kindergarten is not an isolated phenomenon. Almost every company has some kind of incentive program that is insulting and demeaning.

At two of the companies I've worked for, the most stressful time of year was the twice-yearly performance review period. For some reason, the Juno HR department and the Microsoft HR department must have copied their performance review system out of the same Dilbertesque management book, because both programs worked exactly the same way. First, you gave "anonymous" upward reviews for your direct manager (as if that could be done in an honest way). Then, you filled out optional "self-evaluation" forms, which your manager "took into account" in preparing your performance review. Finally, you got a numerical score, in lots of non-scalar categories like "works well with others," from 1 to 5, where the only possible scores were actually 3 or 4. Managers submitted bonus recommendations upwards, which were completely ignored and everybody received bonuses that were almost completely random. The system never took into account the fact that people have different and unique talents, all of which are needed for a team to work well.

Performance reviews were stressful for a couple of reasons. Many of my friends, especially the ones whose talents were very significant but didn't show up on the traditional scales, tended to get lousy performance reviews. For example, one friend of mine was a cheerful catalyst, a bouncy cruise director who motivated everyone else when the going got tough. He was the glue that held his team together. But he tended to get negative reviews, because his manager didn't understand his contribution. Another friend was incredibly insightful strategically; his conversations with other people about how things should be done allowed everyone else to do much better work. He tended to spend more time than average trying out new technologies; in this area he was invaluable to the rest of the team. But in terms of lines of code, he wrote less than average, and his manager was too stupid to notice all his other contributions, so he always got negative reviews, too. Negative reviews, obviously, have a devastating effect on morale. In fact, giving somebody a review that is positive, but not *as* positive as that person expected, also has a negative effect on morale.

The effect of reviews on morale is lopsided: While negative reviews hurt morale a lot, positive reviews have no effect on morale or productivity. The people who get them are already working productively. For them, a positive review makes them feel like they are doing good work in order to get the positive review—as if they were Pavlovian dogs working for a treat, instead of professionals who actually care about the quality of the work they do.

And herein lies the rub. Most people think that they do pretty good work (even if they don't). It's just a little trick our minds play on us to keep life bearable. So if everybody thinks they do good work, and the reviews are merely *correct* (which is not very easy to achieve), then *most people will be disappointed by their reviews*. The cost of this in morale is hard to understate. On teams where performance reviews are done honestly, they tend to result in a week or so of depressed morale, moping, and some resignations. They tend to drive wedges between team members, often because the poorly rated are jealous of the highly rated, in a process that DeMarco and Lister call *teamicide*, the inadvertent destruction of jelled teams.[3]

Alfie Kohn, in a now-classic *Harvard Business Review* article, wrote:

> ...at least two dozen studies over the last three decades have conclusively shown that people who expect to receive a reward for completing a task or for doing that task successfully simply do not perform as well as those who expect no reward at all.[4]

---

3. Tom DeMarco and Timothy Lister, *Peopleware: Productive Projects and Teams, Second Edition* (Dorset House, 1999), p. 132–139.

4. Alfie Kohn, "Why Incentive Plans Cannot Work." *Harvard Business Review,* September 1, 1993. See www.hbsp.harvard.edu/hbsp/prod_detail.asp?93506.

He concludes that *"incentives (or bribes) simply can't work in the workplace."* DeMarco and Lister go further, stating unequivocally that any kind of workplace competition, any scheme of rewards and punishments, and even the old-fashioned trick of "catching people doing something right and rewarding them," all do more harm than good. Giving somebody *positive* reinforcement (such as stupid company ceremonies where people get plaques) implies that they only did it for the Lucite plaque; it implies that they are not independent enough to work unless they are going to get a cookie; and it's insulting and demeaning.

Most software managers have no choice but to go along with performance review systems that are already in place. If you're in this position, the only way to prevent teamicide is to simply give everyone on your team a gushing review. But if you do have any choice in the matter, I'd recommend that you run fleeing from any kind of performance review, incentive bonus, or stupid corporate employee-of-the-month program.

twenty-two

TOP FIVE (WRONG) REASONS YOU DON'T HAVE TESTERS

Sunday, April 30, 2000

In 1992, James Gleick was having a lot of problems with buggy software. A new version of Microsoft Word for Windows had come out, which Gleick, a science writer, considered to be *awful*. He wrote a lengthy article in the Sunday *New York Times Magazine* that could only be described as a flame, skewering the Word team for being unresponsive to the requests of customers and delivering an enormously buggy product.[1]

Later, as a customer of a local Internet provider Panix (which also happens to be my Internet provider), he wanted a way to sort and filter his mail automatically. The UNIX tool for doing this is called procmail, which is really arcane and has the kind of interface that *even* the most hardcore UNIX groupies will admit is obscure.

Anyway, Mr. Gleick inadvertently made some kind of innocent typo in procmail which deleted all his email. In a rage, he decided that he was going to create his own Internet access company. Hiring Uday Ivatury, a programmer, he created Pipeline, which was really quite a bit ahead of its time: It was the first commercial provider of Internet access with any kind of graphical interface.

---

1. James Gleick, "Chasing Bugs in the Electronic Village." *New York Times Magazine*, August 4, 1992. Available online at www.around.com/bugs.html.

~

2. My software is on the Web. I can fix bugs in a second.

Bwa ha ha ha ha! OK, it's true, Web distribution lets you distribute bug fixes much faster than the old days of packaged software. But don't underestimate the cost of fixing a bug, even on a website, after the project has already frozen. For one thing, you may introduce even more bugs when you fix the first one. But a worse problem is that if you look around at the process you have in place for rolling out new versions, you'll realize that it may be quite an expensive proposition to roll out fixes on the Web. Besides the bad impression you will make, which leads to boo-hoo excuse number 3.

~

3. My customers will test the software for me.

Ah, the dreaded "Netscape Defense." This poor company did an almost supernatural amount of damage to its reputation through their "testing" methodology:

1. When the programmers are about halfway done, release the software on the Web without any testing.

2. When the programmers *say* they are done, release the software on the Web without any testing.

3. Repeat six or seven times.

4. Call one of those versions the "final version."

5. Release .01, .02, .03 versions every time an embarrassing bug is mentioned on CNET.

This company pioneered the idea of "wide betas." Literally *millions* of people would download these unfinished, buggy releases. In the first few years, almost everybody using Netscape was using some kind of pre-release or beta version. As a result, most people think that Netscape software is really buggy. Even if the final release was usually reasonably unbuggy, Netscape had so doggone *many* people using buggy versions that the *average* impression that most people have of the software was pretty poor.

Besides, the whole point of letting "your customers" do the testing is that they find the bugs, and you fix them. Unfortunately, neither Netscape, nor any other company on earth, has the manpower to sift through bug reports from 2,000,000 customers and decide what's really important. When I reported bugs in Netscape 2.0, the bug reporting website repeatedly crashed and simply did not let me report a bug (which, of course, would have gone into a black hole anyway). But Netscape doesn't learn. Testers of the current "preview" version, 6.0, have complained in newsgroups that the bug reporting website *still* just doesn't allow submissions. Years later! Same problem!

Of those zillions of bug reports, I would bet that almost all of them were about the same set of five or ten really *obvious* bugs, anyway. Buried in that haystack will be one or two interesting, difficult-to-find bugs that somebody has gone to the trouble of submitting, but nobody is looking at all these reports anyway, so it is lost.

The worst thing about this form of testing is the remarkably bad impression you will make of your company. When UserLand released the first Windows version of their flagship Frontier product, I downloaded it and started working through the tutorial. Unfortunately, Frontier crashed several times. I was literally following the instructions exactly as they were printed in the tutorial, and I just could not get more than two minutes into the program. I felt like nobody at UserLand had even done the *minimum* amount of testing, making sure that the *tutorial* works. The low perceived quality of the product turned me off of Frontier for an awfully long time.

~

4. Anybody qualified to be a good tester doesn't want to work as a tester.

This one is painful. It's very hard to hire good testers. With testers, like programmers, the best ones are *an order of magnitude* better than the average ones. At Juno, we had one tester, Jill McFarlane, who found *three times as many bugs* as *all four other testers, combined.* I'm not exaggerating; I actually measured this. She was more than *twelve times* more productive than the average tester. When she quit, I sent an email to the CEO saying "I'd rather have Jill on Mondays and Tuesdays than the rest of the QA team put together."

Unfortunately, most people who are that smart will tend to get bored with day-to-day testing, so the best testers tend to last for about three or four months and then move on.

The only thing to do about this problem is to recognize that it exists, and deal with it. Here are some suggestions:

- Use testing as a career move up from technical support. Tedious as testing may be, it sure beats dealing with irate users on the phone, and this may be a way to eliminate some of the churn from the technical support side.

- Allow testers to develop their careers by taking programming classes, and encourage the smarter ones to develop automated test suites using programming tools and scripting languages. This is a heck of a lot more interesting than testing the same dialog again and again and again.

- Recognize that you will have a lot of turnover among your top testers. Hire aggressively to keep a steady inflow of people. Don't stop hiring just because you temporarily have a full manifest, 'cause da golden age ain't gonna last.

- Look for "nontraditional" workers: smart teenagers, college kids, and retirees working part time. You could create a stunningly good testing department with two or three top-notch full-timers and an army of kids from Bronx Science (a top-ranked high school in New York) working summers in exchange for college money.

- Hire temps. If you hire about ten temps to come in and bang on your software for a few days, you'll find a tremendous number of bugs. Two or three of those temps are likely to have good testing skills, in which case it's worth buying out their contracts to get them full time. Recognize in advance that some of the temps are likely to be worthless as testers; send them home and move on. That's what temp agencies are for.

Here's one way *not* to deal with it:

- Don't even think of trying to tell college computer science graduates that they can come work for you, but "everyone has to do a stint in QA for a while before moving on to code." I've seen a lot of this. Programmers do not make good testers, and you'll lose a good programmer, who is a lot harder to replace.

And finally, the number one stupid reason people don't hire testers:

$\sim$

5. I can't afford testers!

This is the stupidest, and it's the easiest to debunk. No matter how hard it is to find testers, they are *still* cheaper than programmers. A lot cheaper. And if you don't hire testers, you're going to have programmers doing testing. And if you think it's bad when you have testers churning out, just wait till you see how expensive it is to replace that star programmer, at $100,000 a year, who got sick of being told to "spend a few weeks on testing before we release" and moved on to a more professional company. You could hire three testers for a *year* just to cover the recruiter's fee on the replacement programmer.

Skimping on testers is such an outrageous false economy that I'm simply blown away that more people don't recognize it.

twenty-three

HUMAN TASK SWITCHES CONSIDERED HARMFUL

MONDAY, FEBRUARY 12, 2001

When you're managing a team of programmers, one of the first things you have to learn to get right is task allocation. That's just a five-dollar word for *giving people things to do*. It's known colloquially as "file dumping" in Hebrew (because you dump files in people's laps). And how you decide which files to dump in which laps is one of the areas where you can get incredible productivity benefits if you do it right. Do it wrong, and you can create one of those gnarly situations where nobody gets anything accomplished and everybody complains that "nothing ever gets done around here."

Since this book is for programmers, I'm going to warm up your brains a little bit with a programming problem.

Suppose you have two separate computations to perform, A and B. Each computation requires 10 seconds of CPU time. You have one CPU that, for the sake of this problem, doesn't have anything else in the queue.

On our CPU, multitasking is optional. So you can either do these computations one after the other by using sequential processing:

Computation A   Computation B

1 2 3 4 5 6 7 8 9 10 `11` `12` `13` `14` `15` `16` `17` `18` `19` `20`

Or, you can multitask:

1 `2` 3 `4` 5 `6` 7 `8` 9 `10` 11 `12` 13 `14` 15 `16` 17 `18` 19 `20`

If you multitask, on this particular CPU, tasks run for 1 second at a time, and a task switch takes no time at all.

Which would you rather do? Most people's gut reaction is that multitasking is better. In both cases, you have to wait 20 seconds to get both of your answers. But think about how long it takes to get the results to *each* computation.

In both cases, the results of Computation B (shown in black) take 20 seconds to arrive. But look at Computation A. With multitasking, its results take 19 seconds to arrive...yet with sequential processing they are ready in only 10 seconds.

In other words, in this nice contrived example, the *average time per computation* is lower (15 seconds rather than 19.5 seconds) when you do sequential processing rather than multitasking. (Actually, it's not such a contrived example—it's based on a real problem Jared had to solve at work.)

Method	Computation A takes	Computation B takes	Average
Sequential	10 seconds	20 seconds	15
Multitasking	19 seconds	20 seconds	19.5

Earlier I said that "a task switch takes no time at all." Actually, on real CPUs, a task switch takes a little bit of time—basically enough time to save out the state of the CPU registers and load the CPU registers for the other task. Realistically, this is as close to negligible as possible. But to make life interesting, let's imagine that task switches take half a second. Now things look even worse:

Method	Computation A takes	Computation B takes	Average
Sequential	10 seconds	20 + 1 task switch = 20.5 seconds	15.25
Multitasking	19 + 18 task switches = 28 seconds	20 + 19 task switches = 29.5 seconds	28.75

Now—just humor me, I know this is silly—what if task switches take a whole minute?

Method	Computation A takes	Computation B takes	Average
Sequential	10 seconds	20 + 1 task switch = 80 seconds	45 seconds
Multitasking	19 + 18 task switches = 1099 seconds	20 + 19 task switches = 1160 seconds	almost 19 minutes!

The longer a task switch takes, the worse the multitasking penalty. That, in and of itself, is not so earth shaking, is it? Pretty soon I'm going to be getting irate email from morons accusing me of being "against" multitasking. "Do you want to go back to the days of DOS when you had to exit WordPerfect to run 1-2-3?" they will ask me.

But that's not my point. I just want you to agree with me that in this kind of example:

1. Sequential processing gets you results faster *on average*.

2. The longer it takes to task switch, the bigger the penalty you pay for multitasking.

OK, back to the more interesting topic of managing humans, not CPUs. The trick here is that when you manage *programmers*, specifically, task switches take a really, really, really long time. That's because programming is the kind of task where you have to keep a lot of things in your head at once. The more things you remember at once, the more productive you are at programming. Programmers coding at full throttle are keeping zillions of things in their heads at once: everything, including names of variables, data structures, important APIs, the names of utility functions that they wrote and call a lot, even the name of the subdirectory where they store their source code. If you send that programmer to Crete for a three-week vacation, they will forget it *all*. The human brain seems to move it out of short-term RAM and swaps it out onto a backup tape where it takes forever to retrieve.

How long? Well, my software company recently dropped what we were doing (developing our product CityDesk) to help a client with a bit of an emergency situation for three weeks. When we got back to the office, it seemed to take *another* three weeks to get back to full speed on CityDesk.

On the individual level, have you ever noticed that you can assign one job to one person, and they'll do a great job, but if you assign *two* jobs to that person, they won't really get anything done? They'll either do one job well and neglect the other, or they'll do both jobs so slowly you feel like *slugs* have more zip. That's because programming tasks take so long to task switch. When I have two programming projects on my plate at once, I feel like the task switch time is something like six hours. In an eight-hour day, that means multitasking reduces my productivity to two hours per day. Pretty dismal.

As it turns out, if you give somebody two things to work on, you should be grateful if they "starve" one task and only work on the other, because they're going to get more stuff done and finish the average task sooner. In fact, the real lesson from all this is that you should *never let people work on more than one thing at once*. Make sure they know what it is. Good managers see their responsibility as *removing obstacles* so that people can focus on *one thing* and really get it done. When emergencies come up, think about whether you can handle it yourself before you delegate it to a programmer who is deeply submersed in a project.

twenty-four

THINGS YOU SHOULD
NEVER DO, PART ONE[1]

Thursday, April 6, 2000

Netscape 6.0 is finally going into its first public beta. There never was a version 5.0. The last major release, version 4.0, was released almost three years ago. Three years is an *awfully* long time in the Internet world. During this time, Netscape sat by, helplessly, as their market share plummeted.

It's a bit smarmy of me to criticize them for waiting so long between releases. They didn't do it *on purpose*, now, did they?

Well, yes. They did. They did it by making the *single worst strategic mistake* that any software company can make:

They decided to rewrite the code from scratch.

Netscape wasn't the first company to make this mistake. Borland made the same mistake when they bought Arago and tried to make it into dBase for Windows, a doomed project that took so long that Microsoft Access ate their lunch. Then they made the same mistake in rewriting Quattro Pro from scratch and astonishing people with how few features it had. Microsoft almost made the same mistake, trying to rewrite Word for Windows from scratch in a doomed project called Pyramid, which was shut down, thrown away, and swept under the rug. Lucky for Microsoft, they had never stopped working on the old code base, so they

---

1. There are no other parts. The title is a play on the Mel Brooks movie *History of the World: Part I*, which has absolutely nothing to do with software or this essay.

had something to ship—making it merely a financial disaster, not a strategic one.

We're programmers. Programmers are, in their hearts, architects, and the first thing they want to do when they get to a site is to bulldoze the place flat and build something grand. We're not excited by incremental renovation: tinkering, improving, planting flower beds.

There's a subtle reason why programmers always want to throw away the code and start over. The reason is that they think the old code is a mess. And here is the interesting observation: *They are probably wrong.* The reason that they think the old code is a mess is because of a cardinal, fundamental law of programming:

It's harder to read code than to write it.

This is why code reuse is so hard. This is why everybody on your team has a different function they like to use for splitting strings into arrays of strings. They write their own function because it's easier and more fun than figuring out how the old function works.

As a corollary of this axiom, you can ask almost any programmer today about the code they are working on. "It's a big hairy mess," they will tell you. "I'd like nothing better than to throw it out and start over."

Why is it a mess?

"Well," they say, "look at this function. It is two pages long! None of this stuff belongs in there! I don't know what half of these API calls are for."

Before Borland's new spreadsheet for Windows shipped, Philippe Kahn, the colorful founder of Borland, was quoted a lot in the press bragging about how Quattro Pro would be much better than Microsoft Excel, because it was written from scratch. All new source code! As if source code *rusted.*

The idea that new code is better than old is patently absurd. Old code has been *used.* It has been *tested. Lots* of bugs have been found, and they've been *fixed.* There's nothing wrong with it. It doesn't acquire bugs just by sitting around on your hard drive. *Au contraire,* baby! Is software supposed to be like an old Dodge Dart that rusts just sitting in the garage? Is software like a teddy bear that's kind of gross if it's not made out of *all new material?*

Back to that two-page function. Yes, I know, it's just a simple function to display a window, but it has grown little hairs and stuff on it and nobody knows why. Well, I'll tell you why: Those are bug fixes. One of them fixes that bug that Nancy had when she tried to install the thing on a computer that didn't have Internet Explorer. Another one fixes that bug that occurs in low-memory conditions. Another one fixes that bug that occurred when the file is on a floppy disk and the user yanks out the disk in the middle. That LoadLibrary call is ugly, but it makes the code work on old versions of Windows 95.

Each of these bugs required weeks of real-world usage before being found. The programmer might have spent a couple of days reproducing the bug in the lab and fixing it. If it's like a lot of bugs, the fix might be one line of code, or it might even be a couple of characters, but a lot of work and time went into those two characters.

When you throw away code and start from scratch, you are throwing away all that knowledge. All those collected bug fixes. Years of programming work.

You are throwing away your market leadership. You are giving a gift of two or three years to your competitors, and believe me, that is a *long* time in software years.

You are putting yourself in an extremely dangerous position where you will be shipping an old version of the code for several years, completely unable to make any strategic changes or react to new features that the market demands, because you don't have shippable code. You might as well just close for business for the duration.

You are wasting an outlandish amount of money writing code that already exists.

Is there an alternative? The consensus seems to be that the old Netscape code base was *really* bad. Well, it might have been bad, but you know what? It worked pretty darn well on an awful lot of real-world computer systems.

When programmers say that their code is a holy mess (as they always do), there are three kinds of things that are wrong with it.

First, there are architectural problems. The code is not factored correctly. The networking code is popping up its own dialog boxes from the middle of nowhere; this should have been handled in the UI code. These problems can be solved, one at a time, by carefully moving code, refactoring, changing interfaces. They can be done by one programmer working carefully and checking in his changes all at once, so that

twenty-five

THE ICEBERG SECRET, REVEALED

"I don't know what's wrong with my development team," the CEO thinks to himself. "Things were going so well when we started this project. For the first couple of weeks, the team cranked like crazy and got a great prototype working. But since then, things seem to have slowed to a crawl. They're just not working hard any more." He chooses a Callaway Titanium Driver and sends the caddy to fetch an ice-cold lemonade. "Maybe if I fire a couple of laggards that'll light a fire under them!"

Meanwhile, of course, the development team has *no idea* that anything's wrong. In fact, nothing is wrong. They're right on schedule.

Don't let this happen to you! I'm going to let you in on a little secret about those nontechnical management types that will make your life a million times easier. It's real simple. Once you know my secret, you'll never have trouble working with nontechnical managers again (unless you get into an argument over the coefficient of restitution of their golf clubs).

It's pretty clear that programmers think in one language, and MBAs think in another. I've been thinking about the problem of communication in software management for a while, because it's pretty clear to me that the power and rewards accrue to those rare individuals who know how to translate between Programmerese and MBAese.

Since I started working in the software industry, almost all the software I've worked on has been what might be called "speculative" software. That is, the software is not being built for a particular customer; it's being built in hopes that *zillions* of people will buy it. But many software developers don't have that luxury. They may be consultants developing a project for a single client, or they may be in-house program-mers working on a complicated corporate whatsit for Accounting (or whatever it is you in-house programmers do; it's rather mysterious to me). Have you ever noticed that on these custom projects, the single most common cause of overruns, failures, and general miserableness always boils down to, basically, "the (insert expletive here) customer didn't know what they wanted?"

Here are three versions of the same pathology:

1. "The damn customer kept changing his mind. First he wanted Client/Server. Then he read about XML in Delta Airlines' in-flight magazine and decided he had to have XML. Now we're rewriting the thing to use fleets of small Lego Mindstorms Robots."

2. "We built it *exactly the way they wanted*. The contract speci-fied the whole thing down to the smallest detail. We delivered exactly what the contract said. But when we delivered it, they were crestfallen."

3. "Our miserable sales person agreed to a *fixed-price contract* to build what was basically unspecified, and the customer's lawyers were sharp enough to get a clause in the contract that they don't have to pay us until 'acceptance by customer,' so we had to put a team of nine developers on their project for two years and only got paid $800."

If there's one thing every junior consultant needs to have injected into their head with a heavy-duty 2500 RPM DeWalt drill, it's this:

Customers don't know what they want.
Stop expecting customers to know what they want.

It's just never going to happen. Get over it.

Instead, assume that you're going to have to build something *any-way*, and the customer is going to have to like it, but they're going to be a little bit surprised. *You* have to do the research. *You* have to figure out a design that solves the customer's problem in a pleasing way.

Put yourself in their shoes. Imagine that you've just made $100,000,000 selling your company to Yahoo!, and you've decided that it's about time to renovate your kitchen. So you hire an expert architect with instructions to make it "as cool as Will and Grace's Kitchen." You have no idea how to accomplish this. You don't know that you want a Viking stove and a Subzero refrigerator—these are not words in your vocabulary. You want the architect to do something good; that's why you hired him.

The Extreme Programming folks say that the solution to this is to get the customer *in the room* and involve them in the design process every step of the way, as a member of the development team. This is, I think, a bit *too* "extreme." It's as if my architect made me show up while they were designing the kitchen and asked me to provide input on every little detail. It's boring for me; if I wanted to be an architect, I would have become an architect.

Anyway, you don't really *want* a customer on your team, do you? The customer-nominee is just as likely to wind up being some poor dweeb from Accounts Payable who got sent to work with the programmers because he was the slowest worker over there and they would barely notice his absence. And you're just going to spend all your design time explaining things in words of one syllable.

Assume that your customers don't know what they want. Design it yourself, based on your understanding of the domain. If you need to spend some time learning about the domain or if you need a domain expert to help you, that's fine, but the design of the software is your job. If you do your domain homework and create a good UI, the customer will be pleased.

Now, I promised to tell you a secret about translating between the language of the customers (or nontechnical managers) of your software and the language of programmers.

You know how an iceberg is 90 percent underwater? Well, most software is like that too—there's a pretty user interface that takes about 10 percent of the work, and then 90 percent of the programming work is under the covers. And if you take into account the fact that about half of your time is spent fixing bugs, the UI takes only 5 percent of the work. And if you limit yourself to the *visual* part of the UI, the pixels, what you would see in PowerPoint, now we're talking less than 1 percent.

That's not the secret. The secret is that *people who aren't programmers do not understand this.*

There are some very, very important corollaries to the Iceberg Secret.

~

Important Corollary One

If you show a nonprogrammer a screen that has a user interface that is 90 percent worse, they will think that the program is 90 percent worse.

I learned this lesson as a consultant, when I did a demo of a major Web-based project for a client's executive team. The project was almost 100 percent code complete. We were still waiting for the graphic designer to choose fonts and colors and draw the cool 3-D tabs. In the meantime, we just used plain fonts and black and white, there was a bunch of ugly wasted space on the screen, and basically it didn't look very good at all. But 100 percent of the functionality was there and was doing some pretty amazing stuff.

What happened during the demo? The clients spent the *entire meeting* griping about the graphical appearance of the screen. They weren't even talking about the UI. Just the graphical appearance. *"It just doesn't look slick,"* complained their project manager. That's all they could think about. We couldn't get them to think about the actual functionality. Obviously, fixing the graphic design took about one day. It was almost as if they thought they had hired *painters*.

~

Important Corollary Two

If you show a nonprogrammer a screen with a user interface that is 100 percent beautiful, they will think that the program is almost done.

People who aren't programmers are just looking at the screen and seeing some pixels. And if the pixels look like they make up a program that does something, they think "oh, gosh, how much harder could it be to make it *actually work?*"

The big risk here is that if you mock up the UI first, presumably so you can get some conversations going with the customer, then everybody's going to think you're almost done. And then when you spend the next year working "under the covers," so to speak, nobody will really see what you're doing, and they'll think it's nothing.

~

Important Corollary Three

The dotcom that has the cool, polished-looking website and about four web pages will get a higher valuation than the highly functional dotcom with 3,700 years of archives and a default gray background.

Oh, wait, dotcoms aren't worth anything any more. Never mind.

~

Important Corollary Four

When politics demands that various nontechnical managers or customers "sign off" on a project, give them several versions of the graphic design to choose from.

Vary the placement of some things, change the look and feel and fonts, move the logo and make it bigger or smaller. Let them feel important by giving them noncrucial lipstick-on-a-chicken stuff to muck around with. They can't do much damage to your schedule here. A good interior decorator is constantly bringing their client swatches and samples and stuff to choose from. But they would never discuss dishwasher placement with the client. It goes next to the sink, no matter what the client wants. There's no sense wasting time arguing about where the dishwasher goes, it has to go next to the sink, don't even *bring it up;* let the clients get their design kicks doing some harmless thing like changing their mind 200 times about whether to use Italian granite or Mexican tiles or Norwegian wood butcher block for the countertops.

~

Important Corollary Five

When you're showing off, the only thing that matters is the screen shot. Make it 100 percent beautiful.

Don't, for a minute, think that you can get away with asking *anybody* to *imagine how cool this would be*. Don't think that they're looking at the functionality. They're not. They want to see pretty pixels.

Steve Jobs understands this. Oh *boy* does he understand this. Engineers at Apple have learned to do things that make for great screen shots, like the gorgeous new 1024×1024 icons in the dock, even if they waste valuable real estate. And the Linux desktop crowd goes crazy about semitransparent xterms, which make for good screenshots but are usually annoying to use. Every time Gnome or KDE announces a new release, I go straight to the screenshots and say, "oh, they changed the planet from Jupiter to Saturn. Cool." Never mind what they really did.

~

Manage the Iceberg

Remember the CEO at the beginning of this chapter? He was unhappy because his team had showed him great PowerPoints at the beginning—mockups, created in *Photoshop*, not even VB. And now that they're actually getting stuff done under the covers, it looks like they're not doing anything.

What can you do about this? Once you understand the Iceberg Secret, it's easy to work with it. Understand that any demos you do in a darkened room with a projector are going to be *all about pixels*. If you can, build your UI in such a way that unfinished parts *look* unfinished. For example, use scrawls for the icons on the toolbar until the functionality is there. As you're building your web service, you may want to consider actually leaving out features from the home page until those features are built. That way, people can watch the home page go from 3 commands to 20 commands as you build more things.

More importantly, make sure you control what people think about the schedule. Provide a detailed schedule in Excel format.[1] Every week, send out a self-congratulatory email talking about how you've moved from 32 percent complete to 35 percent complete and are *on track* to ship on December 25th. Make sure that the actual facts dominate any thinking about whether the project is moving forward at the right speed. And don't let your boss use Callaway Titanium Drivers, I don't care how much you want him to win, the USGA has banned them and it's just not fair.

---

1. See Chapter 9.

twenty-six

THE LAW OF LEAKY ABSTRACTIONS

Monday, November 11, 2002

There's a key piece of magic in the engineering of the Internet that you rely on every single day. It happens in the TCP protocol, one of the fundamental building blocks of the Internet.

TCP is a way to transmit data that is *reliable*. By this I mean: If you send a message over a network using TCP, it will arrive, and it won't be garbled or corrupted.

We use TCP for many things like fetching web pages and sending email. The reliability of TCP is why every exciting email from embezzling East Africans arrives in letter-perfect condition. O joy.

By comparison, there is another method of transmitting data, called IP, that is *unreliable*. Nobody promises that your data will arrive, and it might get messed up before it arrives. If you send a bunch of messages with IP, don't be surprised if only half of them arrive, and some of those are in a different order than the order in which they were sent, and some of them have been replaced by alternate messages, perhaps containing pictures of adorable baby orangutans, or more likely just a lot of unreadable garbage that looks like the subject line of Taiwanese spam.

Here's the magic part: TCP is built on top of IP. In other words, TCP is obliged to somehow send data reliably *using only an unreliable tool*.

To illustrate why this is magic, consider the following morally equivalent, though somewhat ludicrous, scenario from the real world.

Imagine that we had a way of sending actors from Broadway to Hollywood that involved putting them in cars and driving them across the country. Some of these cars crashed, killing the poor actors. Sometimes the actors got drunk on the way and shaved their heads or got nasal tattoos, thus becoming too ugly to work in Hollywood, and frequently the actors arrived in a different order than they had set out, because they all took different routes. Now imagine a new service called Hollywood Express, which delivered actors to Hollywood, guaranteeing that they would (a) arrive (b) in order (c) in perfect condition. The magic part is that Hollywood Express doesn't have any method of delivering the actors, other than the unreliable method of putting them in cars and driving them across the country. Hollywood Express works by checking that each actor arrives in perfect condition, and, if he doesn't, calling up the home office and requesting that the actor's identical twin be sent instead. If the actors arrive in the wrong order, Hollywood Express rearranges them. If a large UFO on its way to Area 51 crashes on the highway in Nevada, rendering it impassable, all the actors that went that way are rerouted via Arizona, and Hollywood Express doesn't even tell the movie directors in California what happened. To them, it just looks like the actors are arriving a little bit more slowly than usual, and they never even *hear* about the UFO crash.

That is, approximately, the magic of TCP. It is what computer scientists like to call an *abstraction*: a simplification of something much more complicated that is going on under the covers. As it turns out, a lot of computer programming consists of building abstractions. What is a string library? It's a way to pretend that computers can manipulate strings just as easily as they can manipulate numbers. What is a file system? It's a way to pretend that a hard drive isn't really a bunch of spinning magnetic platters that can store bits at certain locations, but rather a hierarchical system of folders-within-folders containing individual files that in turn consist of one or more strings of bytes.

Back to TCP. Earlier for the sake of simplicity, I told a little fib, and some of you have steam coming out of your ears by now because this fib is driving you crazy. I said that TCP guarantees that your message will arrive. It doesn't, actually. If your pet snake has chewed through the network cable leading to your computer, and *no* IP packets can get through, then TCP can't do anything about it and your message doesn't arrive.

If you were curt with the system administrators in your company and they punished you by plugging you into an overloaded hub, only some of your IP packets will get through, and TCP will work, but everything will be really slow.

This is what I call a *leaky abstraction*. TCP attempts to provide a complete abstraction of an underlying unreliable network, but sometimes the network leaks through the abstraction and you feel the things that the abstraction can't quite protect you from. This is but one example of what I've dubbed the Law of Leaky Abstractions:

All nontrivial abstractions, to some degree, are leaky.

Abstractions fail. Sometimes a little, sometimes a lot. There's leakage. Things go wrong. It happens all over the place when you have abstractions. Here are some examples.

- Something as simple as iterating over a large two-dimensional array can have radically different performance if you do it horizontally rather than vertically, depending on the "grain of the wood"— one direction may result in vastly more page faults than the other direction, and page faults are slow. Even assembly programmers are supposed to be allowed to pretend that they have a big, flat address space, but virtual memory means it's really just an abstraction, which leaks when there's a page fault and certain memory fetches take way more nanoseconds than other memory fetches.

- The SQL language is meant to abstract away the procedural steps that are needed to query a database, instead allowing you to define merely what you want and let the database figure out the procedural steps to query it. But in some cases, certain SQL queries are thousands of times slower than other logically equivalent queries. A famous example of this is that some SQL servers are dramatically faster if you specify "where a=b and b=c and a=c" than if you only specify "where a=b and b=c" even though the result set is the same. You're not supposed to have to care about the procedure, only the specification. But sometimes the abstraction leaks and causes horrible performance, and you have to break out the query plan analyzer and study what it did wrong, and figure out how to make your query run faster.

- Even though network libraries like NFS and SMB let you treat files on remote machines "as if" they were local, sometimes the connection becomes very slow or goes down, and the file stops acting like it was local, and as a programmer you have to write code to deal with this. The abstraction of "remote file is the same as local file" leaks.[1] Here's a concrete example for UNIX sysadmins. If you put users' home directories on NFS-mounted drives (one abstraction), and your users create .forward files to forward all their email somewhere else (another abstraction), and the NFS server goes down while new email is arriving, the messages will not be forwarded because the .forward file will not be found. The leak in the abstraction actually caused a few messages to be dropped on the floor.

- C++ string classes are supposed to let you pretend that strings are first-class data. They try to abstract away the fact that strings are hard[2] and let you act as if they were as easy as integers. Almost all C++ string classes overload the + operator so you can write **s + "bar"** to concatenate. But you know what? No matter how hard they try, there is no C++ string class on Earth that will let you type **"foo" + "bar"**, because string literals in C++ are always char*s, never strings. The abstraction has sprung a leak that the language doesn't let you plug. (Amusingly, the history of the evolution of C++ can be described as a history of trying to plug the leaks in the string abstraction. Why they couldn't just add a native string class to the language itself eludes me at the moment.)

- And you can't drive as fast when it's raining, even though your car has windshield wipers and headlights and a roof and a heater, all of which protect you from caring about the fact that it's raining (they abstract away the weather), but lo, you have to worry about hydroplaning (or aquaplaning in England), and sometimes the rain is so strong that you can't see very far ahead so you go slower in the rain, because the weather can never be completely abstracted away, because of the Law of Leaky Abstractions.

---

1. See Chapter 17.
2. See Chapter 2.

One reason the Law of Leaky Abstractions is problematic is because it means that abstractions do not really simplify our lives as much as they were meant to. When I'm training someone to be a C++ programmer, it would be nice if I never had to teach them about char*s and pointer arithmetic. It would be nice if I could go straight to STL strings. But one day they'll write the code **"foo"** + **"bar"**, and truly bizarre things will happen, and then I'll have to stop and teach them all about char*s anyway. Or one day they'll be trying to call a Windows API function that is documented as having an OUT LPTSTR argument, and they won't be able to understand how to call it until they learn about char*s, and pointers, and Unicode, and wchar_ts, and the TCHAR header files, and all that stuff that leaks up.

In teaching someone about COM programming, it would be nice if I could just teach them how to use the Visual Studio wizards and all the code-generation features, but if anything goes wrong, they will not have the vaguest idea what happened or how to debug it and recover from it. I'm going to have to teach them all about IUnknown and CLSIDs and ProgIDS and . . . oh, the humanity!

In teaching someone about ASP.NET programming, it would be nice if I could just teach them that they can double-click on things and then write code that runs on the server when the user clicks on those things. Indeed, ASP.NET abstracts away the difference between writing the HTML code to handle clicking on a hyperlink (<a>) and the code to handle clicking on a button. Problem: the ASP.NET designers needed to hide the fact that in HTML, there's no way to submit a form from a hyperlink. They do this by generating a few lines of JavaScript and attaching an onclick handler to the hyperlink. The abstraction leaks, though. If the end user has JavaScript disabled, the ASP.NET application doesn't work correctly, and if the programmer doesn't understand what ASP.NET was abstracting away, they simply won't have any clue what is wrong.

The law of leaky abstractions means that whenever somebody comes up with a wizzy new code-generation tool that is supposed to make us all ever-so-efficient, you hear a lot of people saying "learn how to do it manually first, then use the wizzy tool to save time." Code-generation tools that pretend to abstract out something, like all abstractions, leak, and the only way to deal with the leaks competently is to learn about how the abstractions work and what they are abstracting. So, the abstractions save us time working, but they don't save us time learning.

And all this means that paradoxically, even as we have higher and higher level programming tools with better and better abstractions, becoming a proficient programmer is getting harder and harder.

During my first Microsoft internship, I wrote string libraries to run on the Macintosh. A typical assignment: Write a version of strcat that returns a pointer to the end of the new string. A few lines of C code. Everything I did was right from K&R—one thin book about the C programming language.

Today, to work on CityDesk, I need to know Visual Basic, COM, ATL, C++, InnoSetup, Internet Explorer internals, regular expressions, DOM, HTML, CSS, and XML—all high-level tools compared to the old K&R stuff, but I still have to know the K&R stuff, or I'm toast.

Ten years ago, we might have imagined that new programming paradigms would have made programming easier by now. Indeed, the abstractions we've created over the years *do* allow us to deal with new orders of complexity in software development that we didn't have to deal with ten or fifteen years ago, like GUI programming and network programming. And while these great tools, like modern OO forms-based languages, let us get a lot of work done incredibly quickly, suddenly one day we need to figure out a problem where the abstraction leaked, and it takes two weeks. And when you need to hire a programmer to do mostly VB programming, it's not good enough to hire a VB programmer, because they will get completely stuck in tar every time the VB abstraction leaks.

The Law of Leaky Abstractions is dragging us down.

twenty-seven

LORD PALMERSTON ON PROGRAMMING

WEDNESDAY, DECEMBER 11, 2002

There was a time when if you read one book by Peter Norton,[1] you literally knew everything there was to know about programming the IBM-PC. Over the last 20 years, programmers around the world have been hard at work building abstraction upon abstraction on top of the IBM-PC to make it easier to program and more powerful.

But the Law of Leaky Abstractions[2] means that even as they built the abstractions that are supposed to make programming easier, the sheer amount of stuff you have to know to be a great programmer is expanding all the time.

Becoming proficient, really proficient, in just one programming world takes years. Sure, lots of bright teenagers learn Delphi one week and Python the next week and Perl the next week and think they are proficient. Yet they don't have the foggiest clue how much they're missing.

I've been working with ASP and VBScript since it first came out. VBScript is the dinkiest language on earth, and ASP programming consists of learning about five classes, only two of which you use very often. And only now do I finally feel like I know the best way to architect an ASP/VBScript application. I finally think I know where the best place to

---

1. Peter Norton, *Inside the IBM PC: Access to Advanced Features and Programming* (R. J. Brady Co., 1983).
2. See Chapter 26.

put database access code is, the best way to use ADO to get recordsets, the best way to separate HTML and code, etc. And I finally use regexps instead of one-off string manipulation functions. Only last week, I learned how to get COM objects out of memory so you can recompile them (without restarting the whole web server).

Fog Creek is too small to have specialists, so when I needed to write a really good installer[3] for FogBUGZ,[4] our ASP/VBScript-based product, I drew on several years of C++/MFC experience, and years of experience with Windows APIs, and good Corel PHOTO-PAINT skills to create a neat picture in the corner of the wizard. Then to get FogBUGZ to work perfectly with Unicode, I had to write a little ActiveX control using C++ and ATL, which drew upon years of C++ and COM experience and a week or so learning about character encodings when I implemented that code in CityDesk.

So when we had a weird NT 4.0-only bug, it took me three minutes to debug, because I knew how to use VMWare, and I had a clean NT 4.0 machine set up in VMWare, and I knew how to do remote debugging with Visual C++, and I knew to look in the EAX register to get the return value from a function. Someone who was new to this all might have taken an hour or more to debug the same problem, but I already knew a tremendous amount of "stuff" that I've been learning, basically, since 1983 when I got my first IBM-PC and that Norton book.

Leaky abstractions mean that we live with a hockey stick learning curve: You can learn 90 percent of what you use day by day with a week of learning. But the other 10 percent might take you a couple of years catching up. That's where the really experienced programmers will shine over the people who say "whatever you want me to do, I can just pick up the book and learn how to do it." If you're building a team, it's OK to have a lot of less-experienced programmers cranking out big blocks of code using the abstract tools, but the team is not going to work if you don't have some really experienced members to do the really hard stuff.

3. See www.joelonsoftware.com/news/20021002.html.

4. See www.fogcreek.com/FogBUGZ.

There are a lot of programming worlds, each of which requires a tremendous amount of knowledge for real proficiency. Here are the three I personally know best:

- MFC/C++/Windows
- VBScript/ASP
- Visual Basic

All, basically, what you would call Windows programming. Yes, I've written UNIX code and Java code, but not very much. My proficiency in Windows programming comes from knowing not just the basic technologies, but also the whole supporting infrastructure. So, I claim, I'm really good at Windows programming because I also know COM, ATL, C++, 80x86 Assembler, Windows APIs, IDispatch (OLE Automation), HTML, the DOM, the Internet Explorer object model, Windows NT and Windows 95 internals, LAN Manager and NT networking (including security—ACEs, ACLs, and all that stuff), SQL and SQL Server, Jet and Access, JavaScript, XML, and a few other cheerful facts about the square of the hypotenuse. When I can't get the StrConv function in VB to do what I want, I bang out a COM control so I can drop into C++ with ATL and call the MLang functions without dropping a beat. It took me years to get to this point.

There are lots of other programming worlds. There's the world of people developing for BEA WebLogic who know J2EE, Oracle, and all kinds of Java things that I don't even know enough about to enumerate. There are hardcore Macintosh developers who know CodeWarrior, MPW, Toolbox programming in System 6 through X, Cocoa, Carbon, and even nice obsolete things like OpenDoc that don't help anymore.

Very few people, though, know more than one or two worlds, because there's just so much to learn that unless you have to work in one of these worlds for more than a couple of years, you don't really grok it all.

But learn you must.

People get kind of miffed when they go on job interviews and are rejected because, for example, they don't have Win32 (or J2EE, or Mac programming, or whatever) experience. Or they get annoyed because idiot recruiters, who would not know an MSMQ if it bit them in the tail-bone, call them up and ask if they "have ten years MSMQ."

Until you've done Windows programming for a while, you may think that Win32 is just a library, and just as with any other library, you'll read the book and learn it and call it when you need to. You might think that basic programming—say, your expert C++ skills—are the 90 percent, and all the APIs are the 10 percent fluff you can catch up on in a few weeks. To these people I humbly suggest: Times have changed. The ratio has reversed.

Very few people get to work on low-level C algorithms that just move bytes around any more. Most of us spend all our time these days calling APIs, not moving bytes.[5] Someone who is a fantastic C++ coder with no API experience only knows about 10 percent of what you use every day writing code that runs on an API. When the economy is doing well, this doesn't matter.[6] You still get jobs, and employers pay the cost of your getting up-to-speed on the platform. But when the economy is a mess and 600 people apply for every job opening, employers have the luxury of choosing programmers who are already experts at the plat-form in question. Like programmers who can name four ways to FTP a file from Visual Basic code, and the pros and cons of each.

The huge surface area of all these worlds of programming leads to pointless flame wars over whose world is better. Here's a smug comment somebody anonymously made on my discussion board:

> Just one more reason why I'm glad to be living in the "free world."
> Free as in speech (almost) and freedom from pandering to things
> like setup programs and the registry—just to name a few.

I think this person was trying to say that in the Linux world, they don't write setup programs. Well, I hate to disappoint you, but you have something just as complicated: imake, make, config files, and all that

---

5. See www.joelonsoftware.com/articles/fog0000000250.html.
6. See www.joelonsoftware.com/articles/fog0000000050.html.

stuff, and when you're done, you still distribute applications with a 20KB INSTALL file full of witty instructions like "You're going to need zlib" (*what's that?*) or "This may take a while. Go get some runts." (Runts are a kind of candy, I think.) And the registry—instead of one big organized hive of name/value pairs, you have a thousand different file formats, one per application, with .whateverrc and foo.conf files living all over the place. And Emacs wants you to learn how to program lisp if you're going to change settings, and each shell wants you to learn its personal dialect of shell script programming if you want to change settings, and on and on.

People who know only one world get really smarmy, and every time they hear about the complications in the other world, it makes them think that their world doesn't have complications. But they do. You've just moved beyond them because you are proficient in them. These worlds are just too big and complicated to compare any more. Lord Palmerston said: "The Schleswig-Holstein question is so complicated, only three men in Europe have ever understood it. One was Prince Albert, who is dead. The second was a German professor who became mad. I am the third and I have forgotten all about it." The software worlds are so huge and complicated and multifaceted that when I see otherwise intelligent people writing blog entries saying something vacuous like "Microsoft is bad at operating systems," frankly, they just look dumb. Imagine trying to summarize millions of lines of code with hundreds of major feature areas created by thousands of programmers over a decade or two, where no one person can begin to understand even a large portion of it. I'm not even defending Microsoft; I'm just saying that big handwavy generalizations made from a position of deep ignorance is one of the biggest wastes of time on the Net today.

I've been thinking of the problem of how one might deliver an application on Linux, Macintosh, and Windows without paying disproportionately for the Linux and Macintosh versions. For this you need some kind of cross-platform library.

Java attempted this, but Sun didn't grok GUIs well enough to deliver really slick native-feeling applications. Like the space alien in *Star Trek* watching Earth through a telescope; he knew exactly what human food was supposed to *look* like, but he didn't realize it was supposed to *taste* like something.[7] Java apps have menus in the right places, but there are all these keyboard things that don't work the same way as every other Windows app, and their tabbed dialogs look a little scary. And there is no way, no matter how hard you try, to make their menu bars look exactly like Excel's menu bars. Why? Because Java doesn't give you a very good way to drop down to the native facilities whenever the abstraction fails. When you're programming in AWT, you can't figure out the HWND of a window, you can't call the Microsoft APIs, and you certainly can't intercept WM_PAINT and do it differently. And Sun made it plenty clear that if you tried to do that, you weren't Pure. You were Polluted, and to hell with you.

After a number of highly publicized failures to build GUIs with Java (e.g., Corel's Java Office suite and Netscape's Javagator), enough people know to stay away from this world. Eclipse[8] built their own windowing library from the ground up using native widgets just so they could write Java code that had a reasonably native look and feel.

The Mozilla engineers decided to address the cross-platform problem with their own invention called XUL. So far, I'm impressed. Mozilla finally got to the point where it tastes like real food. Even my favorite bugaboo, Alt+Space N to minimize a window, works in Mozilla; it took them long enough, but they did it.

Mitch Kapor, who founded Lotus and created 123, decided for his next application to go with something called wxWindows and wxPython for cross-platform support.[9]

Which is better: XUL, Eclipse's SWT, or wxWindows? I don't know. They are all such huge worlds that I couldn't really evaluate them and tell. It's not enough to read the tutorials. You have to sweat and bleed with the thing for a year or two before you really know it's good enough or realize that no matter how hard you try you can't make your UI taste like real food. Unfortunately, for most projects, you have to decide which world to use before you can write the first line of code, which is precisely the moment when you have the least information. At a previous job, we had to live with some pretty bad architecture because the

---

7. "The Squire of Gothos," *Star Trek* television series (Paramount Studio, January 12, 1967). Read the full transcript, as a poem, at www.voyager.cz/tos/epizody/19squireofgothostrans.htm.

8. See www.eclipse.org/.

9. See blogs.osafoundation.org/mitch/000007.html.

first programmers used the project to teach themselves C++ and Windows programming at the same time. Some of the oldest code was written without any comprehension of event-driven programming. The core string class (of course, we had our own string class) was a textbook example of all the mistakes you could make in designing a C++ class. Eventually, we cleaned up and refactored a lot of that old code, but it haunted us for a while.

So for now, my advice is this: Don't start a new project without at least one architect with several years of solid experience in the language, classes, APIs, and platforms you're building on. If you have a choice of platforms, use the one your team has the most skills with, even if it's not the trendiest or nominally the most productive. And when you're designing abstractions or programming tools, go the extra mile to make them leak-proof.

twenty-eight

MEASUREMENT

Monday, July 15, 2002

"Thank you for calling Amazon.com, may I help you?" Then—Click! You're cut off. That's annoying. You just waited 10 minutes to get through to a human, and you mysteriously got disconnected right away.

Or is it mysterious? According to Mike Daisey, Amazon rated their customer service representatives based on the number of calls taken per hour.[1] The best way to get your performance rating up was to hang up on customers, thus increasing the number of calls you can take every hour.

An aberration, you say?

When Jeff Weitzen took over Gateway, he instituted a new policy to save money on customer service calls. "Reps who spent more than 13 minutes talking to a customer didn't get their monthly bonuses," writes Katrina Brooker.[2] "As a result, workers began doing just about anything to get customers off the phone: pretending the line wasn't working, hanging up, or often—at great expense—sending them new parts or computers. Not surprisingly, Gateway's customer satisfaction rates, once the best in the industry, fell below average."

It seems like any time you try to measure the performance of knowledge workers, things rapidly disintegrate, and you get what Robert D. Austin calls *measurement dysfunction*. His book *Measuring and Managing Performance in Organizations*[3] is an excellent and thorough survey of the subject. Managers like to implement measurement systems, and they like to

---

1. Mike Daisey, *21 Dog Years: Doing Time @ Amazon.com* (Free Press, 2002).

2. *Business 2.0,* April 2000.

3. Robert Austin, *Measuring and Managing Performance in Organizations* (Dorset House, 1996).

tie compensation to performance based on these measurement systems. But in the absence of 100 percent supervision, workers have an incentive to "work to the measurement," concerning themselves solely with the measurement and not with the actual value or quality of their work.

Software organizations tend to reward programmers who a) write lots of code and b) fix lots of bugs. The best way to get ahead in an organization like this is to check in lots of buggy code and fix it all, rather than taking the extra time to get it right in the first place. When you try to fix this problem by penalizing programmers for creating bugs, you create a perverse incentive for them to hide their bugs or not tell the testers about new code they wrote in hopes that fewer bugs will be found. You can't win.

Fortune 500 CEOs are usually compensated with base salary plus stock options. The stock options are often worth tens or hundreds of millions of dollars, which makes the base pay almost inconsequential. As a result, CEOs do everything they can to inflate the price of the stock, even if it comes at the cost of bankrupting or ruining the company (as we're seeing again and again in the headlines this month). They'll do this even if the stock only goes up temporarily, and then sell at the peak. Compensation committees are slow to respond, but their latest brilliant idea is to require the executive to hold the stock until they leave the company. Terrific. Now the incentive is to inflate the price of the stock temporarily and then quit. You can't win, again.

Don't take my word for it; read Austin's book and you'll understand why this measurement dysfunction is inevitable when you can't completely supervise workers (which is almost always).

I've long claimed that incentive pay isn't such a hot idea,[4] even if you *could* measure who was doing a good job and who wasn't, but Austin reinforces this by showing that you can't even measure performance, so incentive pay is even less likely to work.

---

4. See Chapter 21.

part three

Being Joel:
Random Thoughts
on Not-So-Random
Topics

twenty-nine

RICK CHAPMAN IS IN SEARCH OF STUPIDITY[1]

Friday, August 1, 2003

In every high-tech company I've known, there's a war going on between the geeks and the suits.

Before you start reading this great new book full of propaganda from software marketing wizard and über-suit Rick Chapman, let me take a moment to tell you what the geeks think.

Play along with me for a minute, will you?

Please imagine the most stereotypically pale, Jolt-drinking, Chinese-food-eating, video-game-playing, Slashdot-reading, Linux-command-line-dwelling dork. Since this is just a stereotype, you should be free to imagine either a runt or a kind of chubby fellow, but in either case, this is *not* the kind of person who plays football with his high school pals when he visits mom for Thanksgiving. Also, since he's a stereotype, I shall not have to make complicated excuses for making him a *him*.

This is what our stereotypical programmer thinks: "Microsoft makes inferior products, but they have superior marketing, so everybody buys their stuff."

Ask him what he thinks about the marketing people in his own company. "They're really stupid. Yesterday I got into a big argument with this stupid sales chick in the break room and after ten minutes it was totally clear that she had *no clue* what the difference between 802.11*a* and 802.11*b* is. Duh!"

What do marketing people do, young geek? "I don't know. They play golf with customers or something, when they're not making me correct their idiot spec sheets. If it was up to me, I'd fire 'em all."

---

1. This chapter originally appeared as the foreword to Merrill R. (Rick) Chapman, *In Search of Stupidity: Over 20 Years of High-Tech Marketing Disasters* (Apress, 2003).

A nice fellow named Jeffrey Tarter used to publish an annual list of the hundred largest personal computer software publishers called the Soft-letter 100. Here's what the top ten looked like in 1984:[2]

Rank	Company	Annual Revenues
#1	Micropro International	$60,000,000
#2	Microsoft Corp.	$55,000,000
#3	Lotus	$53,000,000
#4	Digital Research	$45,000,000
#5	VisiCorp	$43,000,000
#6	Ashton-Tate	$35,000,000
#7	Peachtree	$21,700,000
#8	MicroFocus	$15,000,000
#9	Software Publishing	$14,000,000
#10	Broderbund	$13,000,000

OK, Microsoft is number 2, but it is one of a handful of companies with roughly similar annual revenues.

Now let's look at the same list for 2001:

Rank	Company	Annual Revenues
#1	Microsoft Corp.	$23,845,000,000
#2	Adobe	$1,266,378,000
#3	Novell	$1,103,592,000
#4	Intuit	$1,076,000,000
#5	Autodesk	$926,324,000
#6	Symantec	$790,153,000
#7	Network Associates	$745,692,000
#8	Citrix	$479,446,000
#9	Macromedia	$295,997,000
#10	Great Plains	$250,231,000

2. Jeffrey Tarter, *Soft*letter*, April 30, 2001, 17:11.

Whoa. Notice, if you will, that *every single company* except Microsoft has disappeared from the top ten. Also notice, please, that Microsoft is *so much larger* than the next largest player, it's not even funny. Adobe would double in revenues if they could just get Microsoft's soda pop budget.

The personal computer software market *is* Microsoft. Microsoft's revenues, it turns out, make up 69 percent of the total revenues of *all the top 100 companies* combined.

This is what we're talking about, here.

Is this just superior marketing, as our imaginary geek claims? Or is this the result of an illegal monopoly? (Which begs the question: How did Microsoft *get* that monopoly? You can't have it both ways.)

According to Rick Chapman, the answer is simpler: Microsoft was the only company on the list that never made a fatal, stupid mistake. Whether this was by dint of superior brainpower or just dumb luck, the biggest mistake Microsoft made was the dancing paperclip. And how bad was that, *really?* We ridiculed them, shut it off, and went back to using Word, Excel, Outlook, and Internet Explorer every minute of every day. But for every other software company that once had market leadership and saw it go down the drain, you can point to one or two giant blunders that steered the boat into an iceberg. Micropro fiddled around rewriting the printer architecture instead of upgrading their flagship product, WordStar. Lotus wasted a year and a half shoehorning 123 to run on 640KB machines; by the time they were done, Excel was shipping and 640KB machines were a dim memory. Digital Research wildly over-charged for CP/M-86 and lost a chance to be the de facto standard for PC operating systems. VisiCorp sued themselves out of existence. Ashton-Tate never missed an opportunity to piss off dBase developers, poisoning the fragile ecology that is so vital to a platform vendor's success.

I'm a programmer, of course, so I tend to blame the marketing peo-ple for these stupid mistakes. Almost all of them revolve around a failure of nontechnical business people to understand basic technology facts. When Pepsi-pusher John Sculley was developing the Apple Newton, he didn't know something that every computer science major in the coun-try knows: Handwriting recognition *is not possible.* This was at the same time that Bill Gates was hauling programmers into meetings beg-ging them to create a single rich text edit control that could be reused in all their products. Put Jim Manzi (the suit who let the MBAs take over Lotus) in that meeting and he would be staring blankly. "What's a rich text edit control?" It never would have occurred to him to take technological leadership because he didn't grok the technology; in fact, the very use of the word *grok* in that sentence would probably throw him off.

If you ask *me*, and I'm biased, *no software company can succeed* unless a programmer is at the helm. So far, the evidence backs me up. But many of these boneheaded mistakes come from the programmers themselves. Netscape's monumental decision to rewrite their browser instead of improving the old code base cost them several years of Internet time, during which their market share went from around 90 percent to about 4 percent, and this was the *programmers' idea*. Of course, the nontechnical and inexperienced management of that company had no idea *why* this was a bad idea. There are still scads of programmers who defend Netscape's ground-up rewrite. "The old code really sucked, Joel!" Yeah, uh-huh. Such programmers should be admired for their love of clean code, but they shouldn't be allowed within 100 feet of any business decisions, since it's obvious that clean code is more important to them than, uh, shipping software.

So I'll concede to Rick a bit and say that if you want to be successful in the software business, you must have a management team that thoroughly understands and loves programming, but they have to understand and love business, too. Finding a leader with strong aptitude in both dimensions is difficult, but it's the only way to avoid making one of those fatal mistakes that Rick catalogs lovingly in this book. So read it, chuckle a bit, and if there's a stupidhead running your company, get your résumé in shape and start looking for a house in Redmond.

thirty

WHAT IS THE WORK OF DOGS IN THIS COUNTRY?

SATURDAY, MAY 5, 2001

How naive *were* we?

We had assumed that Bezos was just *reinvesting* the profits, that's why they weren't showing up on the bottom line.

Last year, about this time, the first big dotcom failures started to hit the news. Boo.com. Toysmart.com. The Get Big Fast mentality was not working. Five hundred 31-year-olds in Dockers discovered that just copying Jeff Bezos wasn't a business plan.

The past few weeks have felt oddly quiet at Fog Creek. We're finishing up CityDesk. I'd like to tell you all about CityDesk, but that will have to wait. I need to tell you about dog food.

Dog food?

Last month Sara Corbett told us about the Lost Boys,[1] Sudanese refugees between 8 and 18 years old separated from their families and forced on a thousand-mile march from Sudan, to Ethiopia, to Sudan, to Kenya. Half died on that trip—of hunger, thirst, alligators. A few were rescued and delivered to places like Fargo, North Dakota, in the middle

---

1. Sara Corbett, "The Long Road From Sudan to America." *The New York Times Magazine,* April 1, 2001. Available online at www.nytimes.com/2001/04/01/magazine/01SUDAN.html? pagewanted=all (free registration required).

of winter. "Are there lions in this bush?" one asked, riding in a car to his new home from the airport. Later at the supermarket:

> Peter touched my shoulder. He was holding a can of Purina dog food. "Excuse me, Sara, but can you tell me what this is?" Behind him, the pet food was stacked practically floor to ceiling. "Um, that's food for our dogs," I answered, cringing at what that must sound like to a man who had spent the last eight years eating porridge. "Ah, I see," Peter said, replacing the can on the shelf and appearing satisfied. He pushed his grocery cart a few more steps and then turned again to face me, looking quizzical. "Tell me," he said, "what is the work of dogs in this country?"

Dogs. Yes, Peter. Fargo has enough food, even for dogs.

It's been a depressing year.

Oh, it started *out* so amusing. We all piled into B2B and B2C and P2P like a happy family getting in the Suburban for a Sunday outing to the Krispy Kreme Donut Shop. But wait, that's not even the amusing part; the amusing part was watching the worst business plans fail, as their stock went from 316 to 3/16. Take that, new economy blabbermouths! Ah, the *schadenfreude.* Ah, the glee, when once again, *Wired* magazine proves that as soon as it puts something on the cover, that thing will be proven to be stupid and wrong within a few short months.

And with this New Economy thing, *Wired really* blew it, because they should have *known* by then what a death kiss their cover was for any technology or company or meme, after years of touting smell-o-rama and doomed game companies and how PointCast was going to replace the Web,[2] no, wait, PointCast *already* replaced the Web, in March 1997. But they tempted fate anyway, and didn't just put the New Economy on the cover, they devoted the *whole goddamn issue* to the New Economy,[3] thus condemning the NASDAQ to plummet like a sheep learning to fly.

---

2. Craig Bicknell, "PointCast Coffin About to Shut." Wired News, March 29, 2000. See www.wired.lycos.com/news/business/0,1367,35208,00.html.

3. Peter Schwartz and Peter Leyden, "The Long Boom: A History of the Future, 1980–2020." *Wired,* July 1997. See www.wired.com/wired/archive/5.07/.

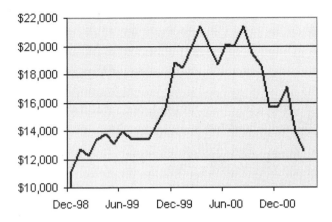

Ooh, sorry. Did you buy the Wired Index?

But joy at others' misfortune can entertain us for only so long. Now it's just getting depressing, and I know the economy is not *officially* in a depression, but I'm depressed, not because so many stupid startups went away, but because the zeitgeist is depressing. And now we have to eat dog food instead of Krispy Kremes.

Which is what we're doing, because life goes on. Even though everybody's walking around with their chins glued to their chests, mourning about the *hours* they devoted, ruining their health and love lives for the sake of stock options in SockPuppet.com, life goes on. And the product development cycle must go on, and we at Fog Creek are reaching the part in the product development cycle where you have to eat your own dog food. So for a while we're Dog Creek Software.

Eating your own dog food is the quaint name that we in the computer industry give to the process of actually *using* your own product. I had forgotten how well it worked, until a month ago, when I took home a build of CityDesk (thinking it was about three weeks from shipping) and tried to build a site with it.

Phew! There were a few bugs that literally made it impossible for me to proceed, so I had to fix those before I could even continue. All the testing we did, meticulously pulling down every menu and seeing if it worked right, didn't uncover the showstoppers that made it impossible to do what the product was intended to allow. Trying to use the product, as a customer would, found these showstoppers in a minute.

And those weren't all. As I worked—not even exercising the features, just quietly trying to build a simple site—I found 45 bugs on one Sunday afternoon. And I am a lazy man; I couldn't have spent more than two hours on this. I didn't even try anything but the most basic functionality of the product.

Monday morning, when I got in to work, I gathered the team in the kitchen. I told them about the 45 bugs. (To be fair, many of these bugs weren't actual defects but simply things that were not as convenient as they should have been.) Then I suggested that everybody build at least one serious site using CityDesk to smoke out more bugs. That's what is meant by eating your own dog food.

Here's one example of the kind of things you find.

I expect that a lot of people will try to import existing web pages into CityDesk by copying and pasting HTML code. That works fine. But when I tried to import a real live page from the *New York Times*, I spent a whole day patiently editing the HTML, finding all the IMG links (referring to outside pictures), downloading the pictures from the Web, importing those pictures into CityDesk, and adjusting the IMG links to refer to the internal pictures. It's hard to believe, but one article on that web site contains about 65 IMG links referring to 35 different pictures, some of which are 1-pixel spacers that are very difficult to download using a web browser. And CityDesk has a funny compulsion to change the name of imported pictures internally into a canonical number, and it doesn't even have a way to find out what that number is, so the long and the short of it was that it took me one full day to import a page into CityDesk.

It was getting a bit frustrating, so I went and weeded the garden for a while. (I don't know *what* we'll do to relieve stress when it's all cleaned up. Thank God we can't afford a landscaping service.) And that's when it hit me. Hey, I'm a programmer! In the time it took me to import one page and adjust the pictures, I could write a subroutine that does it automatically! In fact, it probably took me *less* time to write the subroutine. Now importing a page takes about half a minute instead of one day, and is basically error-free.

Wow.

That's why you eat your own dog food.

And when Michael started importing some sites himself, he found about 10 bugs I had baked in by mistake. For example, we found web sites that use complicated names for pictures that cannot be converted to file names when you import them because they contain question marks, which are legal in URLs but not legal in file names.

Sometimes you download software and you just can't believe how bad it is, or how hard it is to accomplish the very simple tasks that the software tries to accomplish. Chances are, it's because the developers of the software don't use it.

I have an even more amusing example of failing to eat dog food. Guess what email product was used internally at Juno Online Services? (If you're just tuning in, I worked on the Juno client team for a few years.)

Hmm, did you guess Juno? Since that was, uh, *our product*?

No. A couple of people, including the president, used Juno at home. The other 175 of us used Microsoft Outlook.

And for good reasons! The Juno client was just not such a great email client; for two years the only things we worked on were better ways to show ads. A lot of us thought that if we *had to use the product*, we would have to make it better, if only to stop our own pain. The president was very insistent that we show popup ads at six different points in time, until he got home and got six popup ads, and said, "You know what? Maybe just two popups."

AOL was signing up members at a furious rate, in part because it provided a *better user experience* than Juno, and we didn't understand that, because we didn't eat our own dog food. And we didn't eat our own dog food, because it was disgusting, and management was sufficiently dysfunctional that we simply were not allowed to fix it, and at least make it tolerable to eat.

Anyway. CityDesk is starting to look a *lot* better. We've fixed all those bugs, found some more, and fixed them, too. We're adding features we forgot about that became obviously necessary. And we're getting closer to shipping! Hurrah! And thankfully, we no longer have to contend with 37 companies, each with $25 million in VC, competing against us by giving away their product for free in exchange for agreeing to have a big advertisement tattooed on your forehead. In the post-new economy, everybody is trying to figure out how much they can get away with charging. There's nothing *wrong* with the post-new economy, if you're smart. But all the endless news about the "dot coma" says more about the lack of creativity of business press editors than anything else. Sorry, fuckedcompany.com, it was funny for a month or so, now it's just pathetic. We'll focus on improving our product, and we'll focus on staying in business, by listening to our customers and eating our own dog food, instead of flying all over the country trying to raise more venture capital.

thirty-one

GETTING THINGS DONE WHEN YOU'RE ONLY A GRUNT

Tuesday, December 25, 2001

This book is supposed to be about software management. But sometimes you don't have the power to create change in your organization by executive fiat. Obviously, if you're just a grunt programmer at the bottom of the totem pole, you can't exactly order people to start creating schedules or bug databases. And in fact even if you're a manager, you've probably discovered that managing developers is a lot like herding cats, only not as fun. Merely saying "make it so" doesn't make it so.

It can be frustrating when you're working in an organization that scores low on The Joel Test.[1] No matter how good your code is, your coworkers write such bad code that you're embarrassed to be associated with the project. Or management is making bad decisions about what code to write, so you're forced to waste your talent debugging the AS/400 version of a retirement-planning game for kids.

You could just leave, I suppose. But presumably, there's some reason you're stuck there. The stock options haven't quite vested, there's no *better* place to work in Podunk, or perhaps your boss is holding someone you love hostage. In any case, dealing with life on a bad team can be infuriating. But there are strategies for improving your team from the bottom, and I'd like to share a few of them.

---

1. See Chapter 3.

~

Strategy 1: Just Do It

A lot can be done to improve the project just by one person doing it. Don't have a daily build server? Make one. Set up your own machine with a scheduled job to make builds at night and send out email results. Does it take too many steps to make the build? Write the makefile. Nobody does usability tests? Do your own hallway usability tests on the mailroom folks with a piece of paper or a VB prototype.

~

Strategy 2: Harness the Power of Viral Marketing

Many of The Joel Test strategies can be implemented by a single person on an uncooperative team. Some of them, if done well, will spread to the rest of the team.

For example, suppose nobody on your team can be persuaded to use a bug database.[2] Don't let it bother you. Just keep your own. Enter bugs that you find in your own code. If you find a bug that somebody else really should fix, assign the bug to them using the bug database. If you have good bug tracking software, this will send them an email. But now, you can *keep* sending them emails if they don't fix the bug. Eventually, they'll see the value of bug tracking and start to use the system as it was intended. If the QA team refuses to input bugs to the bug tracking system, simply refuse to listen to bug reports through any other channel. About the three-thousandth time that you say to people, "listen, I'd love to fix that, but I'm going to forget. Can you enter a bug in the system?" they'll start using the database.

Nobody on your team wants to use source control? Create your own CVS repository, on your own hard drive if necessary. Even without cooperation, you can check in your code independently from everybody else's. Then, when they have problems that source control can solve

---

2. See www.joelonsoftware.com/articles/fog0000000029.html.

(someone accidentally types **rm** * ~ instead of **rm** *~), they'll come to you for help. Eventually, people will realize that they can have their own checkouts, too.

~

Strategy 3: Create a Pocket of Excellence

The team won't make schedules?[3] Or specs?[4] Write your own. Nobody's going to complain if you take a day or two to write a minimal spec and schedule for the work you're about to do.

Get better people into the team. Get involved in hiring and interviewing,[5] and recruit good candidates to join the team.

Find the people who are willing to improve and are capable of it, and get them on your side. Even on poor teams, you're likely to have some smart people who just don't have the experience to create great code. Help them out. Set them up to learn. Read their code check-ins. If they do something stupid, don't send them a snooty email explaining what's stupid about their check-ins. That will just make them angry and defensive. Instead, innocently report the bug that you know is the result of the check-in. Let them figure out what's causing it. When they find the bug for themselves, they'll remember that lesson a lot better.

~

Strategy 4: Neutralize the Bozos

Even the best teams can have a bozo or two. The frustrating part about having bad programmers on your team is when their bad code breaks your good code, or good programmers have to spend time cleaning up after the bad programmers.

---

3. See Chapter 9.
4. See Chapter 5.
5. See Chapter 20.

As a grunt, your goal is damage-minimization, a.k.a. containment. At some point, one of these geniuses will spend two weeks writing a bit of code that is so unbelievably bad that it can never work. You're tempted to spend the 15 minutes that it takes to rewrite the thing correctly from scratch. Resist the temptation. You've got a perfect opportunity to neutralize this moron for several months. Just keep reporting bugs against their code. They will have no choice but to keep slogging away at it for *months* until you can't find any more bugs. Those are months in which they can't do any damage anywhere else.

~

Strategy 5: Get Away from Interruptions

All happy work environments are alike (private offices, quiet working conditions, excellent tools, few interruptions, and even fewer large meetings). All unhappy work environments are unhappy in their own way.

The bad news is that changing the working environment is almost impossible in virtually any company. Long-term leases may mean that even the CEO can't do anything about it. That's why so few software developers get private offices. This hurts their companies in at least two ways. First, it makes it harder to recruit top-notch developers, who will prefer the firm that gives them cushier conditions (all else being equal). Second, the level of interruptions can dramatically reduce the productivity of developers, who find it impossible to get into the zone and stay in it for any length of time.

Look for ways to get out of this environment. Take a laptop to the company cafeteria, where there are lots of tables that are empty most of the day (and nobody can find you). Book a conference room for the whole day and write code there, and make it clear through the preponderance of check-ins just how much more work you get done when you're in a room by yourself. The next time there's a crunch on and your manager asks you what you need to Get This Done By Tomorrow, you know what to say. They'll find you an office for the day. And pretty soon they'll start wondering what they can do to keep that productive thing going year-round.

Come into work late and leave late. Those hours after the rest of the company goes home can be the most productive. Or, if you're on a team of developers who regularly come in late, get into work at 9 a.m. You'll do more work in the two hours before other people come in and start bothering you than you do in the rest of the day.

Don't keep your email or IM client running. Check your email every hour, if you want, but *don't keep it running.*

~

Strategy 6: Become Invaluable

None of these strategies works if you're not really an excellent contributor. If you don't write good code, and lots of it, you're just going to be resented for messing around with bug databases when you "should be" writing code. There's nothing more deadly to your career than having a reputation of being so concerned with process that you don't accomplish anything.

Once, when I started a new job as a grunt programmer at a new company, I discovered that the company was running somewhere around 2 on The Joel Test, and I was determined to fix it. But I also knew that making a good first impression was crucial. So I allocated the first seven hours of every day to just writing code, as was expected of me. There's nothing like a flurry of check-ins to make you look good to the rest of the development team. But before going home, I reserved another hour every afternoon for improving the process. I used that time to fix things that made it hard to debug our product. I set up a daily build and a bug database. I fixed all the longstanding annoyances that made development difficult. I wrote specs for the work that I was doing during the day. I wrote a document explaining step-by-step how to create a development machine from scratch. I thoroughly documented an important internal language which had been undocumented. Slowly, the process got better and better. Nobody but me (and my team, when I was put in charge of one) ever did schedules or specs, but other than that we hit about 10 on The Joel Test.

You *can* make things better, even when you're not in charge, but you have to be Caesar's wife: above suspicion. Otherwise, you'll make enemies as you go along.

thirty-two

TWO STORIES

Some time in late 1999, Dave Winer opened up an online service called EditThisPage.com and invited people to create their own websites using the same weblog format as he had established with his own site, Scripting News. Coincidentally, I was really pissed off by my experience working at a company with great talent being squandered by ghastly hit-and-run management (definition: intense periods of micromanagement followed by long periods of complete neglect). Thus I wrote this classic Joel rant in the grand tradition of bloggers: a tale of personal bitterness disguised as business management advice.

In those days, thankfully, I had no readers whatsoever, so I could get away with naming names and even risk offending Seattle-area billionaires who have individual cars worth more than all my bank accounts and retirement funds put together. Ah, the golden days.

SUNDAY, MARCH 19, 2000

I want to tell you two stories from my career that I think are classic illustrations of the difference between tech companies that are well-managed and tech companies that are disasters. It comes down to the difference between trusting employees and letting them get things done, versus treating them like burger-flippers who need to be monitored and controlled every minute, lest they wander off and sabotage everything.

My first assignment at my first job was at Microsoft, where I was told to come up with a new macro language strategy for Excel. Pretty soon, I had the first draft of the Excel Basic spec (which later evolved into Visual Basic for Applications, but that's another story). Somehow, this mysterious group of people at Microsoft called the "Application Architecture" group got wind of my spec, which must have concerned them, because for some reason they thought that *they* were in charge of things like macro language strategies, and they asked to see my spec.

I asked around. Who's the Application Architecture group? Nobody seemed to think they were very serious. It turns out that they were a group of just four people, recent hires with PhDs (very unusual for Microsoft). I sent them a copy of my spec and went to meet them, in case they had something interesting to say.

"Blah blah!" said one of them. "Blah blah blah, blah blah blah!" said another. I don't think they quite had anything interesting to say. They were very enamored of the idea of subclassing, and sort of thought that people making macros in Excel wanted to subclass a lot of things. In any case, one of the fellows said, "Well, this is all very interesting. What's next? Who has to approve your spec?"

I laughed. Even though I had only been at Microsoft for a few months, I knew that there was no such thing as somebody *approving* my spec. Hell, nobody had time to *read* my spec, let alone approve it. The programmers were bugging me every day to get them more pages so that they could write more code. My boss (and his boss) made it very clear to me that nobody else understood macros or had time to work on macros, so whatever I did, it better be right. And here this PhD working in a strange research group at Microsoft assumed that things were a bit more formal than that.

I pretty rapidly realized that the App Architecture group knew even less than I did about macros. At least, I had talked to a handful of macro developers and some Excel old-timers to get a grip on what people actually did with Excel macros: things like recalculating a spreadsheet every day, or rearranging some data according to a certain pattern. But the App Architecture group had merely *thought* about macros as an academic exercise, and they couldn't actually come up with any examples of the kind of macros people would want to write. Pressured, one of them came up with the idea that since Excel already had underlining and double-underlining, perhaps someone would want to write a macro to triple underline. Yep. REAL common. So I proceeded to ignore them as diplomatically as possible.

This seemed to piss off a guy named Greg Whitten, who headed up the App Architecture group. Now, Greg was something like Microsoft employee number 6. He had been around forever; nobody could quite point to anything he had done, but apparently he had lunch with Bill Gates a lot and GW-BASIC was named after him. Greg called a Big Meeting and proceeded to complain about how the Excel team (meaning me) was screwing up the macro strategy. We pressured him to come up with some specific reasons, but his arguments just weren't convincing. I thought it was nice that here I was, a new-hire pipsqueak right out of college, arguing with employee number 6 and apparently winning the argument. (Can you imagine that happening at a Gray Flannel Suit company?) My programming team, headed by Ben Waldman (now a VP at Microsoft) backed me up completely, which was all that really mattered, because the programming team wrote the code and thus had the final say on how things got done.

I would have been perfectly happy to leave it at that. If the App Architecture team needed care and feeding and wanted to argue about stuff, that was OK, I would argue with them as much as they wanted as long as they left the programmers alone to do their work. But then something even more interesting happened that blew my mind. I was sitting at lunch with some coworkers, in the Redmond sun, when Pete Higgins came up to me. At that time Pete was the general manager for Office—I knew who he was, of course, but didn't expect that he knew me very well.

"How's it going, Joel?" he asked. "I hear you've been having some issues with the App Architecture group."

"Oh no!" I said. "Nothing I can't handle."

"Say no more," he said, "I understand." He left. By the next day the rumor had gotten back to me: the App Architecture group was disbanded. Not only that, but each member of the group was sent to a different department at Microsoft, as far apart as possible. I never heard from them again.

I was blown away, of course. At Microsoft, if you're the Program Manager working on the Excel macro strategy, even if you've been at the company for less than six months, it doesn't matter—you are the GOD of the Excel macro strategy, and nobody, not even employee number 6, is allowed to get in your way. Period.

This sends a really strong message. For one, it makes everyone that much more conscientious about their jobs. They can't hide behind the idea that "management approved their spec," since management really didn't look too closely at their spec. All management did was hire smart people and gave them something to do. For another, it makes for an extremely nice place to work. Who doesn't want to be king of their own domain? Software, by its nature, is very easy to divide into smaller and smaller components, so it's always possible to divide responsibility among people and let people *own* an area. This is probably *the* reason why software people love working at Microsoft.

Years passed. I found myself working at Juno, an online service and free email provider. This time, the experience was the exact opposite of my work at Microsoft. I had two programmers reporting to me, but my own manager constantly undermined my (limited) authority by going directly to my reports and giving them things to do, often without even telling me. Even for trivial requests like days off, my manager thought that it was his job to approve or disapprove the request.

After a couple of years at Juno, I was working on the new user sign-up feature. For Juno 3.x, a major release, I would be in charge of a complete overhaul of the sign-up process. By this time, I was a relatively senior member of the technical team; I got great performance reviews, and my managers seemed to appreciate the work I was doing. But they just couldn't bring themselves to trust me. Command and control.

One part of the sign-up process asked the users to type in their birthday. This was just one small bit of a lengthy sign-up process that went on for something like 30 screens as Juno grilled you about your income, your favorite sports, how many children you have and how old they were, and about 100 other things. To make the sign-up process a little bit easier, I wanted to change the birthday field to be free format, so you could type "8/12/74" or "August 12, 1974" or "12 Aug 74" or whatever. (Have you used Outlook? It would work like Outlook, where you could type dates in just about any format and it would accept them.)

Without going into too much detail, my manager decided he didn't like this. It became an issue of ego for him. First he yelled at the designer who was working on that page (without even telling me). Then he yelled at me. Then he reminded me every single day that I had to change it to the way *he* wanted it. Then he got the CEO of the company to review it, and made a big show out of getting the CEO of the company to criticize my new design. Even the CEO at Juno is perfectly happy to interfere in work done at the lowest level in the company; in fact, it's standard operating procedure.

I was furious, needless to say. It was a small thing—a matter of taste, really. Some people would prefer my way. Some people would prefer his. In either case, the message was clear: You *will* do as you are told here, dammit. It was a very command-and-conquer mentality that was more of a battle of cojones than a discussion of user interface design.

I won't say that this is the reason I left Juno, but it does illustrate the reason I left Juno: It was the idea that no matter how hard you work, no matter how smart you are, no matter whether you are "in charge" of something or not, you have no authority whatsoever for even the tiniest thing. None. Take your damn ideas, training, brains, and intelligence, all the things we're paying you for, and shove it. And at Juno, there were *plenty* of managers, something like one-quarter of all the employees, and so they had plenty of times to stick their fingers into every single decision and make sure that *they* were in control. The contrast with Microsoft, where VPs descended from Building 9 to make it clear that you have the authority to get things done, was stark.

To some extent, Juno's hopelessly inept management process is a factor of being a New York City company, not a West Coast company, so modern styles of management haven't quite permeated. It's also a problem caused by the deep inexperience of Juno's managers, and it originates at the top—the CEO, a 29-year-old who has never worked outside D. E. Shaw, who interferes in everything he can get his fingers into, including the wording on error messages that come up when things go wrong; the CTO regularly screams at his reports if they dare to question his wisdom;

they take it out on the programmers, who go home and kick their dogs. Compare this to Microsoft, where things are done at the lowest level, and most managers act like their most important job is to run around the room, moving the furniture out of the way, so people can concentrate on their work.

thirty-three

BIG MACS VS. THE NAKED CHEF

THURSDAY, JANUARY 18, 2001

Mystery: Why is it that some of the biggest IT consulting companies in the world do the worst work?

Why is it that the cool upstart consulting companies start out with a string of spectacular successes, meteoric growth, and rapidly degenerate into mediocrity?

I've been thinking about this, and thinking about how my own company should grow. And the best lessons I can find come from McDonald's. Yes, I mean the awful hamburger chain.

The secret of Big Macs is that they're not very good, but every one is not very good in exactly the same way. If you're willing to live with not-very-goodness, you can have a Big Mac with absolutely no chance of being surprised in the slightest.

The other secret of Big Macs is that you can have an IQ that hovers somewhere between "idiot" and "moron" (to use the technical terms), and you'll still be able to produce Big Macs that are exactly as unsurprising as all the other Big Macs in the world. That's because McDonald's *real* secret sauce is its huge operations manual, describing in stunning detail the exact procedure that every franchisee must follow in creating a Big Mac. If a Big Mac hamburger is fried for 37 seconds in Anchorage, Alaska, it will be fried for 37 seconds in Singapore—not 36, not 38. To make a Big Mac, you just follow the damn rules.

The rules have been carefully designed by reasonably intelligent people (back at McDonald's Hamburger University) so that dumdums can follow them just as well as smart people. In fact the rules include all kinds of failsafes, like bells that go off if you keep the fries in the oil too long, which were created to compensate for more than a little human frailty.

There are stopwatches and timing systems everywhere. There is a system to make sure that the janitor checks if the bathrooms are clean every half hour. (Hint: They're not.)

The system basically assumes that everybody will make a bunch of mistakes, but the burgers that come out will be, um, consistent, and you'll always be asked if you want fries with that.

Just for the sake of amusement, let's compare a McDonald's cook, who is following a set of rules exactly and doesn't know anything about food, to a genius like The Naked Chef, the British cutie Jamie Oliver. (If you chose to put down this book now and go to his website[1] to watch the MTV-like videos of making basil aioli, you have my blessing. Go in good health.) Anyway, comparing McDonald's to a gourmet chef is completely absurd, but please suspend disbelief for a moment, because there's something to be learned here.

Now, The Naked Chef doesn't follow no stinkin' Operations Manual. He doesn't measure *anything*. While he's cooking, you see a flurry of food tossed around willy-nilly. "We'll just put a bit of extra rosemary in there, that won't hurt, and give it a good old shake," he says. "Mash it up. Perfect. Just chuck it all over the place." (Yes, it really looks like he's just chucking it all over the place. Sorry, but if *I* tried to chuck it all over the place, it wouldn't work.) It takes about 14 seconds and he's basically improvised a complete gourmet meal with roasted slashed fillet of sea-bass stuffed with herbs, baked on mushroom potatoes with a salsa-verde. Yum.

Well, I think it's pretty obvious that The Naked Chef's food is better than you get at McDonald's. Even if it sounds like a stupid question, it's worth a minute to ask *why*. It's not such a stupid question. Why can't a big company with zillions of resources, incredible scale, access to the best food designers money can buy, and infinite cash flow produce a nice meal?

Imagine that The Naked Chef gets bored doing "telly" and opens a restaurant. Of course, he's a brilliant chef, the food would be incredible, so the place is hopping with customers and shockingly profitable.

When you have a shockingly profitable restaurant, you quickly realize that even if you fill up every night, and even if you charge $19 for an appetizer and $3.95 for a Coke, your profits reach a natural limit,

---

1. See www.jamieoliver.net/.

because one chef can make only so much food. So you hire another chef, and maybe open some more branches, maybe in other cities.

Now a problem starts to develop—what we in the technical fields call the *scalability problem*. When you try to clone a restaurant, you must decide between hiring another great chef of your caliber (in which case, that chef will probably want and expect to keep most of the extra profits that he created, so why bother), or else you'll hire a cheaper, younger chef who's not quite as good, but pretty soon your patrons will figure that out and they won't go to the clone restaurant.

The common way of dealing with the scalability problem is to hire cheap chefs who don't know anything, and give them such precise rules about how to create every dish that they "can't" screw it up. Just follow these here rules, and you'll make great gourmet food!

Problem: It doesn't work exactly right. There are a million things that a good chef does that have to do with *improvisation*. A good chef sees some awesome mangos in the farmer's market and improvises a mango-cilantro salsa for the fish of the day. A good chef deals with a temporary shortage of potatoes by creating some taro chip thing. An automaton chef who is merely following instructions might be able to produce a given dish when everything is working perfectly, but without real talent and skill, will not be able to improvise, which is why you never see jicama at McDonald's.

McDonald's requires a very *particular* variety of potato, which they grow all over the world, and which they precut and freeze in massive quantities to survive shortages. The precutting and freezing means that the french-fries are not as good as they could be, but they are certainly *consistent* and require no chef-skills. In fact, McDonald's does hundreds of things to make sure that their product can be produced with consistent quality, by *any moron you can get in the kitchen,* even if the quality is "a bit" lower.

Summary, so far:

1. Some things need talent to do really well.

2. It's hard to scale talent.

3. One way people try to scale talent is by having the talent create rules for the untalented to follow.

4. The quality of the resulting product is very low.

You can see the *exact same story* playing out in IT consulting. How many times have you heard the following story?

Mike was unhappy. He had hired a huge company of IT consultants to build The System. The IT consultants he hired were incompetents who kept talking about "The Methodology" and who spent millions of dollars and had failed to produce a single thing.

Luckily, Mike found a youthful programmer who was really smart and talented. The youthful programmer built his whole system in one day for $20 and pizza. Mike was overjoyed. He recommended the youthful programmer to all his friends.

Youthful Programmer starts raking in the money. Soon, he has more work than he can handle, so he hires a bunch of people to help him. The good people want too many stock options, so he decides to hire even younger programmers right out of college and "train them" with a six-week course.

The trouble is that the "training" doesn't really produce consistent results, so Youthful Programmer starts creating rules and procedures that are meant to make more consistent results. Over the years, the rule book grows and grows. Soon it's a six-volume manual called The Methodology.

After a few dozen years, Youthful Programmer is now a Huge Incompetent IT Consultant with a capital-M-methodology and a lot of people who blindly obey the Methodology, even when it doesn't seem to be working, because they have no bloody idea whatsoever what else to do, and they're not really talented programmers—they're just well-meaning Poli-Sci majors who attended the six-week course.

And Newly Huge Incompetent IT Consultant starts messing up. Their customers are unhappy. And another upstart talented programmer comes and takes away all their business, and the cycle begins anew.

I don't need to name names, here; this cycle has happened a dozen times. All the IT service companies get greedy and try to grow faster than they can find talented people, and they grow layers upon layers of rules and procedures which help produce "consistent," if not very brilliant, work.

But the rules and procedures only work when nothing goes wrong. Various "data-backed website" consulting companies sprouted up in the last couple of years and filled their ranks by teaching rank amateurs the fourteen things you need to know to create a data-backed website ("here's a select statement, kid, build a website"). But now that dotcoms are imploding and there's suddenly demand for high-end GUI programming, C++ skills, and real computer science, the kids who only have select statements in their arsenal just have too steep a learning curve and can't catch up. But they still keep trying, following the rules in Book III, Chapter 17, Paragraph 29.4*b* about normalizing databases, which mysteriously don't apply to The New World. The brilliant *founders* of these companies could certainly adjust to the new world: they are talented computer scientists who can learn anything, but the *company they built* can't adjust because it has substituted a rulebook for talent, and rulebooks don't adjust to new times.

What's the moral of the story? *Beware of Methodologies.* They are a great way to bring everyone up to a dismal, but passable, level of performance, but at the same time, they are aggravating to more talented people who chafe at the restrictions placed on them. It's pretty obvious to me that a talented chef is not going to be happy making burgers at McDonald's, precisely *because* of McDonald's rules. So why do IT consultants brag so much about their methodologies? (Beats me.)

What does this mean for my company, Fog Creek? Well, our goal has never been to become a huge consulting company. We started out doing consulting as a means to an end—the long-term goal was to be a software company that is always profitable, and we achieved that by doing some consulting work to supplement our software income. After a couple of years in business, our software revenues grew to the point where consulting was just a low-margin distraction, so now we only do consulting engagements that directly support our software. Software, as you know, scales *incredibly* well. When one new person buys FogBUGZ, we make more money without spending any more money.

More important is our obsession with hiring the best...we are perfectly happy to stay small if we can't find enough good people (although with six weeks annual vacation, finding people doesn't seem to pose a problem). And we refuse to grow until the people we already hired have learned enough to become teachers and mentors of the new crowd.

thirty-four

NOTHING IS AS SIMPLE AS IT SEEMS

There are a lot of great ideas that come together under the name
Extreme Programming, *a few not-so-great ideas, and one really dangerous idea: the idea that planning and designing is a waste of time.
Even if the Extreme Programming philosophy advocates a complete
development methodology that seems to make sense, in practice it's
often just used as an excuse by programmers to avoid designing features before they implement them. "The source code is the design!"
they say. But it's not, and if you develop software that way, you'll
find yourself in an endless churn cycle, hunting for software smells
and trying to refactor them away instead of making useful progress.*

MONDAY, MARCH 4, 2002

We had a little usability problem in CityDesk.

Here was the problem: You could import files from the Web by using
a menu command (Import Web Page). And you could import files from a
disk into CityDesk by dragging them with the mouse. But there was no
menu command to import files from a disk. So either people didn't discover that it was possible, or people tried to use the Import Web Page
feature to import from disk, which didn't work right.

I thought that it would be easy to fix with a two-page wizard. Roughly
speaking, page one of the wizard would ask you "Where do you want to
import from?" If you chose "disk," page two would prompt you for a file.
If you chose "Web," page two would prompt you for a URL.

I almost started implementing this, but something stopped me, and
instead, I started to write a mini-spec. Here's the spec, in its entirety:

Page One
Where do you want to import from? (Disk/Web)

Page Two (Disk)
Standard File/Open dialog

Page Two (Web)
URL prompt with mini-web-browser

Suddenly, something occurred to me. Can you put the Windows standard file open dialog, which is usually supplied in toto by the OS, into a wizard?

Hmm.

I investigated. Yes, you can, but it's no fun and takes a few hours of work.[1] How could I make this not be a wizard? I rewrote the spec:

Two Menu Items:

1. **Import Web Page From Internet** > Pops Up URL Dialog

2. **Import Web Page From Disk** > Pops Up File Open Dialog

---

1. See www.vbaccelerator.com/codelib/cmdlgd/cmdlgtp.htm.

Much better. Three minutes of design work saved me hours of coding. If you've spent more than 20 minutes of your life writing code, you've probably discovered a good rule of thumb by now: *nothing is as simple as it seems.*

Something as simple as copying a file is full of perils. What if the first argument is a directory? What if the second argument is a file? What if a file with the same name already exists in the destination? What if you don't have write permission?

What if the copy fails in the middle? What if the destination is on a remote machine which is available, but which requires authentication to continue? What if the files are large and the link is slow and you need to show a progress indicator? What if the transfer speed slows down to almost zero...when do you give up and return an error message?

A good way to interview candidates for testing jobs is to give them a simple operation and ask them to enumerate all the things that can possibly go wrong. A classic Microsoft test interview question: how do you test the File Open dialog box? A good tester will be able to rattle off several dozen weird things to test ("file is deleted by another user between the time it is listed in the box and the time you select it and click Open").

OK, so we have one axiom: Nothing is as simple as it seems.

There's another axiom in software engineering: Always try to reduce risk. One particularly important piece of risk to avoid is schedule risk, when something takes longer than expected. Schedule risk is bad because your boss yells at you, which makes you unhappy. If that's not enough motivation for you, the economic reason why schedule risk is bad is because you decided to do a feature based on information that it would take one week. Now that you realize that it has taken twenty weeks to accomplish, that decision might well have been wrong. Perhaps if you knew it was going to take twenty weeks, you would have made a different decision. The more wrong decisions you make, the more likely all those tote bags with your company logo will end up in the liquidator's warehouse while your ex-CEO mopes that "what sucks is, we weren't even successful enough to get mentioned on fuckedcompany.com when we shut down!"

The combination of the axioms nothing-is-as-simple-as-it-seems and reduce-risk can only lead you to one conclusion:

You have to design things before you implement them.

I'm sorry to disappoint you. Yeah, I know, you read Kent Beck and now you think it's OK to not design things before you implement them. Sorry, it's not OK. You can *not* change things in code "just as easily" as you could change them in the design documents. People say this all the time and it's wrong. "We use high-level tools these days, like Java and XML. We can change things in minutes in the code. Why not design it in code?" My friend, you can put wheels on your mama but that doesn't make her a bus, and if you think you can refactor your wrongly implemented file-copy function to make it preemptive rather than threaded as quickly as I could write that sentence, you're in deep denial.

Anyway, I don't think Extreme Programming really advocates zero design. They just say "don't do any more design than needed," which is fine. But that's not what people hear. Most programmers are looking for any excuse they can find not to do basic design before implementing features. So they latch onto the "no-design" idea like flies in a bug zapper. Dzzzzzzt! It's one of those weird forms of laziness where you end up doing more work than you would have done otherwise. I'm too lazy to design the feature on paper first, so I just write some code, and then it's not right, so I have to fix it, and I spend more time than I would have otherwise. Or, more commonly, I write some code, and then it's not right, but it's too late, and my product is inferior and I spend until the end of time making up excuses for why it "has to be that way." It's just sloppy and unprofessional.

When Linus Torvalds bashed design,[2] he was talking about huge systems, which have to evolve, or they become Multics. He's not talking about your File Copy code. And when you consider that he had a pretty clear road map of exactly where he was going, it's no wonder Linus doesn't see much value in design. Don't fall for it. Chances are it doesn't apply to you. And anyway, Linus is much smarter than we are, so things that work for him don't work for us normal people.

Incremental design and implementation is good. Frequent releases are fine (although for shrinkwrapped or mass-market software, it drives customers crazy, which is never a good idea, so instead do frequent internal milestones). Too much formality in design is a waste of time—I've never seen a project benefit from mindless flowcharting or UMLing or

---

2. See www.uwsg.iu.edu/hypermail/linux/kernel/0112.0/0004.html.

CRCing or whatever the flavor-du-jour is. And those huge 10-million-lines-of-code behemoth systems that Linus is talking about should evolve, because humans don't really know how to design software on that scale.

But when you sit down to write File Copy, or when you sit down to plan the features of the next release of your software, you gotta design. Don't let the Sirens persuade you otherwise.

thirty-five

IN DEFENSE OF NOT-INVENTED-HERE SYNDROME

Sunday, October 14, 2001

Time for a pop quiz.

1. Code Reuse is:

   a) Good

   b) Bad

2. Reinventing the Wheel is:

   a) Good

   b) Bad

3. The Not-Invented-Here Syndrome is:

   a) Good

   b) Bad

Of course, *everybody knows* that you should always leverage other people's work. The correct answers are, *of course*, 1(a) 2(b) 3(b).

Right?

Not so fast, there!

The Not-Invented-Here Syndrome is considered a classic management pathology in which a team refuses to use a technology that they didn't create themselves. People with NIH syndrome are obviously just being petty, refusing to do what's in the best interest of the overall organization because they can't find a way to take credit. (Right?) The Boring Business History Section at your local megabookstore is rife with stories about stupid teams who spend millions of dollars and twelve years building something they could have bought at CompUSA for $9.99. And everybody who has paid any attention *whatsoever* to three decades of progress in computer programming knows that reuse is the Holy Grail of all modern programming systems.

Right. Well, that's what I thought, too. So when I was the program manager in charge of the first implementation of Visual Basic for Applications, I put together a careful coalition of four, count them, four different teams at Microsoft to get custom dialog boxes in Excel VBA. The idea was complicated and fraught with interdependencies. There was a team called AFX that was working on some kind of dialog editor. Then we would use this brand new code from the OLE group which let you embed one app inside another. And the Visual Basic team would provide the programming language behind it. After a week of negotiation, I got the AFX, OLE, and VB teams to agree to this in principle.

I stopped by Andrew Kwatinetz's office. He was my manager at the time and taught me everything I know. "The Excel development team will never accept it," he said. "You know their motto? 'Find the dependencies—and eliminate them.' They'll never go for something with so many dependencies."

In-ter-est-ing. I hadn't known that. I guess that explained why Excel had its own C compiler.

By now I'm sure many of my readers are rolling on the floor laughing. "Isn't Microsoft stupid," you're thinking, "they refused to use other people's code and they even had their own compiler just for one product."

Not so fast, big boy! The Excel team's ruggedly independent mentality also meant that they always shipped on time, their code was of uniformly high quality, and they had a compiler which, back in the 1980s, generated pcode and could therefore run unmodified on Macintosh's 68000 chip as well as Intel PCs. The pcode also made the executable file about half the size that Intel binaries would have been, so it loaded faster from floppy disks and required less RAM.

"Find the dependencies—and eliminate them." When you're working on a really, really good team with great programmers, everybody else's code, frankly, is bug-infested garbage, and nobody else knows how to ship on time. When you're a cordon bleu chef and you *need* fresh lavender, you grow it yourself instead of buying it in the farmers' market, because sometimes they don't have fresh lavender or they have old lavender which they pass off as fresh.

Indeed, during the recent dotcom mania a bunch of quack business writers suggested that the company of the future would be totally virtual—just a trendy couple sipping Chardonnay in their living room outsourcing everything. What these hyperventilating "visionaries" overlooked is that the market pays for value added. Two yuppies in a living room buying an e-commerce engine from company A and selling merchandise made by company B and warehoused and shipped by company C, with customer service from company D, isn't honestly adding much value. In fact, if you've ever had to outsource a critical business function, you realize that outsourcing is hell. Without direct control over customer service, you're going to get nightmarishly bad customer service—the kind people write about in their weblogs when they tried to get someone, *anyone*, from some phone company to do even the most basic thing. If you outsource fulfillment, and your fulfillment partner has a different idea about what constitutes prompt delivery, your customers are not going to be happy, and there's nothing you can do about it, because it took three months to find a fulfillment partner in the first place, and in fact, you won't even *know* that your customers are unhappy, because they can't talk to you, because you've set up an outsourced customer service center with the explicit aim of *not* listening to your own customers. That e-commerce engine you bought? There's no way it's going to be as flexible as what Amazon does with *obidos*, which they wrote themselves. (And if it is, then Amazon has no advantage over their competitors who bought the same thing.) And no off-the-shelf web server is going to be as blazingly fast as what Google does with their hand-coded, hand-optimized server.

This principle, unfortunately, seems to be directly in conflict with the ideal of "code reuse good—reinventing wheel bad."

The best advice I can offer:

If it's a core business function—do it yourself, no matter what.

Pick your core business competencies and goals, and do those in-house. If you're a software company, writing excellent code is how you're going to succeed. Go ahead and outsource the company cafeteria and the CD-ROM duplication. If you're a pharmaceutical company, write software for drug research, but don't write your own accounting package. If you're a Web accounting service, write your own accounting package, but don't try to create your own magazine ads. If you have customers, never outsource customer service.

If you're developing a computer game in which the plot is your competitive advantage, it's OK to use a third-party 3D library. But if cool 3D effects are going to be your distinguishing feature, you had better roll your own.

The only exception to this rule, I suspect, is if your own people are more incompetent than everyone else, so whenever you try to do anything in house, it's botched up. Yes, there are plenty of places like this. If you're in one of them, I can't help you.

thirty-six

STRATEGY LETTER I: BEN & JERRY'S VS. AMAZON

FRIDAY, MAY 12, 2000

Building a company? You've got one very important decision to make, because it affects everything else you do: No matter what else you do, you absolutely *must* figure out which camp you're in, and gear everything you do accordingly, or you're going to have a disaster on your hands.

The decision? Whether to grow slowly, organically, and profitably, or whether to have a big bang with very fast growth and lots of capital.

The organic model is to start small, with limited goals, and slowly build a business over a long period of time. I'm going to call this the Ben & Jerry's model, because Ben & Jerry's fits this model pretty well.

The other model, popularly called Get Big Fast (a.k.a. Land Grab), requires you to raise a lot of capital, and work as quickly as possible to get big fast without concern for profitability. I'm going to call this the Amazon model, because Jeff Bezos, the founder of Amazon, has practically become the celebrity spokesmodel for Get Big Fast.

Let's look at some of the differences between these models. The first thing to ask is: Are you going into a business that has competition, or not?

Ben & Jerry's	Amazon
Lots of established competitors	New technology, no competition at first

If you don't have any real competition, as with Amazon, there is a chance that you can succeed at a Land Grab—that is, get as many customers as quickly as possible so that later competitors will have a serious barrier to entry. But if you're going into an industry that has a well-established set of competitors, the Land Grab idea doesn't make sense, because you'd need to create your customer base by getting customers to switch over from competitors.

In general, venture capitalists aren't too enthusiastic about the idea of going into a market with pesky competitors. Personally, I'm not so scared of established competition, perhaps because I worked on Microsoft Excel during a period when it almost completely took over Lotus 123, which virtually had the market to itself. The number-one word processor, Word, displaced WordPerfect, which displaced WordStar, all of which had been near monopolies at one time or another. And Ben & Jerry's grew to be a fabulous business, even though it's not like you couldn't get ice cream before they came along. It's not impossible to displace a competitor, if that's what you want to do. (I'll talk about how to do that in the next chapters.)

Another question about displacing competitors has to do with network effects and lock-in:

Ben & Jerry's	Amazon
No network effect, weak customer lock-in	Strong network effect, strong customer lock-in

A *network effect* is a situation where the more customers you have, the more customers you will get. It's based on Metcalfe's Law:[1] The value of a network is equal to the number of users squared.

A good example is eBay. If you want to sell your old Patek Philippe watch, you're going to get a better price on eBay, because there are more buyers there. If you want to buy a Patek Philippe watch, you're going to look on eBay, because there are more sellers there.

Another extremely strong network effect is created by proprietary chat systems like ICQ or AOL Instant Messenger. If you want to chat with people, you have to go where they are, and ICQ and AOL have the

---

1. See www.mgt.smsu.edu/mgt487/mgtissue/newstrat/metcalfe.htm.

most people by far. Chances are, your friends are using one of those services, not one of the smaller ones like MSN Instant Messenger. With all of Microsoft's muscle, money, and marketing skill, they are just not going to be able to break into auctions or instant messaging, because the network effects there are so strong.

Lock-in is the characteristic of the business that makes people not want to switch. Nobody wants to switch their Internet provider, even if the service isn't very good, because of the hassle of changing your email address and notifying everyone. People don't want to switch word processors if their old files can't be read by the new word processor.

Even better than lock-in is the sneaky version I call *stealth lock-in*: services that lock you in without your even realizing it. For example, all those new services like PayMyBills.com, which receive your bills for you, scan them in, and show them to you on the Internet. They usually come with three months free service. But when the three months are up, if you don't want to continue with the service, you have no choice but to contact every single bill provider and ask them to change the billing address back to your house. The sheer chore of doing this is likely to prevent you from switching away from PayMyBills.com—better just to let them keep sucking $8.95 out of your bank account every month. Gotcha!

If you are going into a business that has natural network effects and lock-in, and there are no established competitors, then you *better* use the Amazon model, or somebody else will, and you simply won't be able to get a toehold.

Quick case study. In 1998, AOL was spending massively to grow at a rate of a million customers every five weeks. AOL has nice features, like chat rooms and instant messaging, that provide stealth lock-in. Once you've found a group of friends you like to chat with, you are simply *not* going to switch Internet providers. That's like trying to get all new friends. In my mind, that's the key reason AOL can charge around $22 a month when there are plenty of $10-a-month Internet providers.

While I was working at Juno, management just failed to understand this point, and they missed their best opportunity to overtake AOL during a Land Grab when everyone was coming on-line: they didn't spend strongly enough on customer acquisition because they didn't want to dilute existing shareholders by raising more capital, and they didn't think strategically about chat and IM, so they never developed any software features to provide the kind of stealth lock-in that AOL has. Now

Juno has around 3 million people paying them an average of $5.50 a month, while AOL has around 21 million people paying them an average of $17 a month. Oops.

Ben & Jerry's	Amazon
Little capital required; break even fast	Outrageous amounts of capital required; profitability can take years

Ben & Jerry's–style companies start on somebody's credit card. In their early months and years, they must use a business model that becomes profitable extremely quickly, which may not be the ultimate business model that they want to achieve. For example, you may *want* to become a giant ice cream company with $200,000,000 in annual sales, but for now, you're going to have to *settle* for opening a little ice cream shop in Vermont, hope that it's profitable, and, if it is, reinvest the profits to expand business steadily. The Ben & Jerry's corporate history says they started with a $12,000 investment. ArsDigita says that they started with an $11,000 investment. These numbers sound like a typical MasterCard credit limit. Hmmm.

Amazon companies raise money practically as fast as anyone can spend it. There's a reason for this. They are in a terrible rush. If they are in a business with no competitors and network effects, they better get big super fast. Every day matters. And there are *lots* of ways to substitute money for time. Nearly all of them are fun:

- Use prebuilt, furnished executive offices instead of traditional office space. Cost: about three times as much. Time saved: several months to a year, depending on market.

- Pay outrageous salaries or offer programmers BMWs as starting bonuses. Cost: about 25 percent extra for technical staff. Time saved: you can fill openings in three weeks instead of the more typical six months.

- Hire consultants instead of employees. Cost: about three times as much. Time saved: you can get consultants up and running right away. (Having trouble getting your consultants to give you the time and attention you need? Bribe them with cash until they want to work only for you.)

- Spend cash freely to spot-solve problems. If your new star programmer isn't getting a lot of work done because they are busy setting up their new house and relocating, hire a high-class relocation service to do it for them. If it's taking forever to get phones installed in your new offices, buy a couple dozen cellular phones. Internet access problems slowing people down? Just get two redundant providers. Provide a concierge available to all employees for picking up dry cleaning, getting reservations, arranging for limos to the airport, etc.

Ben & Jerry's companies just can't afford to do this, so they have to settle for growing slowly.

Ben & Jerry's	Amazon
Corporate culture is important.	Corporate culture is impossible.

When your company is growing faster than about 100 percent per year, it is simply impossible for mentors to transmit corporate values to new hires. If a programmer is promoted to manager and suddenly has five new reports, hired just yesterday, it is simply impossible to have much mentoring. Netscape is the most egregious example of this, growing from 5 to about 2,000 programmers in one year. As a result, their culture was a mishmash of different people with different values about the company, all tugging in different directions.

For some companies, this might be OK. For other companies, the corporate culture is an important part of the raison d'être of the company. Ben & Jerry's *exists* because of the values of the founders, who would not accept growing faster than the rate at which that culture can be promulgated.

Let's take a hypothetical software example. Suppose you want to break into the market for word processors. Now, this market seems to be pretty sewn up by Microsoft, but you see a niche for people who, for whatever reason, absolutely cannot have their word processors crashing on them. You are going to make a super-robust, industrial-strength word processor that just won't go down, and you sell it at a premium to people who simply depend on word processors for their *lives*. (OK, it's a stretch. I *said* this was a hypothetical example.)

Now, your corporate culture probably includes all kinds of techniques for writing highly robust code: unit testing, formal code reviews, coding conventions, large QA departments, and so on. These techniques are not trivial; they must be learned over a period of time. While a new programmer is learning how to write robust code, they must be mentored and coached by someone more experienced.

As soon as you try to grow so fast that mentoring and coaching is impossible, you are simply going to stop transmitting those values. New hires won't know better and will write unreliable code. They won't check the return value from malloc(), and their code will fail in some bizarre case that they never thought about, and nobody will have time to review their code and teach them the right way to do it, and your entire competitive advantage over Microsoft Word has been squandered.

Ben & Jerry's	Amazon
Mistakes become valuable lessons.	Mistakes are not really noticed.

A company that is growing too fast will simply not notice when it makes a big mistake, especially of the spend-too-much-money kind. Amazon buys Junglee, a comparison shopping service, for around $180,000,000 in stock, and then suddenly realizes that comparison shopping services are not very good for their business, so they just shut it down. Having piles and piles of cash makes stupid mistakes easy to cover up.

Ben & Jerry's	Amazon
It takes a long time to get big.	You get big very fast.

Getting big fast gives the *impression* (if not the reality) of being successful. When prospective employees see that you're hiring 30 new people a week, they will feel like they are part of something big and exciting and successful which will IPO. They may not be as impressed by a "sleepy little company" with 12 employees and a dog, even if the sleepy company is profitable and is building a better long-term company.

As a rule of thumb, you can make a nice place to work, or you can promise people they'll get rich quick. But you have to do one of those, or you won't be able to hire.

Some of your employees will be impressed by a company with a high chance of an IPO that gives out lots of stock options. Such people will be willing to put in three or four years at a company like this, even if they hate every minute of their working days, because they see the pot at the end of the rainbow.

If you're growing slowly and organically, the pot may be further off. In that case, you have no choice but to make a work environment where the journey is the reward. It can't be hectic 80-hour workweeks. The office can't be a big noisy loft jammed full of folding tables and hard wooden chairs. You have to give people decent vacations. People have to be friends with their coworkers, not just coworkers. Sociology and community at work matter. Managers have to be enlightened and get off people's backs, they can't be Dilbertesque micromanagers. If you do all this, you'll attract plenty of people who have been fooled too many times by dreams of becoming a millionaire in the next IPO; now they are just looking for something *sustainable*.

Ben & Jerry's	Amazon
You'll probably succeed. You certainly won't lose *too* much money.	You have a tiny chance of becoming a billionaire, and a high chance of just failing.

With the Ben & Jerry's model, if you're even reasonably smart, you're going to succeed. It may be a bit of a struggle, there may be good years and bad years, but unless we have another Great Depression, you're certainly not going to lose *too* much money, because you didn't put in too much to begin with.

The trouble with the Amazon model is that all anybody thinks about is Amazon. And there's only one Amazon. You have to think of the other 95 percent of the companies that spend an astonishing amount of venture capital and then simply fail because nobody wants to buy their products. At least, if you follow the Ben & Jerry's model, you'll know that nobody wants your product long before you spend more than one MasterCard's-worth of credit limit on it.

~

The Worst Thing You Can Do

The worst thing you can do is fail to decide whether you're going to be a Ben & Jerry's company or an Amazon company.

If you're going into a market with no existing competition, lock-in, and network effects, you *better* use the Amazon model, or you're going the way of Wordsworth.com, which started two years before Amazon, and nobody's ever heard of them. Or even worse, you're going to be a ghost site like MSN Auctions[2] with virtually no chance of ever overcoming eBay.

If you're going into an established market, getting big fast is a fabulous way of wasting tons of money, as did BarnesandNoble.com. Your best hope is to do something *sustainable* and *profitable*, so that you have years to slowly take over your competition.

Still can't decide? There are other things to consider. Think of your personal values. Would you rather have a company like Amazon or a company like Ben & Jerry's? Read a couple of corporate histories—Amazon[3] and Ben & Jerry's[4] for starters, even though they are blatant hagiographies—and see which one jibes more with your set of core values. Actually, an even better model for a Ben & Jerry's company is Microsoft, and there are lots of histories of Microsoft. Microsoft was, in a sense, "lucky" to land the PC-DOS deal, but the company was profitable and growing all along, so they could have hung around indefinitely waiting for their big break.

Think of your risk/reward profile. Do you want to take a shot at being a billionaire by the time you're 35, even if the chances of doing that make the lottery look like a good deal? Ben & Jerry's companies are not going to do that for you.

---

2. See auctions.msn.com/.

3. Robert Spector, *amazon.com—Get Big Fast: Inside the Revolutionary Business Model that Changed the World* (HarperCollins, 2000).

4. Fred Lager, *Ben & Jerry's: The Inside Scoop: How Two Real Guys Built a Business With a Social Conscience and a Sense of Humor* (Crown, 1994).

Probably the worst thing you can do is to decide that you have to be an Amazon company, and then act like a Ben & Jerry's company (while in denial all the time). Amazon companies absolutely *must* substitute cash for time whenever they can. You may think you're smart and frugal by insisting on finding programmers who will work at market rates. But you're not so smart, because that's going to take you six months, not two months, and those four months might mean you miss the Christmas shopping season, so now it cost you a year, and probably made your whole business plan unviable. You may think that it's smart to have a Mac version of your software, as well as a Windows version, but if it takes you twice as long to ship while your programmers build a compatibility layer, and you only get 15 percent more customers, well, you're not going to look so smart, then, are you?

Both models work, but you've got to pick one and stick to it, or you'll find things mysteriously going wrong and you won't quite know why.

thirty-seven

STRATEGY LETTER II: CHICKEN-AND-EGG PROBLEMS

WEDNESDAY, MAY 24, 2000

The idea of advertising is to lie without getting caught. Most companies, when they run an advertising campaign, simply take the most unfortunate truth about their company, turn it upside down ("lie"), and drill that lie home. Let's call it "proof by repeated assertion." For example, plane travel is cramped and uncomfortable and airline employees are rude and unpleasant, indeed the whole commercial air *system* is designed as a means of torture. So almost all airline ads are going to be about how *comfortable* and *pleasant* it is to fly and how *pampered* you will be every step of the way. When British Airways showed an ad with a businessman in a plane seat dreaming that he was a baby in a basket, all sense of reasonableness was gone for good.

Need another example? Paper companies are completely devastating our national forests, clear-cutting old growth forest that they don't even own. So when they advertise, they inevitably show some nice old pine forest and talk about how much they care about the environment. Cigarettes cause death, so their ads show life, like all the ads with happy smiling healthy people exercising outdoors. And so on.

When the Macintosh first came out, no software was available for it. So obviously, Apple created a giant glossy catalog listing all the great software that was "available." Half of the items listed said, in fine print, "under development," and the other half couldn't be had for love or money. Some were such lame products that nobody would buy them. But even having a thick, glossy catalog with one software "product" per page described in glowing prose couldn't disguise the fact that you just could not buy a word processor or spreadsheet to run on your 128KB Macintosh. There were similar "software product guides" for NeXT and BeOS. (Attention, NeXT and BeOS bigots: I don't need any flak about your poxy operating systems, OK? Write your own column.) The only thing a software product guide tells you is that no software is available for the system. When you see one of these beasts, run fleeing in the opposite direction.

Amiga, Atari ST, Gem, IBM TopView, NeXT, BeOS, Windows CE, General Magic—the list of failed "new platforms" goes on and on. Because they are *platforms*, they are, by definition, not very interesting in and of themselves without juicy software to run on them. But, with very few exceptions (and I'm sure I'll get a whole *host* of email from tedious supporters of arcane and unloved platforms like the Amiga or RSTS-11), no software developer with the least bit of common sense would intentionally write software for a platform with 100,000 users on a *good* day, like BeOS, when they could do the same amount of work and create software for a platform with 100,000,000 users, like Windows. The fact that anybody writes software for those oddball systems at all proves that the profit motive isn't everything; religious fervor is still alive and well. Good for you, darling. You wrote a nice microEmacs clone for the Timex Sinclair 1000. Bravo. Here's a quarter, buy yourself a treat.

So. If you're in the platform-creation business, you probably will suffer from what is commonly known as the *chicken-and-egg problem*: Nobody is going to buy your platform until there's good software that runs on it, and nobody is going to write software until you have a big installed base. Ooops. It's sort of like a Gordian Knot, although a Gordian Death Spiral might be more descriptive.

The chicken-and-egg problem, and variants thereof, is *the* most important element of strategy to understand. Well, OK, you can probably live without understanding it: Steve Jobs practically made a *career* out of not understanding the chicken-and-egg problem, *twice*. But the rest of us don't have Jobs's Personal Reality Distortion Field at our disposal, so we'll have to buckle down and study hard.

The classic domain of chicken-and-egg problems is in software platforms. But here's another chicken-and-egg problem: Every month, *millions* of credit card companies mail out *zillions* of bills to consumers in the mail. People write paper checks, stuff them in trillions of envelopes, and mail them back. The envelopes are put in big boxes and taken to countries where labor is cheap to be opened and processed. But the whole operation costs quite a bit: the last figure I heard was that it is more than $1 per bill.

To us Internet wise-guys, that's a joke. "Email me my bill," you say. "I'll pay it online!" You say. "It'll only cost, say, 1/10,0000th of a penny. You'll save *millions*." Or something like that.

And you're right. So a lot of companies have tried to get into this field, which is technically known as *bill presentment*. One example is (guess who) Microsoft. Their solution, TransPoint,[1] looks like this: It's a website. You go there, and it shows you your bills. You pay them.

So, now, if you get your bills on this Microsoft system, you have to visit the web page every few days to see if any bills have arrived so you don't miss them. If you get, say, ten bills a month, this might not be too big a hassle. Therein lies the other problem: Only a small handful of merchants will bill you over this system. So for all your other bills, you'll have to go elsewhere.

End result? It's not worth it. I would be surprised if 10,000 people are using this system. Now, Microsoft has to go to merchants and say, "Bill your customers over our system!" And the merchants will say, "OK! How much will it cost?" And Microsoft will say, "50 cents! But it's a lot cheaper than $1!" And the merchants will say, "OK. Anything else?" And Microsoft will say, "Oh yes, it will cost you about $250,000 to set up the software, connect our systems to your systems, and get everything working."

And since Microsoft has so few dang users on this system, it's hard to imagine why anyone would pay $250,000 to save 50 cents on 37 users. Aha! The chicken-and-egg problem has reared its ugly head! Customers won't show up until you have merchants, and merchants won't show up until you have customers! Eventually, Microsoft is just going to spend their way out of this predicament.[2] For smaller companies, that's not an option. So what can you do?

Software platforms actually gives us some nice hints as to how to roast your chicken-and-egg problem. Let's look a bit at the history of

1. TransPoint is long gone. I guess I was right.
2. I guess I was wrong.

personal computer software platforms in the years since the IBM-PC came out; maybe we'll discover something!

Most people think that the IBM-PC required PC-DOS. Not true. When the IBM-PC first came out, you had a choice of three operating systems: PC-DOS, XENIX (a wimpy 8-bit version of UNIX published by, and I am not making this up, Microsoft), and something called UCSD P-System,[3] which was, if you can believe this, just like Java: nice, slow, portable bytecodes, about 20 years before Java.

Now, most people have never heard of XENIX or UCSD's weirdo stuff. You kids today probably think that this is because Microsoft took over the market for dinky operating systems through marketing muscle or something. Absolutely not true; Microsoft was tiny in those days. The company with the marketing muscle was Digital Research, which had a different operating system. So, why was PC-DOS the winner of the three-way race?

Before the PC, the only real operating system you could get was CP/M, although the market for CP/M-based computers, which cost about $10,000, was too small. They were cranky and expensive and not very user-friendly. But those who did buy them did so to use as word processors, because you could get a pretty good word processor called WordStar for CP/M, and the Apple II just could *not* do word processing (it didn't have lower case, to begin with).

Now, here's a little-known fact: Even DOS 1.0 was designed with a CP/M backward-compatibility mode *built in*. Not only did it have its own spiffy new programming interface, known to hard-core programmers as INT 21, but it fully supported the old CP/M programming interface. It could *almost* run CP/M software. In fact, WordStar was ported to DOS by changing *one single byte* in the code. (Real Programmers can tell you what that byte was; I've long since forgotten.) That bears mentioning again. WordStar was ported to DOS by changing *one single byte* in the code. Let that sink in.

There.

Got it?

---

3. See www.threedee.com/jcm/psystem/.

DOS was popular *because it had software from day one*. And it had software because Tim Paterson had thought to include a CP/M compatibility feature in it, because way back in the dark ages, somebody was smart about chicken-and-egg problems.

Fast forward. In the entire *history* of the PC platform, there have only been two major paradigm shifts that took along almost every PC user: We all switched to Windows 3.x, and then we all switched to Windows 95. Only a tiny number of people ever switched to anything else on the way. Microsoft conspiracy to take over the world? Fine, you're welcome to think that. I think it's for another, more interesting reason, which just comes back to the chicken and the egg.

We all switched to Windows 3.x. The important clue in that sentence is the *3*. Why didn't we all switch to Windows 1.0? Or Windows 2.0? Or Windows 286 or Windows 386 which followed? Is it because it takes Microsoft five releases to "get it right"? *No.*

The actual reason was even more subtle than that, and it has to do with a very arcane hardware features that first showed up on the Intel 80386 chip, which Windows 3.0 required.

- Feature one: Old DOS programs put things on the screen by writing directly to memory locations that corresponded to character cells on the screen. This was the only way to do output fast enough to make your program look good. But Windows ran in graphics mode. On older Intel chips, the Microsoft engineers had no choice but to flip into full-screen mode when they were running DOS programs. But on the 80386, they could set up virtual memory blocks and set interrupts so that the operating system was *notified* whenever a program tried to write to screen memory. Windows could then write the equivalent text into a graphical window on the screen instantly.

- Feature two: Old DOS programs assumed they had the run of the chip. As a result, they didn't play well together. But the Intel 80386 had the ability to create "virtual" PCs, each of them acting like a complete 8086, so old PC programs could pretend like they had the computer to themselves, even while other programs were running and, themselves, pretending they had the whole computer to themselves.

So Windows 3.x on Intel 80386s was the first version that could run multiple DOS programs respectably. (Technically, Windows 386 could too, but 80386s were rare and expensive until about the time that Windows 3.0 came out.) Windows 3.0 was the first version that could actually do a reasonable job running all your old software.

Windows 95? No problem. Nice new 32-bit API, but it still ran old 16-bit software perfectly. Microsoft obsessed about this, spending a big chunk of change testing every old program they could find with Windows 95. Jon Ross, who wrote the original version of SimCity for Windows 3.x, told me that he accidentally left a bug in SimCity where he read memory that he had just freed. Yep. It worked fine on Windows 3.x, because the memory never went anywhere. Here's the amazing part: On beta versions of Windows 95, SimCity wasn't working in testing. Microsoft tracked down the bug and *added specific code to Windows 95 that looks for SimCity*. If it finds SimCity running, it runs the memory allocator in a special mode that doesn't free memory right away. That's the kind of obsession with backward compatibility that made people willing to upgrade to Windows 95.

You should be starting to get some ideas about how to break the chicken-and-egg problem: Provide a backward-compatibility mode that either delivers a truckload of chickens, or a truckload of eggs, depending on how you look at it, and sit back and rake in the bucks.

Ah. Now back to bill presentment. Remember bill presentment? The chicken-and-egg problem is that you can only get your Con Ed bills, so you won't use the service. How can you solve it? Microsoft couldn't figure it out. PayMyBills.com (and a half-dozen other Silicon Valley startups) all figured it out at the same time. You provide a *backward-compatibility mode*: If the merchant won't support the system, just get the merchant to mail their damn paper bills to University Avenue, in Palo Alto, where a bunch of actual human beings will open them and scan them in. Now you can get *all* your bills on their website. Since every merchant on Earth is available on the system, customers are happy to use it, even if it is running in this weird backward-compatibility mode where stupid Visa member banks send the bill electronically to a printer, print it out on paper, stuff it in an envelope, ship it 1,500 miles to California, where it is cut open, the stupid flyers harping worthless "free" AM clock radios that actually cost $9.95 are thrown into a landfill somewhere, and the paper bill is scanned back into a computer and stuck up on the

Web where it should have been sent in the first place. But the stupid backward-compatibility mode will eventually go away, because PayMyBills.com, unlike Microsoft, can actually get customers to use their system, so pretty soon they'll be able to go to the stupid Visa member banks and say, "hey, I've got 93,400 of your customers. Why don't you save yourselves $93,400 each month with a direct wire connection to me?" And suddenly PayMyBills.com is very profitable while Microsoft is still struggling to sign up their second electric utility, maybe one serving Georgia would be a nice change of pace.

Companies that fail to recognize the chicken-and-egg problem can be thought of as *boil the ocean* companies: Their business plan requires 93,000,000 humans to cooperate with their crazy business scheme before it actually works. One of the most outrageously stupid ideas I ever encountered was called ActiveNames.[4] Their boneheaded idea was that everybody in the world would install a little add-in to their email client, which looked up people's names on their central servers to get the actual email address. Then instead of telling people that your email address is kermit@sesame-street.com, you would tell them that your ActiveName is "spolsky," and if they want to email you, they need to install this special software. Bzzzzt. Wrong answer. I can't even *begin* to list all the reasons this idea is never going to work.

Conclusion: If you're in a market with a chicken-and-egg problem, you *better* have a backward-compatibility answer that dissolves the problem, or it's going to take you a loooong time to get going (like, forever).

A lot of other companies recognized the chicken-and-egg problem face-on and defeated it intelligently. When Transmeta unveiled their new CPU, it was the first time in a *long* time that a company that was *not* Intel finally admitted that if you're a CPU, and you want a zillion people to buy you, you gotta run x86 code. This after Hitachi, Motorola, IBM, MIPS, National Semiconductor, and who knows how many other companies deceived themselves into thinking that they had the right to invent a new instruction set. The Transmeta architecture assumes from day one that any business plan that calls for making a computer that doesn't run Excel is just not going anywhere.

---

4. ActiveNames didn't make it. See Patricia Odell, "ActiveNames Shutters Business." DIRECT Newsline, April 17, 2001. See www.directmag.com/ar/ marketing_activenames_shutters_business/.

thirty-eight

STRATEGY LETTER III: LET ME GO BACK!

SATURDAY, JUNE 3, 2000

When you're trying to get people to switch from a competitor to your product, you need to understand *barriers to entry*, and you need to understand them a lot better than you think, or people won't switch, and you'll be waiting tables.

A couple of chapters back, I wrote about the difference between two kinds of companies: the Ben & Jerry's kind of company that is trying to take over from established competition, versus the Amazon.com kind of company that is trying a "land grab" in a new field where there is no established competition. When I worked on Excel in the early 1990s, Microsoft was a card-carrying member of the Ben & Jerry's camp. Lotus 123, the established competitor, had an almost complete monopoly in the market for spreadsheets. Sure, some new users were buying computers and starting out with Excel, but for the most part, if Microsoft wanted to sell spreadsheets, they were going to have to get people to switch.

The most important thing to do when you're in this position is to *admit it*. Some companies can't even do this. The management at my last employer, Juno, was unwilling to admit that AOL had already achieved a dominant position. They spoke of the "millions of people not yet online." They said that "in every market, there is room for two players: Time and Newsweek, Coke and Pepsi, etc." The only thing they wouldn't say is "we have to get people to switch away from AOL." I'm not sure what they were afraid of. Perhaps they thought they were afraid to "wake up the sleeping bear." One of Juno's star programmers (no, not me) had the *chutzpah*, the unmitigated *gall*, to ask a simple question at a company meeting: "Why aren't we doing more to get AOL users to switch?" They hauled him off, screamed at him for an hour, and denied him a promotion he had been promised. (Guess who took his talent elsewhere?)

There's nothing wrong with being in a market that has established competition. In fact, even if your product is radically new, like eBay, you probably have competition: garage sales! Don't stress too much. If your product *is* better in some way, you actually have a pretty good chance of getting people to switch. But you must think strategically about it, and thinking strategically means thinking *one step beyond* the obvious.

The *only strategy* in getting people to switch to your product is to *eliminate barriers*. Imagine that it's 1991. The dominant spreadsheet, with 100-percent market share, is Lotus 123. You're the product manager for Microsoft Excel. Ask yourself: What are the barriers to switching? What keeps users from becoming Excel customers tomorrow? Here were some barriers to potential Excel users:

Barrier	
1. They have to know about Excel and know that it's better.	
2. They have to buy Excel.	
3. They have to buy Windows to run Excel.	
4. They have to convert their existing spreadsheets from 123 to Excel.	
5. They have to rewrite their keyboard macros, which won't run in Excel.	
6. They have to learn a new user interface.	
7. They need a faster computer with more memory.	

And so on and so on. Think of these barriers as an obstacle course that people have to run before you can count them as your customers. If you start out with a field of 1,000 runners, about half of them will trip on the tires; half of the survivors won't be strong enough to jump the wall; half of *those* survivors will fall off the rope ladder into the mud, and so on, until only one or two people actually overcome all the obstacles. With eight or nine barriers, *everybody* will have one nonnegotiable deal killer.

This calculus means that *eliminating barriers to switching* is the most important thing you have to do if you want to take over an existing market, because eliminating *just one barrier* will likely *double* your sales. Eliminate two barriers, and you'll double your sales again. Microsoft looked at the list of barriers and worked on *all of them*:

Barrier	Solution
1. They have to know about Excel and know that it's better.	Advertise Excel, send out demo disks, and tour the country to show it off.
2. They have to buy Excel.	Offer a special discount for former 123 users to switch to Excel.
3. They have to buy Windows to run Excel.	Make a runtime version of Windows that ships free with Excel.
4. They have to convert their existing spreadsheets from 123 to Excel.	Give Excel the capability to read 123 spreadsheets.
5. They have to rewrite their keyboard macros, which won't run in Excel.	Give Excel the capability to run 123 macros.
6. They have to learn a new user interface.	Give Excel the ability to understand Lotus keystrokes, in case you were used to the old way of doing things.

And it worked pretty well. By incessant pounding on barrier elimination, they slowly pried some market share away from Lotus.

One thing you see a lot during a transition from an old monopoly to a new monopoly is a magic "tipping point": one morning, you wake up and your product has 80 percent market share instead of 20 percent market share. This flip tends to happen *very* quickly (VisiCalc to 123 to Excel, WordStar to WordPerfect to Word, Mosaic to Netscape to Internet

Explorer, dBase to Access, and so on). It usually happens because the very last barrier to entry has fallen, and suddenly it's logical for everyone to switch.

Obviously, it's important to work on fixing the obvious barriers to entry, but once you think you've addressed those, you need to figure out what the not-so-obvious ones are. And this is where strategy becomes tricky, because there are some non-obvious things that keep people from switching.

Here's an example. This summer I'm spending most of my time in a house near the beach, but my bills still go to the apartment in New York City. And I travel a lot. There's a nice Web service, PayMyBills.com, which is supposed to simplify your life; you have *all* your bills sent to them, and they scan them and put them on the Web for you to see wherever you may be.

Now, PayMyBills costs about $9 a month, which sounds reasonable, and I would consider using it, but in the past, I've had pretty bad luck with financial services on the Internet, like Datek, which made so many *arithmetic* mistakes in my statements, I couldn't believe they were licensed. So I'm willing to *try* PayMyBills, but if I don't like it, I want to be able to go back to the old way.

The trouble is, after I use PayMyBills, if I don't like it, I need to call every damn credit card company and change my address *again*. That's a lot of work. And so the *fear* of how hard it will be *to switch back* is keeping me from using their service. Earlier I called this *stealth lock-in,*[1] and sort of praised it, but if potential customers figure it out, oh boy are you in trouble.

That's the barrier to entry. Not how hard it is to switch *in*: it's how hard it might be to switch *out*.

And this reminded me of Excel's tipping point, which happened around the time of Excel 4.0. And the biggest reason was that Excel 4.0 was the first version of Excel that could *write* Lotus spreadsheets transparently.

Yep, you heard me. *Write.* Not read. It turns out that what was stopping people from switching to Excel was that everybody else they

---

1. See Chapter 36.

worked with was still using Lotus 123. They didn't want a product that would create spreadsheets that nobody else could read: a classic chicken-and-egg problem.[2] When you're the lone Excel fan in a company where everyone else is using 123, even if you love Excel, you can't switch until you can participate in the 123 ecology.

To take over a market, you have to address *every* barrier to entry. If you forget just one barrier that trips up 50 percent of your potential customers, then *by definition*, you can't have more than 50 percent market share, and you will never displace the dominant player, and you'll be stuck on the sad (omelet) side of chicken-and-egg problems.

The trouble is that most managers only think about strategy one step at a time, like chess players who refuse to think one move ahead. Most of them will say, "it's important to let people convert *into* your product, but why should I waste my limited engineering budget letting people convert *out?*"

That's a childish approach to strategy. It reminds me of independent booksellers, who said "why should I make it comfortable for people to read books in my store? I want them to buy the books!" And then one day Barnes and Nobles puts *couches* and *cafes* in the stores and practically *begged* people to read books in their store without buying them. Now you've got all these customers sitting in their stores for *hours* at a time, *mittengrabben* all the books with their filthy hands, and the probability that they find something they want to buy is linearly proportional to the amount of time they spend in the store, and even the dinkiest Barnes and Nobles superstore in Iowa City rakes in hundreds of dollars a *minute* while the independent booksellers are going out of business. Honey, Shakespeare and Company on Manhattan's Upper West Side did *not* close because Barnes and Nobles had cheaper prices; it closed because Barnes and Nobles had *more human beings in the building.*

The mature approach to strategy is not to try to force things on potential customers. If somebody *isn't even your customer yet,* trying to lock them in just isn't a good idea. When you have 100 percent market share, come talk to me about lock-in. Until then, if you try to lock them in now, it's too early, and if any customer catches you in the act, you'll

---

2. See Chapter 37.

just wind up locking them *out*. Nobody wants to switch to a product that is going to eliminate their freedom in the future.

Let's take a more current example: ISPs, a highly competitive market. Something that virtually no ISP offers is the ability to get your email forwarded to another email address *after you quit their service*. This is small-minded thinking of the worst sort, and I'm pretty surprised nobody has figured it out. If you're a small ISP trying to get people to switch, they are going to be worrying about the biggest barrier: telling all their friends their new email address. So they won't even want to try your service. If they do try it, they won't tell their friends the new address for a while, just in case it doesn't work out. Which means they won't be getting much email at the new address, which means they won't really be trying out the service and seeing how much better they like it. Lose-lose.

Now suppose one brave ISP would make the following promise: "Try us. If you don't like us, we'll keep your email address functioning, and we'll forward your email for free to any other ISP. For life. Hop around from ISP to ISP as many times as you want, just let us know, and we'll be your permanent forwarding service."

Of course, the business managers would have fits. Why should we make it *easy* for customers to leave the service? That's because they are shortsighted. These are *not your customers now*. Try to lock them in *before* they become your customers, and you'll just lock them *out*. But if you make an honest promise that it will be easy to back out of the service if they're not happy, and suddenly you eliminate one more barrier to entry. And, as we learned, eliminating even a single barrier to entry can have a dramatic effect on conversions, and over time, when you knock down that last barrier to entry, people will start flooding in, and life will be good for a while. Until somebody does the same thing to you.

thirty-nine

STRATEGY LETTER IV: BLOATWARE AND THE 80/20 MYTH

Friday, March 23, 2001

Version 5.0 of Microsoft's flagship spreadsheet program Excel came out in 1993. It was positively *huge*; it required a whole *15MB* of hard drive space. In those days we could still remember our first 20MB PC hard drives (around 1985), so 15MB sure seemed like a lot.

By the time Excel 2000 came out, it required a whopping 146MB— almost a tenfold increase! Dang those sloppy Microsoft programmers, right?

Wrong.

I'll bet you think I'm going to write one of those boring articles you see all over the net bemoaning "bloatware." Whine whine whine, this stuff is so bloated, oh woe is me, edlin and vi are *so* much better than Word and Emacs because they are svelte, etc.

Ha ha! I tricked you! I'm not going to write that article again, because it's not true.

In 1993, given the cost of hard drives in those days, Microsoft Excel 5.0 took up about $36 worth of hard drive space.

In 2000, given the cost of hard drives in 2000, Microsoft Excel 2000 takes up about $1.03 in hard drive space.[1]

In real terms, it's almost like Excel is actually *getting smaller*!

---

1. These figures are adjusted for inflation and based on hard drive price data from
   www.littletechshoppe.com/ns1625/winchest.html.

What is bloatware, exactly? The Jargon File[2] snidely defines it as "software that provides minimal functionality while requiring a disproportionate amount of disk space and memory. Especially used for application and OS upgrades. This term is very common in the Windows/NT world. So is its cause."

I guess those guys just hate Windows. I haven't run out of memory in more than a decade, ever since virtual memory appeared in Windows 386 (1989). And hard drive space is down to $0.0071 per megabyte and still plummeting like a sheep learning to fly by jumping out of a tree.

Maybe Linus Åkerlund can explain it. On his web page, he writes, "The big disadvantage of using these bloated programs is that you have to load this very large program, even if you just want to accomplish one tiny little thing. It eats up all your memory... you're not using your system in an efficient way. You make the system seem more inefficient than it really is, and this is totally unnecessary."[3]

Ohhh. It eats up all your memory. I see. Actually, well, no, it doesn't. Ever since Windows 1.0, in 1987, the operating system only loads pages as they are used. If you have a 15MB executable and you only use code that spans 2MB worth of pages, you will only ever load 2MB from disk to RAM. In fact, if you have a modern version of Windows, the OS will automatically rearrange those pages on the hard drive so that they're consecutive, which makes the program start even faster next time.

And I don't think anyone will deny that on today's overpowered, under-priced computers, loading a huge program is still faster than loading a small program was even five years ago. So what's the problem?

A programmer who shall remain anonymous gives us a clue. It looks like he spent *hours* dissecting a small Microsoft utility, apparently enraged that it was a whole megabyte in size. (That's $0.0315 of hard drive space at the time he wrote the article.) In his opinion, the program should have been around 95 percent smaller. The joke is that the utility he dissected is something called RegClean, which you've probably never heard of. This is a program that goes through your Windows registry looking for things that aren't being used and deleting them. You have to be a little bit on the obsessive-compulsive side to care about cleaning up

2. See www.catb.org/~esr/jargon/

3. Linus Åkerlund, "Why I don't like bloatware: A perfectly normal rant." Linus's Home Page, 1998. See user.tninet.se/~uxm165t/bloatware.html.

unused parts of your registry. So I'm starting to suspect that fretting about bloatware is more of a mental health problem than a software problem.

In fact there are lots of great reasons for bloatware. For one, if programmers don't have to worry about how large their code is, they can ship it sooner. And that means you get more features, and features make your life better (when you use them) and don't usually hurt (when you don't). If your software vendor stops, before shipping, and spends two months squeezing the code down to make it 50 percent smaller, the net benefit to you is going to be imperceptible. Maybe, just maybe, if you tend to keep your hard drive full, that's one more Duran Duran MP3 you can download. But the loss to you of waiting an extra two months for the new version *is* perceptible, and the loss to the software company that has to give up two months of sales is even worse.

A lot of software developers are seduced by the old "80/20" rule. It *seems* to make a lot of sense: 80 percent of the people use 20 percent of the features. So you convince yourself that you only need to implement 20 percent of the features, and you can still sell 80 percent as many copies.

Unfortunately, it's never the same 20 percent. Everybody uses a *different* set of features. In the last ten years I have probably heard of *dozens* of companies who, determined not to learn from each other, tried to release "lite" word processors that only implement 20 percent of the features. This story is as old as the PC. Most of the time, what happens is that they give their program to a journalist to review, and the journalist reviews it by writing their review using the new word processor, and then the journalist tries to find the "word count" feature which they need because most journalists have precise word count requirements, and it's not there, because it's in the "80 percent that nobody uses," and the journalist ends up writing a story that attempts to claim simultaneously that lite programs are good, bloat is bad, and I can't use this damn thing 'cause it won't count my words.[4] If I had a dollar for every time[5] this has happened, I would be very happy.

4. David Coursey, "Want a cheap alternative to MS Office? Here's why you should try ThinkFree." ZDNet, February 2, 2001. See www.zdnet.com/anchordesk/stories/story/0,10738,2681437,00.html.

5. Charles Bermant, "Yeah Write." WashingtonPost.com, June 27, 1997. See washingtonpost.com/wp-srv/tech/reviews/finder/rev_1030.htm.

When you start marketing your "lite" product, and you tell people, "hey, it's lite, only 1MB," they tend to be very happy. Then they ask you if it has *their* crucial feature, and it doesn't, so they don't buy your product.

Bottom line: If your strategy is 80/20, you will have trouble selling software. That's just reality. This strategy is as old as the software industry itself, and it just doesn't pay; what's surprising is how many executives at "fast companies" think that it's going to work.

Jamie Zawinski says it best, discussing the original version of Netscape that changed the world.[6] "Convenient though it would be if it were true, Mozilla [Netscape 1.0] is not big because it's full of useless crap. Mozilla is big because your needs are big. Your needs are big because the Internet is big. There are lots of small, lean web browsers out there that, incidentally, do almost nothing useful. But being a shining jewel of perfection was not a goal when we wrote Mozilla."

---

6. Jamie Zawinski, "easter eggs." www.jwz.org/doc/easter-eggs.html, 1998.

forty

STRATEGY LETTER V: THE ECONOMICS OF OPEN SOURCE

WEDNESDAY, JUNE 12, 2002

When I was in college I took two intro economics courses: macroeconomics and microeconomics. Macro was full of theories like "low unemployment causes inflation" that never quite stood up to reality. But the micro stuff was both cool and useful. It was full of interesting concepts about the relationships between supply and demand that really did work. For example, if you have a competitor who lowers their prices, the demand for your product will go down unless you match them.

In today's episode, I'll show how one of those concepts explains a lot about some familiar computer companies. Along the way, I noticed something interesting about open source software, which is this: Most of the companies spending big money to develop open source software are doing it because it's a good business strategy for them, not because they suddenly stopped believing in capitalism and fell in love with freedom-as-in-speech.[1]

Every product in the marketplace has *substitutes* and *complements*. A substitute is another product you might buy if the first product is too expensive. Chicken is a substitute for beef. If you're a chicken farmer and the price of beef goes up, the people will want more chicken, and you will sell more.

---

1. "Freedom-as-in-speech" has a very specific technical meaning among the advocates of free software; see www.gnu.org/philosophy/free-sw.html for discussion. Basically, they're saying that you are free to do things with the software, not that you don't have to pay for it.

A complement is a product that you usually buy together with another product. Gas and cars are complements. Computer hardware is a classic complement of computer operating systems. And babysitters are a complement of dinner at fine restaurants. In a small town, when the local five-star restaurant has a two-for-one Valentine's day special, the local babysitters double their rates. (Actually, the nine-year-olds get roped into early service.)

All else being equal, demand for a product increases when the prices of its complements decrease.

Let me repeat that because you might have dozed off, and it's important. Demand for a product increases when the prices of its complements decrease. For example, if flights to Miami become cheaper, demand for hotel rooms in Miami goes up—because more people are flying to Miami and need a room. When computers become cheaper, more people buy them, and they all need operating systems, so demand for operating systems goes up, which means the price of operating systems can go up.

At this point, it's pretty common for people to try to confuse things by saying, "aha! But Linux is *free*!" OK. First of all, when an economist considers price, they consider the total price, including some intangible things like the time it takes to set up, reeducate everyone, and convert existing processes. All the things that we like to call "total cost of ownership."

Secondly, by using the free-as-in-beer argument, these advocates try to believe that they are not subject to the rules of economics because they've got a nice zero they can multiply everything by. Here's an example. When Slashdot asked Linux developer Moshe Bar if future Linux kernels would be compatible with existing device drivers, he said that they didn't need to be. "Proprietary software goes at the tariff of US$50–200 per line of debugged code. No such price applies to OpenSource software."[2] Moshe goes on to claim that it's OK for every Linux kernel revision to make all existing drivers obsolete, because the cost of rewriting all those existing drivers is zero. This is completely wrong. He's basically claiming that spending a small amount of programming time making the kernel backward compatible is equivalent to spending a huge amount of programming time rewriting every driver,

---

2. Slashdot interview with Moshe Bar, June 7, 2002. See http://interviews.slashdot.org/interviews/02/06/07/1255227.shtml?tid=156.

because both numbers are multiplied by their "cost," which he believes to be zero. This is a prima facie fallacy. The thousands or millions of developer hours it takes to revise every existing device driver are going to have to come at the expense of something. And until that's done, Linux will be once again handicapped in the marketplace because it doesn't support existing hardware. Wouldn't it be better to use all that "zero cost" effort making Gnome better? Or supporting new hardware?

Debugged code is *not* free, whether proprietary or open source. Even if you don't pay cash dollars for it, it has opportunity cost, and it has time cost. There is a finite amount of volunteer programming talent available for open source work, and each open source project competes with each other open source project for the same limited programming resource, and only the sexiest projects really have more volunteer developers than they can use. To summarize, I'm not very impressed by people who try to prove wild economic things about free-as-in-beer software, because they're just getting divide-by-zero errors as far as I'm concerned.

Open source is not exempt from the laws of gravity or economics. We saw this with Eazel, ArsDigita, The Company Formerly Known as VA Linux, and a lot of other attempts. But something is still going on that very few people in the open source world really understand: a lot of very large public companies, with responsibilities to maximize shareholder value, are investing a lot of money in supporting open source software, usually by paying large teams of programmers to work on it. And that's what the principle of complements explains.

Once again: Demand for a product increases when the price of its complements decreases. In general, a company's strategic interest is going to be to get the price of their complements as low as possible. The lowest theoretically sustainable price would be the "commodity price"—the price that arises when you have a bunch of competitors offering indistinguishable goods. So:

Smart companies try to commoditize their products' complements. If you can do this, demand for your product will increase and you will be able to charge more and make more.

When IBM designed the PC architecture, they used off-the-shelf parts instead of custom parts, and they carefully documented the interfaces between the parts in the (revolutionary) IBM-PC Technical Reference Manual. Why? So that other manufacturers could join the party. As long as you match the interface, you can be used in PCs. *IBM's goal was to commoditize the add-in market,* which is a complement of the PC market, and they did this quite successfully. Within a short time, scrillions of companies sprung up offering memory cards, hard drives, graphics cards, printers, etc. Cheap add-ins meant more demand for PCs.

When IBM licensed the operating system PC-DOS from Microsoft, Microsoft was very careful not to sell an exclusive license. This made it possible for Microsoft to license the same thing to Compaq and the other hundreds of OEMs who had legally cloned the IBM-PC using IBM's own documentation. *Microsoft's goal was to commoditize the PC market.* Very soon, the PC itself was basically a commodity, with ever decreasing prices, consistently increasing power, and fierce margins that make it extremely hard to make a profit. The low prices, of course, increase demand. Increased demand for PCs meant increased demand for their complement, MS-DOS. All else being equal, the greater the demand for a product, the more money it makes for you. And that's why Bill Gates can buy Sweden and you can't.

This year, Microsoft's trying to do it again: their new game console, the XBox, uses commodity PC hardware instead of custom parts. The theory was that commodity hardware gets cheaper every year, so the XBox could ride down the prices.[3] Unfortunately, it seems to have backfired. Apparently, commodity PC hardware has already been squeezed down to commodity prices, and so the price of making an XBox isn't declining as fast as Microsoft would like. The other part of Microsoft's XBox strategy was to use DirectX, a graphics library that can be used to write code that runs on all kinds of video chips. The goal here is to make the video chip a commodity to lower its price, so that more games are sold, which is where the real profits occur. And why don't the video chip vendors of the world try to commoditize the games somehow? That's a *lot* harder. If the game *Halo* is selling like crazy, it doesn't really *have* any substitutes. You're not going to go to the movie theater to see *Star Wars: Attack of the Clones* and decide instead that you would be satisfied with a Woody Allen movie. They may both be great movies, but they're not perfect substitutes. Now, who would you rather be, a game publisher or a video chip vendor?

---

3. Dean Takahashi, *Opening the Xbox: Inside Microsoft's Plan to Unleash an Entertainment Revolution* (Prima Lifestyles, 2002).

Commoditize your complements.

Understanding this strategy actually goes a long, long way in explaining why many commercial companies are making big contributions to open source. Let's go over these.

∿

Headline: IBM Spends Millions to Develop Open Source Software

Myth: They're doing this because Lou Gerstner read the GNU Manifesto and decided he doesn't actually like capitalism.

Reality: They're doing this because IBM is becoming an IT consulting company. IT consulting is a complement of enterprise software. Thus IBM needs to commoditize enterprise software, and the best way to do this is by supporting open source. Lo and behold, their consulting division is winning big with this strategy.

∿

Headline: Netscape Open Sources Their Web Browser

Myth: They're doing this to get free source code contributions from people in cybercafés in New Zealand.

Reality: They're doing this to commoditize the web browser.

This has been Netscape's strategy *from day one*. Have a look at the very first Netscape press release:[4] the browser is "freeware." Netscape gave away the browser so they could make money on servers. Browsers and servers are classic complements. The cheaper the browsers, the more servers you sell. This was never as true as it was in October 1994. (Netscape was actually surprised when MCI came in the door and

---

4. Netscape Communications News Release, "Netscape Communications Offers New Network Navigator Free on the Internet." Netscape.com, 1999. See http://wp.netscape.com/newsref/pr/newsrelease1.html.

dumped so much money in their laps that they realized they could make money off of the browser, too.[5] This wasn't required by the business plan.)

When Netscape released Mozilla as open source, it was because they saw an opportunity to lower the cost of developing the browser. So they could get the commodity benefits at a lower cost.

Later, AOL/Time Warner acquired Netscape. The server software, which was supposed to be the beneficiary of commodity browsers, wasn't doing all that well, and was jettisoned. Now, why would AOL/Time Warner continue to invest anything in open source?

AOL/Time Warner is an entertainment company. Entertainment companies are the complement of entertainment delivery platforms of all types, including web browsers. This giant conglomerate's strategic interest is to make entertainment delivery—web browsers—a commodity for which nobody can charge money.

My argument is a little bit tortured by the fact that Internet Explorer is free-as-in-beer. Microsoft wanted to make web browsers a commodity, too, so they can sell desktop and server operating systems. They went a step further and delivered a collection of components that anyone could use to throw together a web browser. Neoplanet, AOL, and Juno used these components to build their own web browsers. Given that IE is free, what is the incentive for Netscape to make the browser "even cheaper"? It's a preemptive move. They need to prevent Microsoft from getting a complete monopoly in web browsers, even free web browsers, because that would theoretically give Microsoft an opportunity to increase the cost of web browsing in other ways—say, by increasing the price of Windows.

(My argument is even more shaky because it's pretty clear that Netscape in the days of Barksdale didn't exactly know what it was doing.[6] A more likely explanation for what Netscape did is that upper management was technologically inept, and they had no choice but to go

---

5. Netscape Communications News Release, "MCI Selects Netscape Communications' Secure Software for New InternetMCI Service." Netscape.com, 1999. See http://wp.netscape.com/newsref/pr/newsrelease4.html.

6. Charles Ferguson, *High Stakes, No Prisoners: A Winner's Tale of Greed and Glory in the Internet Wars* (Crown Business, 1999).

along with whatever scheme the developers came up with. The developers were hackers, not economists, and only coincidentally came up with a scheme that serves their strategy. But let's give them the benefit of the doubt.)

~

Headline: Transmeta Hires Linus, Pays Him to Hack on Linux

Myth: They just did it to get publicity. Would you have heard of Transmeta otherwise?

Reality: Transmeta is a CPU company. The natural complement of a CPU is an operating system. Transmeta wants OSs to be a commodity.

~

Headline: Sun and HP Pay Ximian to Hack on Gnome

Myth: Sun and HP are supporting free software because they like Bazaars, not Cathedrals.

Reality: Sun and HP are hardware companies. They make boxen. In order to make money on the desktop, they need windowing systems, which are a complement of desktop computers, to be a commodity. Why don't they take the money they're paying Ximian and use it to develop a proprietary windowing system? They tried this (Sun had NeWS and HP had New Wave), but these are really hardware companies at heart with pretty crude software skills, and they need windowing systems to be a *cheap commodity*, not a proprietary advantage which they must pay for. So they hired the nice guys at Ximian to do this for the same reason that Sun bought StarOffice and open sourced it: to commoditize software and make more money on hardware.

~

Headline: Sun Develops Java; New "Bytecode" System Means Write Once, Run Anywhere

The bytecode idea is not new; programmers have always tried to make their code run on as many machines as possible. (That's how you commoditize your complement.) For years Microsoft had its own pcode compiler and portable windowing layer, which let Excel run on Mac, Windows, and OS/2, and on Motorola, Intel, Alpha, MIPS and PowerPC chips. Quark has a layer that runs Macintosh code on Windows. The C programming language is best described as a hardware-independent assembler language. It's not a new idea to software developers.

If you can run your software anywhere, that makes hardware more of a commodity. As hardware prices go down, the market expands, driving more demand for software (and leaving customers with extra money to spend on software which can now be more expensive.)

Sun's enthusiasm for WORA is, um, *strange*, because Sun is a hardware company. Making hardware a commodity is the *last* thing they want to do.

Ooooooooooooooooooooooooops!

Sun is the loose cannon of the computer industry. Unable to see past their raging fear and loathing of Microsoft, they adopt strategies based on anger rather than self-interest. Sun's two strategies are 1) make software a commodity by promoting and developing free software (Star Office, Linux, Apache, Gnome, etc.), and 2) make hardware a commodity by promoting Java, with its bytecode architecture and WORA. OK, Sun, pop quiz: When the music stops, where are you going to sit down? Without proprietary advantages in hardware or software, you're going to have to take the commodity price, which barely covers the cost of cheap factories in Guadalajara, not your cushy offices in Silicon Valley.

"But Joel!" Jared says. "Sun is trying to commoditize the operating system, like Transmeta, not the hardware." Maybe, but the fact that Java bytecode also commoditizes the hardware is some pretty significant collateral damage to sustain.

An important thing you notice from all these examples is that it's easy for software to commoditize hardware (you just write a little hardware abstraction layer, like Windows NT's HAL, which is a tiny piece of code), but it's incredibly hard for hardware to commoditize software. Software is not interchangeable, as the StarOffice marketing team is learning. Even when the price is zero, the cost of switching from Microsoft Office is non-zero. Until the switching cost becomes zero, desktop office software is not truly a commodity. And even the smallest differences can make two software packages a pain to switch between. Despite the fact that Mozilla has all the features I want and I'd love to use it if only to avoid the whack-a-mole pop-up-ad game, I'm too used to hitting Alt+D to go to the address bar. So sue me. One tiny difference, and you lose your commodity status. But I've pulled hard drives out of IBM computers and slammed them into Dell computers and, boom, the system comes up perfectly and runs as if it were still in the old computer.

Amos Michelson, the CEO of Creo,[7] told me that every employee in his firm is required to take a course in what he calls "economic thinking." Great idea. Even simple concepts in basic microeconomics go a long way to understanding some of the fundamental shifts going on today.

---

7. See www.creo.com/.

forty-one

A WEEK OF MURPHY'S LAW GONE WILD

~

Chapter One

The Linux server hosting our CVS repository (all our source code) fails. No big deal; it is automatically mirrored (using rsync) to a remote location. It takes a few hours to compress and transmit the mirrored data. We discover that we forgot the option to rsync that removes deleted files, so the mirror isn't perfect: it includes files that were deleted. These have to be manually removed.

When this is all done I decide to check out the whole source tree from scratch and compare it to what I already have, as a final sanity check. But I don't have enough disk space on my laptop to do this. Time to upgrade. I order a 60GB laptop hard drive and a PCMCIA/hard drive connector that is supposed to allow you to clone the old hard drive on the new one. This process takes something like six hours and fails when it is 50 percent complete, instructing me to "run scandisk." Which takes a couple of hours. Start another copy. Six hours more. At 50 percent, it fails again. Only now, the *original* hard drive is toast, taking my entire life with it. It takes a couple of hours fiddling around, putting the drive into different computers, etc., to discover that it is indeed lost.

OK, not too big a deal, we have daily backups (NetBackup Pro). I put the new 60GB drive into the laptop, format it, and install Windows XP Pro. I instruct NetBackup Pro to restore that machine to its precrash state. I'll lose a day of work, but it was a day in which I hardly got anything done, anyway. A day of email was lost, so if you sent me something this week and I didn't respond, resend.

NetBackup Pro works for a few hours. I go home, to let it finish overnight. In the morning, the system is completely toast and won't even boot. I hypothesize that it must be because I tried to restore a Win2K image on top of an XP Pro OS. So I start again, this time installing Win 2K (format hard drive: one hour; install Win 2K: one hour; then install the NetBackup Pro Client). And I start the restore again. Five hours later, it's only halfway done, and I go home.

The next morning, the system doesn't *quite* boot, it blue-screens, but a half hour of fiddling around with Safe Mode and I get it to boot happily. And behold, everything is restored, except, for some reason, a few files that I let Windows encrypt for me (using EFS) are inaccessible. This has something to do with public keys and certificates. When you restore a file that was encrypted, I guess you can't read it. I still haven't found the solution to this. If you know how to fix this I will be forever indebted to you. [1/26: I fixed this problem after a few hours of tearing out my hair.]

Lesson Learned

This is not the first time that a hard drive failure has led to a series of other problems that wound up wasting days and days of work. Notice that I had a very respectable backup strategy, everything was backed up daily, offsite. In fact, I believe this is the third time that a hard drive failure has led to a series of mishaps that wasted days. Conclusion: Backups aren't good enough. I want RAID mirroring from now on. When a drive dies, I want to spend 15 minutes putting in a new drive and resume working exactly where I left off. New policy: All non-laptops at Fog Creek will have RAID mirroring.

~

Chapter Two

Did you notice that our web server was down? On Friday around noon, a fire in a local Verizon switch knocked out all our phone lines and our Internet connectivity. Verizon got the phone lines working in a couple of hours, but the T1 was a bit more problematic. We purchased the T1 from Savvis, which, in turn, hired MCI to run the local loop, which is now called WorldCom, and of course WorldCom doesn't actually *run* any loops, God forbid they should get their hands *dirty*, they just buy the local loop from Verizon.

So from Friday at noon until Saturday at midnight, Michael and I, working as a tag team, call Savvis every hour or so to see what's going on. We're pushing on Savvis, who, occasionally, push on WorldCom, who have decided that some kind of SQL Server DDOS attack can be blamed for everything, so they kind of ignore Savvis, who don't tell us that WorldCom is ignoring them, and we push on Savvis *again*, and *they* push on WorldCom again, and around the third time, WorldCom agrees to call Verizon, who send out a tech who fixes the thing. Honestly, it's like pushing on *string*. Just like the last time Savvis made our T1 go down for a day, the technical problem was relatively trivial and could have been diagnosed and fixed in minutes if we weren't dealing with so many idiot companies.

Lesson Learned

When you're buying a service from a company that's just outsourcing that service, one level deep, it's difficult to get decent customer service. When there are two levels of outsourcing, it's nearly impossible. Much as I hate to encourage monopolistic local telcos, the only thing worse than dealing with a local telco directly is dealing with another idiot bureaucratic company who themselves have no choice but to deal with the local telco. Our next office space will be wired by Verizon DSL, thank you very much.

Incidentally, none of you would have noticed this outage at all if Dell had delivered our damn server on time. We were supposed to be up and running in a nice Peer 1 Network highly redundant secure colocation facility a month ago. Did I mention that I have a fever? I always get sick when things are going wrong.

~

Chapter Three

For the thousandth time, the heat on the fourth floor of the Fog Creek brownstone is out. Heat is supplied by hot water pipes running through the walls. These pipes were frozen solid. How did they get a chance to freeze? Oh, that's because the furnace went off last week, because it was installed by an idiot moron, probably unlicensed, who put in a 25-foot-long *horizontal* chimney segment, which prevents ventilation and has, so far, hospitalized one tenant and caused the furnace to switch off dozens of times. Finally, someone at the heating company admitted that it was possible to install a draft inducer forcing the chimney to ventilate, which they did, but not before the hot water pipes had frozen. Of course, the pipes are inadequately insulated because of another incompetent in the New York City construction trade, but this wouldn't have mattered if the furnace had kept running.

Lesson Learned

Weak systems may appear perfectly healthy until neighboring systems break down. People with allergies *and* back problems may go for months without suffering from either one, but suddenly an attack of hay fever makes them sneeze hard enough to throw out their back. You see this in systems administration *all the time*. Use these opportunities to *fix all the problems at once*. Get RAID on *all* your PCs *and* do backups, and don't use EFS and always get hard drives that are way too large so you'll never have to stop to upgrade them, and double-check the command-line options to rsync. Install the draft inducer *and* insulate the pipes. Move your important servers to a secure colo facility *and* switch the office T1 to Verizon.

forty-two

HOW MICROSOFT LOST THE API WAR

Sunday, June 13, 2004

Here's a theory you hear a lot these days: "Microsoft is finished. As soon as Linux makes some inroads on the desktop and web applications replace desktop applications, the mighty empire will topple."

Although there is some truth to the fact that Linux is a huge threat to Microsoft, predictions of the Redmond company's demise are, to say the least, premature. Microsoft has an incredible amount of cash money in the bank and is still incredibly profitable. It has a long way to fall. It could do everything wrong for a decade before it started to be in remote danger, and you never know—they could reinvent themselves as a shaved-ice company at the last minute. So don't be so quick to write them off. In the early 1990s everyone thought IBM was completely over: mainframes were history! Back then, Robert X. Cringely predicted that the era of the mainframe would end on January 1, 2000, when all the applications written in COBOL would seize up, and rather than fix those applications, for which, allegedly, the source code had long since been lost, everybody would rewrite those applications for client-server platforms.

Well, guess what. Mainframes are still with us, nothing happened on January 1, 2000, and IBM reinvented itself as a big ol' technology consulting company that also happens to make cheap plastic telephones. So extrapolating from a few data points to the theory that Microsoft is finished is really quite a severe exaggeration.

However, there is a less understood phenomenon that is going largely unnoticed: Microsoft's crown strategic jewel, the Windows API, is lost.

The cornerstone of Microsoft's monopoly power and incredibly profitable Windows and Office franchises, which account for virtually all of
Microsoft's income and covers up a huge array of unprofitable or marginally profitable product lines, the Windows API is no longer of much
interest to developers. The goose that lays the golden eggs is not quite
dead, but it does have a terminal disease, one that nobody noticed yet.

Now that I've said that, allow me to apologize for the grandilo-
quence and pomposity of that preceding paragraph. I think I'm starting
to sound like those editorial writers in the trade rags who go on and on
about Microsoft's strategic asset, the Windows API. It's going to take me
a few pages, here, to explain what I'm really talking about and justify
my arguments. Please don't jump to any conclusions until I explain what
I'm talking about. This will be a long chapter. I need to explain what the
Windows API is; I need to demonstrate why it's the most important
strategic asset to Microsoft; I need to explain how it was lost and what
the implications of that are in the long term. And because I'm talking
about big trends, I need to exaggerate and generalize.

~

Developers, Developers, Developers, Developers

Remember the definition of an operating system? It's the thing that
manages a computer's resources so that application programs can
run. People don't really care much about operating systems; they care
about those application programs that the operating system makes possible. Word Processors. Instant Messaging. Email. Accounts Payable.
Web sites with pictures of Paris Hilton. By itself, an operating system is
not that useful. People buy operating systems because of the useful
applications that run on it. And therefore the most useful operating system is the one that has the most useful applications.

The logical conclusion of this is that if you're trying to sell operating
systems, the most important thing to do is make software developers
want to develop software for your operating system. That's why Steve
Ballmer was jumping around the stage shouting "Developers, developers,

developers, developers."[1] It's so important for Microsoft that the only reason they don't outright *give away* development tools for Windows is because they don't want to inadvertently cut off the oxygen to competitive development tools vendors (well, those that are left), because having a variety of development tools available for their platform makes it that much more attractive to developers. But they really *want* to give away the development tools. Through their Empower ISV[2] program, you can get five complete sets of MSDN Universal (otherwise known as "basically every Microsoft product except Flight Simulator") for about $375. Command-line compilers for the .NET languages are included with the free .NET runtime, also free. The C++ compiler is now free.[3] Anything to encourage developers to build for the .NET platform, and holding just short of wiping out companies like Borland.

~

Why Apple and Sun Can't Sell Computers

Well, of course, that's a little bit silly; of course Apple and Sun can sell computers, but not to the two most lucrative markets for computers, namely, the corporate desktop and the home computer. Apple is still down there in the very low single digits of market share, and the only people with Suns on their desktops are at Sun. (Please understand that I'm talking about large trends here, and therefore when I say things like "nobody," I really mean "fewer than 10,000,000 people," and so on and so forth.)

Why? Because Apple and Sun computers don't run Windows programs, or, if they do, it's in some kind of expensive emulation mode that doesn't work so great. Remember, people buy computers for the applications that they run, and there's so much more great desktop software available for Windows than Mac that it's very hard to be a Mac user.

---

1. See www.ntk.net/ballmer/mirrors.html.

2. See members.microsoft.com/partner/competency/isvcomp/empower/default.aspx.

3. See msdn.microsoft.com/visualc/vctoolkit2003/.

And that's why the Windows API is such an important asset to Microsoft.

(I know, I know, at this point the 2.3 percent of the world that uses Macintoshes are warming up their email programs to send me a scathing letter about how much they love their Macs. Once again, I'm speaking in large trends and generalizing, so don't waste your time. I know you love your Mac. I know it runs everything *you* need. I love you, you're a Pepper, but you're only 2.3 percent of the world, so this article isn't about you.)

What is this "API" thing?

If you're writing a program, say, a word processor, and you want to display a menu or write a file, you have to ask the operating system to do it for you, using a very specific set of function calls that are different on every operating system. These function calls are called the API: it's the interface that an operating system, like Windows, provides to application developers, like the programmers building word processors and spreadsheets and whatnot. It's a set of thousands and thousands of detailed and fussy functions and subroutines that programmers can use, which cause the operating system to do interesting things like display a menu, read and write files, and more esoteric things like find out how to spell out a given date in Serbian, or extremely complex things like display a web page in a window. If your program uses the API calls for Windows, it's not going to work on Linux, which has different API calls. Sometimes they do approximately the same thing. That's one important reason Windows software doesn't run on Linux. If you wanted to get a Windows program to run under Linux, you'd have to reimplement the entire Windows API,[4] which consists of thousands of complicated functions; this is almost as much work as implementing Windows itself, something that took Microsoft thousands of person-years. And if you make one tiny mistake or leave out one function that an application needs, that application will crash.

---

4. See, for example, Wine, an open source attempt to do just that: www.winehq.com/.

The Two Forces at Microsoft

There are two opposing forces inside Microsoft, which I will refer to, somewhat tongue-in-cheek, as The Raymond Chen Camp and The MSDN Magazine Camp.

Raymond Chen is a developer on the Windows team at Microsoft. He's been there since 1992, and his weblog The Old New Thing[5] is chock-full of detailed technical stories about why certain things are the way they are in Windows, even silly things, which turn out to have very good reasons.

The most impressive things to read on Raymond's weblog are the stories of the incredible efforts the Windows team has made over the years to support backward compatibility:

Look at the scenario from the customer's standpoint. You bought programs X, Y and Z. You then upgraded to Windows XP. Your computer now crashes randomly, and program Z doesn't work at all. You're going to tell your friends, "Don't upgrade to Windows XP. It crashes randomly, and it's not compatible with program Z." Are you going to debug your system to determine that program X is causing the crashes, and that program Z doesn't work because it is using undocumented window messages? Of course not. You're going to return the Windows XP box for a refund. (You bought programs X, Y, and Z some months ago. The 30-day return policy no longer applies to them. The only thing you can return is Windows XP.)

I first heard about this from one of the developers of the hit game SimCity, who told me that there was a critical bug in his application: it used memory right after freeing it, a major no-no that *happened* to work OK on DOS but would not work under Windows, where memory that

---

5. Raymond Chen, The Old New Thing. See weblogs.asp.net/oldnewthing/.

is freed is likely to be snatched up by another running application right away. The testers on the Windows team were going through various popular applications, testing them to make sure they worked OK, but SimCity kept crashing. They reported this to the Windows developers, who disassembled SimCity, stepped through it in a debugger, found the bug, and added special code that checked if SimCity was running, and if it did, ran the memory allocator in a special mode in which you could still use memory after freeing it.

This was not an unusual case. The Windows testing team is huge and one of their most important responsibilities is guaranteeing that everyone can safely upgrade their operating system, no matter what applications they have installed, and those applications will continue to run, even if those applications do bad things or use undocumented functions or rely on buggy behavior that happens to be buggy in Windows *n* but is no longer buggy in Windows *n+1*. In fact if you poke around in the AppCompatibility section of your registry, you'll see a whole list of applications that Windows treats specially, emulating various old bugs and quirky behaviors so they'll continue to work. Raymond Chen writes, "I get particularly furious when people accuse Microsoft of maliciously breaking applications during OS upgrades. If any application failed to run on Windows 95, I took it as a personal failure. I spent many sleepless nights fixing bugs in third-party programs just so they could keep running on Windows 95."

A lot of developers and engineers don't agree with this way of working. If the application did something bad, or relied on some undocumented behavior, they think it should just break when the OS gets upgraded. In the early days of the Macintosh, the developers of the Macintosh OS at Apple were of this camp (although Apple got much better at backward compatibility as time went on). It's why so few applications from the early days of the Macintosh still work. If the company that made the application went out of business (and most of them did), well, tough luck, bubby.

To contrast, I've got DOS applications that I wrote in 1983 for the very original IBM-PC that still run flawlessly, thanks to The Raymond Chen Camp at Microsoft. I know, it's not just Raymond, of course; it's the whole *modus operandi* of the core Windows API team. But Raymond has publicized it the most through his excellent website The Old New Thing, so I'll name it after him.

That's one camp. The other camp is what I'm going to call The MSDN Magazine Camp, which I will name after the developer's magazine full of exciting articles about all the different ways you can shoot yourself in the foot by using esoteric combinations of Microsoft products in your own software. The MSDN Magazine Camp is always trying to convince you to use new and complicated external technology like COM+, MSMQ, MSDE, Microsoft Office, Internet Explorer and its components, MSXML, DirectX (the very latest version, please), Windows Media Player, and Sharepoint (Sharepoint! which *nobody* has)—a veritable panoply of *external dependencies* each one of which is going to be a huge headache when you ship your application to a paying customer and it doesn't work right. The technical name for this is DLL Hell. It works here; why doesn't it work there?

The Raymond Chen Camp believes in making things easy for developers by making it easy to write once and run anywhere (well, on any Windows box). The MSDN Magazine Camp believes in making things easy for developers by giving them really powerful chunks of code that they can leverage, if they are willing to pay the price of incredibly complicated deployment and installation headaches, not to mention the huge learning curve. The Raymond Chen Camp is all about consolidation. Please, don't make things any worse, let's just keep making what we already have *still work*. The MSDN Magazine Camp needs to keep churning out new gigantic pieces of technology that nobody can keep up with.

Here's why this matters.

~

Microsoft Lost the Backward Compatibility Religion

Inside Microsoft, The MSDN Magazine Camp has won the battle. The first big win was making Visual Basic .NET not backward compatible with VB 6.0. This was literally the first time in living memory that when you bought an upgrade to a Microsoft product, your old data (i.e., the code you had written in VB6) could not be imported perfectly and silently. It was the first time a Microsoft upgrade did not respect the work that users did using the previous version of a product.

And the sky didn't *seem* to fall, not inside Microsoft. VB6 developers were up in arms, but they were disappearing anyway, because most of them were corporate developers who were migrating to web development anyway. The real long-term damage was hidden.

With this major victory under their belts, The MSDN Magazine Camp took over. Suddenly it was OK to change things. IIS 6.0 came out with a different threading model that broke some old applications. I was shocked to discover that our customers with Windows Server 2003 were having trouble running FogBUGZ. Then .NET 1.1 was not perfectly backward compatible with 1.0. And now that the cat was out of the bag, the OS team got into the spirit and decided that instead of adding features to the Windows API, they were going to completely replace it. Instead of Win32, we are told, we should now start getting ready for WinFX: the next generation Windows API.[6] All different. Based on .NET with managed code. XAML. Avalon. Yes, vastly superior to Win32, I admit it. But not an upgrade: a break with the past.

Outside developers, who were never particularly happy with the complexity of Windows development, have defected from the Microsoft platform *en masse* and are now developing for the Web. Paul Graham, who created Yahoo! Stores in the early days of the dotcom boom, summarized it eloquently: "There is all the more reason for startups to write Web-based software now, because writing desktop software has become a lot less fun. If you want to write desktop software now you do it on Microsoft's terms, calling their APIs and working around their buggy OS. And if you manage to write something that takes off, you may find that you were merely doing market research for Microsoft."[7]

Microsoft got big enough, with too many developers, and they were too addicted to upgrade revenues, so they suddenly decided that reinventing *everything* was *not* too big a project. Heck, we can do it twice. The old Microsoft, the Microsoft of Raymond Chen, might have implemented things like Avalon, the new graphics system, as a series of DLLs that can run on any version of Windows and which could be bundled

6. Mark Driver, "Microsoft WinFX Accelerates Need for .NET Adoption," Gartner Research, November 3, 2003. See www.gartner.com/DisplayDocument?doc_cd=118261.

7. Paul Graham, "The Other Road Ahead," September 2001. See www.paulgraham.com/road.html.

with applications that need them. There's no technical reason not to do this. But Microsoft needs to give you a reason to buy Longhorn, and what they're trying to pull off is a sea change, similar to the sea change that occurred when Windows replaced DOS. The trouble is that Longhorn is not a very big advance over Windows XP—not nearly as big as Windows was over DOS. It probably won't be compelling enough to get people to buy all new computers and applications like they did for Windows. Well, maybe it will, Microsoft certainly needs it to be, but what I've seen so far is not very convincing. A lot of the bets Microsoft made are the wrong ones. For example, WinFS, advertised as a way to make searching work by making the file system be a relational database, ignores the fact that the real way to make searching work is by making searching work.[8] Don't make me type metadata for all my files that I can search using a query language. Just do me a favor and search the damned hard drive, quickly, for the string I typed, using full-text indexes and other technologies that were boring in 1973.

~

Automatic Transmissions Win the Day

Don't get me wrong; I think .NET is a great development environment, and Avalon with XAML is a tremendous advance over the old way of writing GUI apps for Windows. The biggest advantage of .NET is the fact that it has automatic memory management.

A lot of us thought in the 1990s that the big battle would be between procedural and object-oriented programming, and we thought that object-oriented programming would provide a big boost in programmer productivity. I thought that, too. Some people still think that. It turns out we were wrong. Object-oriented programming is handy dandy, but it's not really the productivity booster that was promised. The *real* significant productivity advance we've had in programming has been from languages that manage memory for you automatically. It can be with

---

8. John Udell, "Questions about Longhorn, part 1: WinFS," iDiscuss: Jon Udell's Weblog, InfoWorld, June 2, 2004. See weblog.infoworld.com/udell/2004/06/02.html#a1012.

reference counting or garbage collection; it can be Java, Lisp, Visual Basic (even 1.0), Smalltalk, or any of a number of scripting languages. If your programming language allows you to grab a chunk of memory without thinking about how it's going to be released when you're done with it, you're using a managed-memory language, and you are going to be much more efficient than someone using a language in which you have to explicitly manage memory. Whenever you hear someone bragging about how productive their language is, they're probably getting most of that productivity from the automated memory management, even if they mis-attribute it.

Why Memory Management?

Why does automatic memory management make you so much more productive? 1) Because you can write f(g(x)) without worrying about how to free the return value from g, which means you can use functions that return interesting complex data types and functions that transform interesting complex data types, in turn allowing you to work at a higher level of abstraction. 2) Because you don't have to spend any time writing code to free memory or tracking down memory leaks. 3) Because you don't have to carefully coordinate the exit points from your functions to make sure things are cleaned up properly.

Racing car aficionados will probably send me hate mail for this, but my experience has been that there is only one case, in normal driving, where a good automatic transmission is inferior to a manual transmission. Similarly in software development: In almost every case, automatic memory management is superior to manual memory management and results in far greater programmer productivity.

If you were developing desktop applications in the early years of Windows, Microsoft offered you two ways to do it: writing C code that calls the Windows API directly and managing your own memory, or using Visual Basic and getting your memory managed for you. These are the two development environments I have used the most, personally, over the last 13 years or so, and I know them inside-out, and my experi-ence has been that Visual Basic is *significantly* more productive. Often

I've written *the same code*, once in C++ calling the Windows API and once in Visual Basic, and C++ always took three or four times as much work. Why? Memory management. The easiest way to see why is to look at the documentation for any Windows API function that needs to return a string. Look closely at how much discussion there is around the concept of who allocates the memory for the string, and how you negotiate how much memory will be needed. Typically, you have to call the function *twice*—on the first call, you tell it that you've allocated zero bytes, and it fails with a "not enough memory allocated" message and conveniently also tells you how much memory you need to allocate. That's if you're lucky enough not to be calling a function which returns a *list of strings* or a whole variable-length structure. In any case, simple operations like opening a file, writing a string, and closing it using the raw Windows API can take a page of code. In Visual Basic, similar operations can take three lines.

So, you've got these two programming worlds. Everyone has pretty much decided that the world of managed code is far superior to the world of unmanaged code. Visual Basic was (and probably remains) the number-one bestselling language product of all time, and developers preferred it over C or C++ for Windows development, although the fact that "Basic" was in the name of the product made hardcore programmers shun it even though it was a fairly modern language with a handful of object-oriented features and very little leftover gunk (line numbers and the LET statement having gone the way of the hula hoop). The other problem with VB was that deployment required shipping a VB runtime, which was a big deal for shareware distributed over modems, and, worse, let other programmers see that your application was developed in (the shame!) Visual Basic.

~

One Runtime to Rule Them All

And along came .NET. This was a grand project, the super-duper unifying project to clean up the whole mess once and for all. It would have memory management, of course. It would still have Visual Basic, but it would gain a new language, one which is in spirit virtually the same as Visual Basic but with the C-like syntax of curly braces and semi-colons. And best of all, the new Visual Basic/C hybrid would be called Visual C#, so you would not have to tell anyone you were a "Basic" programmer any more. All those horrid Windows functions with their tails and hooks and backward-compatibility bugs and impossible-to-figure-out string-returning semantics would be wiped out, replaced by a single clean object-oriented interface that only has one kind of string. One runtime to rule them all. It was beautiful. And they pulled it off, technically. .NET is a great programming environment that manages your memory and has a rich, complete, and consistent interface to the operating system and a rich, super complete, and elegant object library for basic operations.

And yet, people aren't really using .NET much.

Oh sure, some of them are.

But the idea of unifying the mess of Visual Basic and Windows API programming by creating a *completely new, ground-up* programming environment with not one, not two, but three languages (or are there four?) is sort of like the idea of getting two quarreling kids to stop arguing by shouting "shut up!" louder than either of them; it only works on TV. In real life when you shout "shut up!" to two people arguing loudly, you just create a louder three-way argument.

(By the way, for those of you who follow the arcane but politically charged world of blog syndication feed formats, you can see the same thing happening over there. RSS became fragmented with several different versions, inaccurate specs, and lots of political fighting, and the attempt to clean everything up by creating *yet another format* called Atom has resulted in several different versions of RSS plus one version of Atom, inaccurate specs, and lots of political fighting. When you try to unify two opposing forces by creating a third alternative, you just end up with three opposing forces. You haven't unified anything and you haven't really fixed anything.)

So now instead of .NET unifying and simplifying, we have a big six-way mess, with everybody trying to figure out which development strategy to use and whether they can afford to port their existing applications to .NET.

No matter how consistent Microsoft is in their marketing message ("just use .NET—trust us!"), most of their customers are still using C,

C++, Visual Basic 6.0, and classic ASP, not to mention all the other development tools from other companies. And the ones using .NET are using ASP.NET to develop web applications, which run on a Windows server but *don't require Windows clients*, which is a key point I'll talk about more when I talk about the Web.

~

Oh, Wait, There's More Coming!

Now Microsoft has so many developers cranking away that it's not enough to reinvent the entire Windows API; they have to reinvent it *twice*. At last year's PDC they preannounced the next major version of their operating system, codenamed Longhorn, which will contain, among other things, a completely new user interface API, codenamed Avalon, rebuilt from the ground up to take advantage of modern computers' fast display adapters and real-time 3D rendering. And if you're developing a Windows GUI app today using Microsoft's "official" latest-and-greatest Windows programming environment, WinForms, you're going to have to start over again in two years to support Longhorn and Avalon. Which explains why WinForms is completely stillborn. Hope you haven't invested too much in it. Jon Udell found a slide from Microsoft labeled "How Do I Pick Between Windows Forms and Avalon?" and asks, "Why do I have to pick between Windows Forms and Avalon?" A good question, and one to which he finds no great answer.[9]

So you've got the Windows API, you've got VB, and now you've got .NET, in several language flavors, and don't get too attached to any of that, because we're making Avalon, you see, which will only run on the newest Microsoft operating system, which nobody will have for a *loooong* time. And personally I still haven't had time to learn .NET very deeply, and we haven't ported Fog Creek's two applications from classic

---

9. John Udell, "Questions about Longhorn, part 3: Avalon's enterprise mission," iDiscuss: Jon Udell's Weblog, InfoWorld, June 9, 2004. See weblog.infoworld.com/udell/2004/06/09.html#a1019.

ASP and Visual Basic 6.0 to .NET because there's no return on investment for us. None. It's just Fire and Motion[10] as far as I'm concerned:
Microsoft would love for me to stop adding new features to our bug
tracking software and content management software and instead waste
a few months porting it to another programming environment, something which will not benefit a single customer and therefore will not gain
us one additional sale, and therefore which is a complete waste of several months, which is great for Microsoft, because they have content
management software and bug tracking software, too, so they'd like
nothing better than for me to waste time spinning cycles catching up
with the flavor du jour, and then waste another year or two doing an
Avalon version, too, while they add features to their own competitive
software. *Riiiight.*

No developer with a day job has time to keep up with all the new
development tools coming out of Redmond, if only because there are *too
many dang employees at Microsoft making development tools!*

~

It's Not 1990

Microsoft grew up during the 1980s and 1990s, when the growth in
personal computers was so dramatic that every year there were
more new computers sold than the entire installed base. That meant that
if you made a product that only worked on new computers, within a
year or two it could take over the world even if nobody *switched* to your
product. That was one of the reasons Word and Excel displaced
WordPerfect and Lotus so thoroughly: Microsoft just waited for the next
big wave of hardware upgrades and sold Windows, Word, and Excel to
corporations buying their next round of desktop computers (in some
cases their first round). So in many ways Microsoft never needed to
learn how to get an installed base to switch from product n to product
$n+1$. When people get new computers, they're happy to get all the latest

---

10. See Chapter 15.

Microsoft stuff on the new computer, but they're far less likely to upgrade. This didn't matter when the PC industry was growing like wildfire, but now that the world is saturated with PCs, most of which are Just Fine, Thank You, Microsoft is suddenly realizing that it takes much longer for the latest thing to get out there. When they tried to "End Of Life" Windows 98, it turned out there were still so many people using it they had to promise to support that old creaking grandma for a few more years.[11]

Unfortunately, these Brave New Strategies, things like .NET and Longhorn and Avalon, trying to create a *new* API to lock people into, can't work very well if everybody is still using their good-enough computers from 1998. Even if Longhorn ships when it's supposed to, in 2006, which I don't believe for a minute, it will take a couple of years before enough people have it that it's even worth considering as a development platform. Developers, developers, developers, and developers are not buying into Microsoft's multiple-personality-disordered suggestions for how we should develop software.

~~~

Enter the Web

I'm not sure how I managed to get this far without mentioning the Web. Every developer has a choice to make when they plan a new software application: they can build it for the Web, or they can build a "rich client" application that runs on PCs. The basic pros and cons are simple: Web applications are easier to deploy, while rich clients offer faster response time enabling much more interesting user interfaces.

Web applications are easier to deploy because there's no installation involved. Installing a web application means typing a URL in the address bar. Today I installed Google's new email application by typing Alt+D, gmail, Ctrl+Enter. There are far fewer version compatibility problems and problems coexisting with other software. Every user of your product

---

11. See www.windows-help.net/microsoft/98-lifecycle.html.

is using the same version, so you never have to support a mix of old versions. You can use any programming environment you want, because you only have to get it up and running on your own server. Your application is automatically available at virtually every reasonable computer *on the planet.* Your customers' data, too, is automatically available at virtually every reasonable computer on the planet.

But there's a price to pay in the smoothness of the user interface. Here are a few examples of things you can't really do well in a web application:

1. Create a fast drawing program.

2. Build a real-time spell checker with wavy red underlines.

3. Warn users that they are going to lose their work if they hit the close box of the browser.

4. Update a small part of the display based on a change that the user makes without a full roundtrip to the server.

5. Create a fast keyboard-driven interface that doesn't require the mouse.

6. Let people continue working when they are not connected to the Internet.

These are not all big issues. Some of them will be solved very soon by witty JavaScript developers. Two new web applications, Gmail[12] and Oddpost,[13] both email apps, do a really decent job of working around or completely solving some of these issues. And users don't seem to care about the little UI glitches and slowness of web interfaces. Almost all the normal people I know are perfectly happy with web-based email, for some reason, no matter how much I try to convince them that the rich client is, uh, richer.

So the Web user interface is about 80 percent there, and even without new web browsers, we can probably get 95 percent there. This is Good

12. See gmail.google.com/.

13. See www.oddpost.com/.

Enough for most people, and it's certainly good enough for developers, who have voted to develop almost every significant new application as a web application.

Which means, suddenly, Microsoft's API doesn't matter so much. Web applications don't require Windows.

It's not that Microsoft didn't notice this was happening. Of course they did, and when the implications became clear, they slammed on the brakes. Promising new technologies like HTAs[14] and DHTML were stopped in their tracks. The Internet Explorer team seems to have disappeared; they have been completely missing in action for several years. There's no way Microsoft is going to allow DHTML to get any better than it already is; it's just too dangerous to their core business, the rich client. The big meme at Microsoft these days is: *"Microsoft is betting the company on the rich client."* You'll see that somewhere in every slide presentation about Longhorn. Joe Beda, from the Avalon team, says that "Avalon, and Longhorn in general, is Microsoft's stake in the ground, saying that we believe power on your desktop, locally sitting there doing cool stuff, is here to stay. We're investing on the desktop, we think it's a good place to be, and we hope we're going to start a wave of excitement... "[15]

The trouble is, it's too late.

~

I'm a Little Bit Sad About This, Myself

I'm actually a little bit sad about this, myself. To me the Web is great, but web-based applications with their sucky, high-latency, inconsistent user interfaces are a huge step backward in daily usability. I love my rich client applications and would go nuts if I had to use web versions of the applications I use daily: Visual Studio, CityDesk, Outlook, Corel PHOTO-PAINT, QuickBooks. But that's what developers are going to

---

14. Microsoft, *Introduction to HTML Applications (HTAs)*, Microsoft Corporation. See msdn.microsoft.com/workshop/author/hta/overview/htaoverview.asp.

15. Joe Beda, "Is Avalon a way to take over the Web?" Channel 9, April 7, 2004. See http://channel9.msdn.com/ShowPost.aspx?PostID=948.

give us. Nobody (by which, again, I mean "fewer than 10,000,000 people") wants to develop for the Windows API any more. Venture capitalists won't invest in Windows applications because they're so afraid of competition from Microsoft. And most users don't seem to care about crappy Web UIs as much as I do.

And here's the clincher: I noticed (and confirmed this with a recruiter friend) that Windows API programmers here in New York City who know C++ and COM programming earn about $130,000 a year, while typical Web programmers using managed-code languages (Java, PHP, Perl, even ASP.NET) earn about $80,000 a year. That's a huge difference, and when I talked to some friends from Microsoft Consulting Services about this, they admitted that Microsoft had lost a whole generation of developers. The reason it takes $130,000 to hire someone with COM experience is because nobody bothered learning COM programming in the last eight years or so, so you have to find somebody really senior, usually they're already in management, and convince them to take a job as a grunt programmer, dealing with (God help me) marshalling and monikers and apartment threading and aggregates and tearoffs and a million other things that, basically, only Don Box ever understood, and even Don Box can't bear to look at them any more.

Much as I hate to say it, a huge chunk of developers have long since moved to the Web and refuse to move back. Most .NET developers are ASP.NET developers, developing for Microsoft's web server. ASP.NET is brilliant; I've been working with web development for ten years, and it's really just a generation ahead of everything out there. But it's a server technology, so clients can use any kind of desktop they want. And it runs pretty well under Linux using Mono.[16]

None of this bodes well for Microsoft and the profits it enjoyed thanks to its API power. The new API is HTML, and the new winners in the application development marketplace will be the people who can make HTML sing.

---

16. See www.go-mono.com/.

part four

A Little Bit Too Much Commentary on .NET

forty-three

MICROSOFT GOES BONKERS

*In the old days, Microsoft sold developer tools to programmers.
I remember a great advertisement for Microsoft C, probably version 3.0, consisting of a dense four-page white paper describing the
new optimization techniques that compiler used in great detail.*

*At some point in time when I wasn't paying close attention, the
marketers in Microsoft's developer products realized that the really
big budgets are controlled by executive managers, not programmers. These managers, presumably, love to hear pseudobabble like
"manage performance and scalability throughout your .NET application life cycle to reduce risk and lower total cost of ownership."
(Yes, that's a direct quote from the Visual Studio home page.[1]) The
old days of marketing to developers themselves are long gone. It
first hit me in July 2000 when Microsoft announced .NET to a great
deal of fanfare, and accompanied by a lot of the usual PR happy
talk, about three years before .NET actually shipped, apparently to
create FUD around Java.*

SATURDAY, JULY 22, 2000

Microsoft's latest announcement, called Microsoft .NET, while touted by
the likes of *Fortune* magazine as a huge "revolution," is really nothing but
vaporware, and I think it proves that something has gone very, very
wrong in Redmond.

---

1. Microsoft Visual Studio Development Center, http://msdn.microsoft.com/vstudio (accessed
    May 25, 2004).

With vaporware, you promise all kinds of features and products that you simply can't sell because you don't really have them. But .NET is worse than vaporware. In their blasé loftiness, Microsoft isn't even bothering to provide the *vapor itself*.

Read the white paper[2] closely, and you'll see that for all the hoopla, .NET is just a thin cloud of FUD. There's no there there. Try as you might to grasp onto something, the entire white paper *does not say anything*. The harder you grasp, the more it slips right through your fingers.

I'm not saying that there's nothing *new* in .NET. I'm saying that there's *nothing there at all*.

Look at some of this:

Everyone believes the Web will evolve, but for that evolution to be truly empowering for developers, businesses and consumers, a radical new vision is needed. Microsoft's goal is to provide that vision and the technology to make it a reality.

How about this:

The Microsoft .NET vision means empowerment for consumers, businesses, software developers and the entire industry. It means unleashing the full potential of the Internet. And it means the Web the way you want it.

What's going on here? I couldn't find *one single idea* that could actually be implemented in a software product in that entire white paper. Instead of providing a list of features, Microsoft provides a list of amorphous "benefits" like this one:

---

2. "Microsoft .NET: Realizing the Next Generation Internet." Microsoft, June 22, 2000. This is no longer available on Microsoft's website, but a copy is available at web.archive.org/web/20001027183304/http://www.microsoft.com/business/vision/netwhitepaper.asp.

Web sites become flexible services that can interact, and exchange and leverage each other's data.

That's a "feature" of this exciting .NET architecture. The fact that it is so broad, vague, and high level that it doesn't mean *anything at all* doesn't seem to be bothering anyone. Or how about:

Microsoft .NET makes it possible to find services and people with which to interact.

Oh, joy! *Five years* after Altavista went live, and two years after Larry Page and Sergei Brin actually invented a radically better search engine (Google), Microsoft is pretending like there's no way to search on the Internet and *they're* going to solve this problem for us. The whole document is exactly like that.

There are two things going on here. Microsoft has some great thinkers. When great thinkers think about problems, they start to see patterns. They look at the problem of people sending each other word-processor files, and then they look at the problem of people sending each other spreadsheets, and they realize that there's a general pattern: sending files. That's one level of abstraction already. Then they go up one more level: people *send* files, but web browsers also "*send*" requests for web pages. Those are both *sending* operations, so our clever thinker invents a new, higher, broader abstraction called *messaging*, but now it's getting *really* vague and nobody really knows what they're talking about any more.

And if you go too far up, abstraction-wise, you run out of oxygen. Sometimes smart thinkers just don't know when to stop, and they create these absurd, all-encompassing, high-level pictures of the universe that are all good and fine, but don't actually mean anything at all.

And that seems to be what happened here:

> The next generation of the Windows desktop platform, Windows .NET supports productivity, creativity, management, entertainment and much more, and is designed to put users in control of their digital lives.

This stuff is so abstract it's impossible to criticize. Who doesn't want an operating system that supports productivity? Great feature! Get me one of those spiffy new operating systems with the productivity feature! Problem: How exactly is Microsoft going to do it? For the last 20 years of software, productivity improvements have been gradual and incremental. Have they suddenly discovered a new chemical compound that will make their operating system more productive? I don't think they have. I think they're bluffing. FUD and vaporware.

~

The Scary Thing Is, They're *Earnest*

I know Microsoft—worked there for three years. I know the kind of people who wrote this document. Bill Gates almost certainly had a very significant role in it; that's why he gave up the CEO position, so he could work on this stuff. I don't think that Microsoft created this document because they needed some vaporware. These are supersmart people.

I actually think that they earnestly think they're inventing the future, as well as they know how. They've looked at every Microsoft product, from Hotmail to SQL Server, and tried to fit them into a Bold New Vision Thing. But the trouble is that nobody there is actually inventing anything earthshaking. Which isn't surprising—not because Microsoft is stupid, which they're not, but because earthshaking new inventions are so rare, and Microsoft only has a finite number of smart people. Only one person in the whole world invented Napster, and he didn't work for Microsoft. Microsoft desperately wants to believe that it can manufacture revolution, but even in the Cambrian explosion of the Internet, there are only a handful of truly revolutionary ideas per year, and the chances that one of them will happen inside the tiny world of Bill Gates and the knights of the Redmond table are vanishingly small. The chances are even smaller when you consider that a typical smart programmer, working in the bowels of Microsoft on display drivers for Windows NT, who has a great idea is probably not going to get his idea listened to.

The only thing concrete that you *can* discern from the white paper is that software should be a subscription service you get over the Internet, not something you install from a CD-ROM.

To a customer, getting your word processor via Internet subscription rather than via a CD-ROM might be a *small* benefit, but, um, no, not really. It doesn't really solve any customer problem. Getting bug fixes over the Internet? Great. I can already do that. I've been downloading patches for Microsoft products for seven years, and now it's quite automatic. Getting new versions? What's the point, if the only thing that the new version does is make it easier to get new versions! They've hardly added a single new feature to Word for the last three releases, except that at some point, they did something bizarre to make it "easy" to position pictures, and I can never get pictures to go where I want them.

The truth is, Microsoft noticed way back in 1991 that an increasing amount of their revenue came from upgrades, and that it's hard to get everybody to upgrade, and they've been trying to get their customers to agree to a subscription model for buying software for almost a decade. But it hasn't worked because the customers don't want it. Microsoft sees .NET as a way to finally enforce the subscription model which suits their bottom line.

It almost seems as if Microsoft .NET doesn't fill a single customer need, it only fills Microsoft's need to find something for 10,000 programmers to do for the next ten years. We all know it's been a long time since they've thought of a new word processing feature that anybody needs, so what else are all those programmers going to do?

~

The Bright Side of the "Vision Thing"

Old joke: A man goes to the psychiatrist. The shrink shows him a picture of a bird and says "What does this make you think of?" The man says: "Sex." The shrink shows him a picture of a tree. "OK, what does *this* make you think of?" The man says: "Sex." Picture of a train. "Sex." A house. "Sex."

"My God!" says the shrink. "You're obsessed with sex!"

"*I'm* obsessed with sex!?" says the man. "*You're* the one who keeps showing me dirty pictures!"

Ya see, the bright side of vague documents like the .NET white paper is that they are a kind of Rorschach test. People read them with preconceived ideas, and since the document is so vague, they think that Microsoft is reiterating their ideas. Dave Winer,[3] president of UserLand Software,[4] has many interesting, innovative ideas about software. When he read about Microsoft .NET, he assumed that Microsoft was finally recognizing the same ideas that he'd been talking about for two years. Dave, you give them too much credit. They are completely clueless compared to you. They are playing the trick of psychic hotlines and newspaper horoscopes; by feeding you cloudy, meaningless generalizations, you fall into their trap of thinking that they read your mind. "Today the planetary alignment is such that you will take a big step forward to achieve your goals." The difference is that Dave has real, concrete ideas that can translate into real software, while Microsoft is still in the kind of lalaland they were in six years ago when they were talking about how "Cairo" would provide "Information At Your Fingertips," a vision that the Internet fulfilled and Cairo didn't.

So hopefully, all this meaningless blah blah will actually get somebody's creative juices going (as it has at UserLand) and lead to some real innovations. But these innovations are probably more likely to come from outside Microsoft than inside.

---

3. See www.scripting.com/.
4. See www.userland.com/.

⌣

Postcript: *After this article appeared, the next version of almost every product at Microsoft was renamed with the ".NET" moniker...for a while, until the confusion was just too much to bear. At great cost and difficulty, Windows Server 2003 was renamed from ".NET Server," and the label .NET was restricted to refer to the new programming environment of "managed code." Which, incidentally, is really quite good. The combination of C# and the .NET common language framework is really a fantastic programming environment. It even reduces risk and lowers total cost of ownership! Nirvana!*

forty-four

OUR .NET STRATEGY

Here are my current thoughts on the gradual migration to .NET development tools at Fog Creek.

The status quo: Most of CityDesk is written in Visual Basic 6.0, with parts written in Visual C++ 6.0. Most of FogBUGZ is written in VBScript for ASP, with parts written in C++. Almost all of our internal tools and our web presence (FogShop, Discussions, etc.) are written in VBScript for ASP.

Why bother moving to .NET at all? Simply put, it's because .NET appears so far to be one of the most brilliant and productive development environments ever created. ASP.NET really makes it incredibly easy to create useful web applications; over the last couple of days I've been creating some applications we use internally at incredible speed. All the grungy stuff that takes 75 percent of the time creating web applications with ASP (such as form validation and error reporting) becomes trivial. ASP.NET is as big a jump in productivity over ASP as Java is to C. Wow.

C# has most of the good stuff from Java, with a few small improvements like automatic boxing. Although we have always done what we can to create reasonably object-oriented code in ASP and VB6 in the past, switching to C# will be nice.

Finally, the class libraries that ship with .NET are great. The fact that *everything*, from data access to web development to GUI development, was redesigned means that there is incredible consistency from top to bottom. When you look at the old Win32 APIs, it is simply amazing how many different ways there are to get a string back from a function call, for example. Every two years, they changed their mind about what a good way is to do this. .NET has cleaned that all up. I love the fact that you can use an ASP.NET calendar widget, which generates HTML that selects a date on a monthly calendar, and be confident that the "date" class you get back from that thing (System.DateTime, I believe) will be the exact same date class that the SQL Server classes expect. You would not believe how much time we wasted in the past doing things like reformatting dates for SQL statements, or converting COleDateTimes to someOtherKindOfDateTime. And finally—a string data type that works everywhere! Just last week I was writing ATL code and messing around with BSTRs and OLECHARs and char*s and LPSTRs and what a mess that was. Good riddance.

OK, I admit it—.NET violated the Never Rewrite From Scratch rule.[1] Microsoft got away with it because they had two things. First, they had the world's best language designer, the man who was responsible for 90 percent of the productivity gains in software development in the last 20 years, Anders Hejlsberg,[2] who gave us Turbo Pascal (thank you!), Delphi (thank you!), WFC (nice try!) and now .NET (smacked the ball outta the park). Second, they put about a zillion engineers on it for about three years, during a period where much of their competition was more-or-less stalled. Remember, just because Microsoft can do something, doesn't mean you can. *Microsoft makes their own gravity.* Normal rules don't apply to them.

A few dozen people will now proceed to compose angry emails praising some other development environment, or asking why we don't just use Java and get Write Once Run Anywhere (giggle), or Delphi (the talent has left the building. .NET *is* Delphi 7.0, and 8.0, and 9.0), or Lisp, or whatever. "I am getting locked in the Microsoft Trunk!" they will say. Regrettably, I don't have time to get into religious discussions right now and I usually find them quite boring. I don't *care* if Japanese is a better language than English. It just doesn't matter. Let me finish describing our strategy.

First problem: We don't know enough about .NET to write good code. As usual in any development environment, there are many ways to do any given thing, and we haven't quite learned the first way, let alone

1. See Chapter 24.
2. John Osborn, "Deep Inside C#: An Interview with Microsoft Chief Architect Anders Hejlsberg." O'Reilly.com, August 1, 2000. See windows.oreilly.com/news/hejlsberg_0800.html.

the second way. So the quality of .NET code that we can write is not good enough to ship. Until Bill Vaughn's *first* ADO book came out, we didn't even know the optimal ways to do basic SQL queries. So our first priority is education, which we will accomplish by doing all future in-house and web-based development in .NET—basically, all the software that nobody is paying money for. We can migrate parts of the FogShop to .NET and certainly use .NET for all kinds of internal stuff. (Today I wrote a FogShop Coupon Generator in ASP.NET. It's kind of messy, but it works!)

Second problem: the obese 20MB CLR (runtime). It's bad enough that about 6MB of the 8MB CityDesk download comes from runtimes and data access libraries; we just can't expect every CityDesk Starter Edition home user to download another 20MB. The hope is that in a year or two or three, lots of people will have the CLR from somewhere else (too bad it didn't make it into Windows XP). We'll keep an eye on that.

The bottom line is that neither CityDesk nor FogBUGZ can be ported to .NET today. We will port some future version of CityDesk when the CLR has about 75 percent penetration. The plan is to:

1. Port existing code and forms using Microsoft's conversion tools.

2. Fix problems by brute force until it's working again.

3. Create new forms and classes using C#.

4. Port old forms and classes to C# gradually—whenever they need major work, anyway.

5. Let many old forms and classes remain in VB.NET forever (using the ugly backward compatibility string functions, etc.) as long as they work properly.

FogBUGZ also needs to wait for greater CLR penetration on server computers; we need to survey our customers and find out how bad it would be if FogBUGZ required the CLR.

We have another product in the works that we haven't talked about publicly; this one will share a large portion of its code base with FogBUGZ (a subset we are going to name "Dispatcho") so it will remain VBScript/ASP at heart until we port FogBUGZ.

For FogBUGZ/Dispatcho/SecretNewProduct, the plan is:

1. Wait until it's OK to require CLR.

2. Port existing "business logic" classes to C#.

3. Keep current web forms in ASP.

4. Create new web forms in ASP.NET.

forty-five

PLEASE SIR MAY I HAVE A LINKER?

If I were paranoid, I'd say that Microsoft doesn't really want to make development tools for systems or application developers who might compete with their core business; they really just want to make development tools for IT departments building custom vertical software where there's no potential business for Microsoft. But that would be paranoid. Please sir may I have a tin foil hat?

WEDNESDAY, JANUARY 28, 2004

For some reason, Microsoft's brilliant and cutting-edge .NET development environment left out one crucial tool . . . a tool that has been common in software development environments since, oh, about 1950, and taken so much for granted that it's incredibly strange that nobody noticed that .NET doesn't really have one.

The tool in question? *A linker.* Here's what a linker does. It combines the compiled version of your program with the compiled versions of all the library functions that your program uses. Then, it removes any library functions that your program does not use. Finally, it produces a single executable binary program that people can run on their computers.

Instead, .NET has this idea of a "runtime," a big 22MB steaming heap of code that is linked dynamically and that everybody has to have on their computers before they can use .NET applications.

Runtimes are a problem, much like DLLs, because you can get into trouble when application version 1 was designed to work with runtime version 1, and then runtime version 2 comes out, and suddenly application version 1 doesn't work right for some unpredictable reason. For example, right now for some reason our internal company control panel is rounding sales figures to four decimal points as a result of upgrading from 1.0 to 1.1 of the runtime. Usually the incompatibilities are worse.

In fact .NET includes an extensive technology system called "manifests," which are manifestly complicated and intended to ensure that somehow *only* the right runtime will be used with a given application, but nobody I know can figure out how to use them.

This calls for a story. At the Fog Creek New Year's Eve party, we wanted a bunch of computer screens in the main room to display a countdown until midnight. Michael wrote an application to do this in C# with WinForms in about 60 seconds. It's a great development environment.

My job was to get countdown.exe to run on three computers. Sounds easy.

Nope. Double-click the EXE, and I got a ridiculously user-hostile error message about mscoree.dll or something, followed by a gratuitous dump of my path. No mention of the fact that the problem was simply that the .NET runtime was not installed. Luckily, I'm a programmer and I figured that must be the problem.

How do you install the runtime? The "easiest" way is through Windows Update. But Windows Update really wanted me to get all the critical updates *first* before I installed the runtime. That's reasonable, right? Two of the "critical" updates were a Windows service pack and a new version of Internet Explorer, both of which required a reboot.

All told, for each computer I needed to run this little .NET application on, I had to download something like 70 or 80MB (good thing we have a fast Net connection) and reboot three or four times. And this is at a software company! I know how long it took, because the first time it started downloading, I put *Office Space* on the big-screen TV, and by the time the movie was over, the installation process was *almost* finished. Every ten minutes during the movie, I had to jump up, go to each computer, and hit OK to some stupid dialog box.

This is frustrating enough for our in-house apps. But think about our product CityDesk. Almost all of our users download a free trial version before buying the product.[1] The download is around 9MB and has no additional requirements. Almost none of these users has the .NET runtime yet.

---

1. See www.fogcreek.com/CityDesk/Starter.html for more information.

If we asked our trial users, usually small organizations and home users, to go through a movie-length installation hell just to try our app, I think we'd probably lose 95 percent of them. These are not customers *yet*; they're prospects, and I can't afford to give up 95 percent of my prospects just to use a nicer development environment.

"But Joel," people say, "eventually enough people will have the runtime and this problem will go away."

I thought that too, then I realized that every six or twelve months, Microsoft ships a *new version* of the runtime, and the gradually increasing number of people that have it deflates again to zero. And I'll be damned if I'm going to struggle to test my app on three different versions of the runtime just so I can get the benefit of the 1.2 percent of the installed base that has one of the three.

I just want to link everything I need in a single static EXE that runs without any installation prerequisites. I don't mind if it's a bit bigger. All I would need is the functions that I actually *use*, the bytecode interpreter, and a little bit of runtime stuff. I don't need the entire C# compiler that is a part of the runtime. I promise that CityDesk doesn't need to compile any C# source code. I don't need all 22MB. What I need is probably 5 or 6MB, *at most*.

I know of companies that have the technology to do this, but they can't do it without permission from Microsoft to redistribute bits and pieces of the runtime like the bytecode interpreter. So Microsoft: Wake up, get us some nice 1950s-era linker technology, and let me make a single EXE that runs on any computer with Win 98 or later and *no other external dependencies*. Otherwise, .NET is fatally flawed for consumer, downloaded software.

part five

Appendix

appendix

THE BEST OF ASK JOEL

For a while I hosted a discussion forum on my website called "Ask Joel," in which I invited readers to ask questions that I attempted to answer. Here are some of my favorites.

Q My organization has in recent years been overrun with program managers who seem better equipped to make decisions about polo shirts and khaki pants than about technical matters.

They foment confusion by misusing distinct technical terms as if they were interchangeable. They're oblivious to technical nuance. Worst of all, they have no natural defenses against the influence of weak engineers. (Hmmm, maybe the weak engineers are the real problem here—maybe software companies don't need technical PMs.)

Obviously, I'm a bitter curmudgeon whose judgment is a bit skewed by personal frustrations and nostalgia for the days when a little flame mail went a long way to nip a bad idea in the bud. But what's the more tempered perspective? How technical do PMs really need to be, relative to the technical depth of their environment? Am I way off-base here?

—Anonymous

A Ah, polo shirts and khaki pants. I miss Redmond. Where else can you go to the Gap on Sunday, come back to work the next day, and find twelve other program managers wearing the exact same thing you just bought?

I used to say that program managers who do not have the respect of developers are not going to be effective, because they won't get anything done. In my day on the Excel team, the developers ate untechnical program managers for breakfast. It sounds from your anecdotes that you've seen some teams with the worst of both worlds: weak program managers and weak developers.

The truth is that the Program Management gene and the Software Development gene are mutually exclusive. The perfect program manager is a software developer with user empathy, organizational skills, and the people skills of a sorority leader—and there just aren't enough of those to keep 45 buildings under control. At some point someone decided that coding was an expendable skill for this job, and, guess what? Who interviews potential program managers at Microsoft? Other program managers. Remember As hires As, but Bs hires Cs?

The only reason I had any success at all as a program manager was because I have two—that's right, two—complete sets of DNA. It's called the quadruple helix, and only I have it. And I avoided the Gap entirely; after one terrifying oh-my-god-did-I-just-pass-MYSELF-in-the-hall? incident too many involving a boldly colored striped sweater, I resolved to choose my polo shirts and khaki pants from the other 27 perfectly good polo shirt stores at Bellevue Square Mall.

Talk to Microsoft program managers about their roles. They'll always tell you things like "our job is not just to run with the ball, but to find the ball in the first place!" or something grandiose like that. OK. So the programmers think they're deciding everything and the program managers think they're deciding everything. How can they both be deciding everything? They can't. Who is really deciding, then? Let me give you a hint. Of the program managers and developers you know, on the whole, who has better people skills? Eh? Speak up boy, I can't hear you. Duh! Of course it's the program managers. You knew that. Developers couldn't people-skill their way out of a summer intern party at BillG's lakeside mansion. Developers have such weak people skills they can't even imagine what people skills could be used for, other than the purely theoretical concept of getting a theoretical date ("I...like...big *butts* and I cannot *lie...*"), so it's no wonder they're not even aware of the secret that I can finally reveal today.

You know how the really good program managers make you feel like you're doing all the important design work, and they're just a gopher, taking care of dumb bureaucracy like "dealing with users" and "dealing with marketing shit" and "writing lame-ass specs?"

Guess what. Number-one required skill in a program manager is learning to make software developers do what you want by making them think *it was their own idea*. Yes, it requires a polo shirt to pull this off, but an average program manager does it three, four times a day and for the most part pulls it off. I've read entire self-published "books" by ex-Microsoft developers who detailed their sophomoric Microsoft careers in insanely boring detail, including an entire chapter about how stupid and irrelevant program managers are, and yet they never once realized they were being manipulated the whole time—the sign of a brilliant program manager. A brilliant program manager makes it all look effortless! Which is not hard when you're dealing with a person whose favorite comeback is, "I didn't give you the wrong answer, you asked the wrong question!"

Can you imagine the phat skilz it takes to manipulate a developer into doing what you want, while simultaneously appearing to be just an airhead Club Med *Gentil Organisateur*? Not only do you have to erase your ego ("oh, what a smart idea you just had, Mr. Developer!"), but you have to do so *while appearing to be a self-centered preppy*. Sean Penn couldn't pull off a role like this as well as a merely average Microsoft program manager can.

Q Right now the "hot new thing" is .NET. And Longhorn is coming. Woo-hoo.

But where do you see the software development business going in, say, 10 years? What will the profession of development look like in a decade? What new concepts will be have to be embraced? What break-throughs do you think will come about?

—*Norrick*

A We will have robots in our kitchens to wash the dishes! And robots in elevators to operate the elevator controls!

Instead of tellers in banks, there will be rows of ultramodern computers that dispense stacks of crisp, new dollar bills. (Although in the future even common laborers will make enough money to take out ten, twenty, or even forty dollars each time they go to the bank!)

Flying machines will whisk us in comfortable pressurized air from city to city. Perhaps you might even be served a simple hot meal, high above the clouds!

The world's largest encyclopedia—bigger, indeed, than a school library—will be instantly available in homes by means of pneumatic tubes or perhaps electrical wires.

A special telephotograph-machine will enable the spread of education throughout the world, giving even the poorest dustbin-cleaner an opportunity to better themselves by learning the classics, eliminating hunger and suffering.

Oh, and C# will have anonymous methods, allowing the code associated with a delegate to be written in-line where the delegate is used, conveniently tying the code directly to the delegate instance.

Q My company is just about to finish development of our first product. Our idea isn't terribly original, but there are only one or two other players in our niche and we think we can do better. We also added an additional feature or two that the competitors didn't have that we feel adds quite a bit of value. However, we just found out that our main competitor will be launching a new version of their product with new features very similar to our own.

Needless to say we're a bit discouraged. We think our product does a lot of things better, but it's very similar to existing products that have had more time to mature.

What should our top priority be at this point? Find some new features that give us a clear competitive advantage? Work on refining our existing product and feature-set to a level beyond the competition? Any advice would be helpful.

—*Sam Thomas*

A Stop paying attention to your competitors. Repeat after me: Listen to your customers, not your competitors!
Listen to your customers, not your competitors!
Listen to your customers, not your competitors!

There are dozens of competitors for our bug tracking software, and I have no idea what they do or why they're better or worse than ours. I couldn't care less. All I care about is what my customers tell me, which gives me plenty of work to keep busy.

Ship your thing, ignore the competition. You're going to get some customers who just haven't *heard* of the competition. Maybe not a lot, but it's a start. Talk to your customers regularly and make sure there's an email address on every page of your website. You'll start to notice trends—features that keep coming up that explain why some people are not choosing your products. With FogBUGZ 1.0, it was the ability to attach files to bugs. We added that for FogBUGZ 2.0. Do our competitors have that feature? Beats me, I have no idea. It's not worth the ten minutes it would take to find out. All I cared about was that people were telling us that they wouldn't buy our software until you could attach files to bugs. So now you can.

Strategy Letter III has some discussion of understanding the business of getting users to switch from an entrenched competitor.[1] But for now your action item is to ship, then listen to your customers and almost-customers to figure out what to do next.

Q A followup...
What methods are you using to solicit meaningful feedback from customers? What about prospects? Do you do any outbound calls/emails/etc. for this purpose?

—dir

A Nothing outbound. Our three best sources for feedback:

- the "Send Feedback" menu item in CityDesk. Goes right into our bug tracking database, and generates so much (excellent) feedback that we simply can't reply to any of it; we're lucky if we have time to tally votes for feature requests.
- a general policy that there should be an email link at the bottom of every page on our website
- online discussion forums

These three methods get us more than enough feedback. I generally tell Dmitri (who handles most of our technical support) to keep an eye out for things of the form "I like your product but I can't buy it because X."

These are much more important feedback points than "Why doesn't your product have X?" which does not necessarily represent a "final objection," but might just be general ranting or creativity. For example,

---

1. See Chapter 38.

someone read one of my articles linked from Slashdot and now they want to know whether CityDesk runs on Linux; this does not necessarily represent a person who is sitting with his credit card in hand. Or someone might use the software and have a "great idea" for some clever new feature, which is good to hear, but not as important as "I like your product but I can't buy it because X."

Q From a logistics perspective, I'm puzzled over something so simple. Why is it that every grocery store double-bags? Why don't they just make the bags stronger?

Even what appears to be a more sturdy bag from Duane Reade, for larger items, was just doubled up for my bottle of water…um, am I missing something obvious?

—Curious in NYC

A Because the cashiers don't get to specify the bags. The accountants at Gristede's World Headquarters live in outer Queens and drive to the supermarket in SUVs, so they don't even understand the concept of carrying home your groceries. They just go for the cheapest possible per-unit cost even though this ends up costing more in the long run, because they haven't been to Manhattan since the big blackout and the riots in the mid-1970s, except for a brief visit to see the matinee of *Oh! Calcutta!* one last time before it closed in the 1980s, and they couldn't in their wildest dreams imagine what it's like to carry 12 bottles of Margarita Mix three long city blocks and then up six flights of stairs to your walkup $1700 studio in Hell's Kitchen.

Q What percentage/amount of time needs to be kept as buffer time while doing estimation and on what basis/criteria?

—Vani

A If your estimates are based on very fine-grained tasks (each task is about one day in length) and you have enough experience to include *everything* in the estimates (including vacation, holidays, sick days, integration time, "new features" time for the new features that are invented during development, time to go to stupid management meetings, time to interview people, etc.) then you're only going to need 10 percent buffer.

Rather than having buffer time, which is just a way to wave your hands, you should have types of buffer and allocate time to each one based on priorities:

- Buffer for unexpected features we thought up during development.
- Buffer for unexpected competitive responses needed because our competitor did something.
- Buffer to allow code written by different developers to be integrated so it works together. (Depending on the experience of your team, this can be 25–100 percent.)
- Buffer to find and fix bugs during testing.
- Buffer for nondevelopment tasks that employees must perform, e.g. "one day mandatory diversity training," "emergency company meeting," fire drills, birthday cake for the boss, etc. etc.
- Buffer because things took longer than estimated.
- Buffer because things needed to be done for which no estimates had been provided.

Break it down like this and you can track it carefully. If you're 80 percent done and you've only used 20 percent of the boss-birthday-cake budget, you can remove hours from that line and put them on something else more urgent.

Q Would it be possible for somebody to have software run in a restricted environment such that clever social engineering worm messages can't propagate?

It seems like a losing battle to me to keep saying "upgrade your antivirus software" and "don't run random attachments" when people *don't* keep antivirus software up to date and *do* run random attachments.

The most obvious option would be to not allow execution of binaries, but some people would simply save, then execute. Plus advertising the message as a security update or game makes people want to run it anyway.

The problem is that people just can't be trusted to make smart decisions about what binaries are safe to execute on their machine.

Could a "jail" environment be designed such that worms are so restricted (or obviously flagged as malicious) that serious propagation isn't likely anymore?

—*Eric Seppanen*

A That's the age-old sandbox problem.
The short answer is: probably not.

I recently switched to Sprint PCS for my cell service because their phones could be programmed in Java. I had all kinds of ideas for applets I wanted to write:

1. An applet to synchronize the phone list in my phone with my Outlook contact list.

2. An applet so I could easily switch my phone between "modes" that combined ringing and voicemail behavior. So I could tell the phone I was at the gym and it would switch to an outgoing voicemail message saying, "please leave a voicemail, I'll get it within an hour," or I could tell it I was in the subway and the voicemail would say, "I'm in the subway and will get your message within 20 minutes."

Then I started looking into J2ME and discovered that a) I did not have access to the phone numbers stored on the phone, b) I did not have access to any of the phone settings such as ringer volume, c) I did not have the ability to make outgoing phone calls, d) I did not have the ability to use the GPS built into the phone to determine my location, e) I did not have the ability to access the phone's built-in camera, f) and on and on.

Basically, this reflects Sun's attitude toward sandboxing, which is, err on the side of safety, even if it means your development environment is completely useless. And the same thing will happen to J2ME that happened to applets in the browser: The only thing the sandbox lets you do is write really slow games (Ms. PacMan is decent, even if it does take 53 seconds to load), and the technology is virtually worthless for anything else.

Microsoft's attitude toward sandboxing is quite different—infinitely more dangerous, but a lot more fun. At the PDC, they showed a demo where somebody used a .NET-powered cell phone and about 10 lines of mobile .NET code to take a picture, take coordinates with the GPS and convert them to a street address, take a sound recording with some notes, and upload the whole thing to a database (the proverbial "insurance adjuster's app"). All stuff you can't do with J2ME even though the phone clearly has the capability to do it.

Now—the reason I mentioned the age-old sandbox problem goes back to Applets. When Applets first appeared there was a lot of George Gilder talk about how the next word processor would be a big ol' Java Applet. The trouble is that a Java Applet couldn't read or write files on the hard drive. It was in the sandbox. If it wanted persistence, it had to upload the files to some hard drive in the sky. Someone thought it was OK to allow data to persist *inside* the sandbox, as long as you can't get to data *outside* the sandbox. The trouble is . . . your data is on the outside. But never mind that. Even in a brave new world in which you have all your data *inside* the sandbox, well, now you don't have much security do you? Because everything you care about is inside the sandbox. Face it: If you want the ability to run arbitrary code which modifies your pictures, so you can put Bill Clinton's face on Marky Mark's body, you're going to have to have the ability to run arbitrary code which modifies your pictures, and if that code decides to do something bad to your pictures, you lose. Sorry bubby.

Microsoft and Sun are both moving to a "fine-grained" security model where you give individual apps fine-grained permission to do certain things. Ms. PacMan can read and write files, but only the high score table, and she certainly can't access the Net. You can set up infinitely complex security policies.

As anyone who knows anything about security will tell you, This Is Not Going To Work. The more complicated a security system is, the more likely it is to be misconfigured. Humans can only deal with so much complexity, and nobody has time to manage the permissions for all their apps on a fine-grained basis.

So all in all, it seems like a depressing world. That said, there's nothing we can do to keep thugs from hitting old ladies over the heads with baseball bats and taking their purses. We can threaten them with punishment and we can lock up thugs, but right now I assure you that if you were determined to hit an old lady over the head with a baseball bat, you'd probably succeed. Similarly, there's nothing to stop you from driving your car off a cliff. Get in your car, go to a cliff, try to drive off—nothing will stop you.

People expect the computer world to be so much safer than the real world and they expect it to "protect you from yourself," but it just ain't going to happen, just like car makers are never going to figure out how to make cars that refuse to drive off cliffs, and little old ladies will not start wearing hardhats in public. And yet life goes on, so I for one am going to find something else to lose sleep over.

Q What's the big deal with expensing stock options? It seems like it's a good idea to give your employees a stake in the success of the company. Why does expensing them make them less attractive?

—*Jason*

A Let's say you're a big software company with a stock price that's going up 100 percent every year. By tossing your employees a few stock options, you can give them the equivalent of thousands or millions of dollars in compensation without spending any cash. In fact, you can lower their base salary at the same time and they won't really mind because they're making so much money off the stock options. Indeed in the late 1980s Microsoft salaries were probably 30 or 40 percent lower than the competition—those were the years where every employee became a millionaire.

Where do all these options come from if you don't spend any cash for them? Usually, you issue more stock. This has the effect of diluting the existing shareholders. To take a simple example, if you have a million shares outstanding, and you issue another million shares for the purpose of giving stock to your employees at a below-market price (when they exercise their options), now there are two million shares outstanding. If the company is worth as much as it was before, each share has just halved in value. Effectively, you have taken money out of your shareholders' pockets to pay your employees.

Why is this even legal? It's not, unless the shareholders agree to it, and they do, because to the shareholder, they can either pay the employees by having money come out of the company bank account, which reduces the value of each share of the company, or they can pay the employees by increasing the number of shares outstanding, which reduces the value of each share of the company.

Did you catch that? Pay close attention—I'll give you another example. This is the critical insight. Are you paying attention? Good.

I'm a big software company worth two million dollars. There are a million shares outstanding. Each share is thus worth $2.

Now I need to pay my employees. They need $1 million in salary.

Scenario 1: I pay them cash out of the bank account. My company that was worth $2m is now worth $1m, by definition, because we just paid out $1m in cash. When that million went out the door the value of the company had to be reduced by a million, right? So each share goes down in value from $2 to $1.

Scenario 2: Instead of paying them in cash, I get permission from the shareholders and issue another million shares of stock and give those to the employees. Now there are two million in shares outstanding instead of one million. And the company is still worth $2 million because I haven't spent any money—nothing has gone out of the company. So each share goes down in value from $2 to $1 just because there are twice as many shares around.

Notice the common theme? In both cases the underlying value of the share went from $2 to $1.

What's the difference between Scenario 1 and 2?

- In both scenarios, the employees get $1 million.
- In both scenarios, the shareholders see the value of their shares go down by 50 percent, from $2 each to $1 each.
- In Scenario 2, the company is theoretically happier because they have more cash on hand.

And the clincher:

- Under the old accounting rules, if you don't have to expense options, with Scenario 2 you show an extra million dollars in profit that you don't show in Scenario 1.

So far we haven't mentioned profit at all. Profit is income minus outgo. Income is the same in both scenarios. The only difference is whether that $1m flowed out of the company or not.

Since Scenario 1 and 2 are really the same thing, for all intents and purposes, it's not really fair that companies following Scenario 2 should report an extra million dollars in profit that the company following Scenario 1 didn't have.

In other words, we're really doing the same thing vis-à-vis the employees and vis-à-vis the shareholders in both scenarios. So why should the profit be a million dollars more in the second scenario? It doesn't make sense that you're suddenly more "profitable" because you chose to pay employees by diluting shareholders rather than depleting the bank account. To the shareholder, it's the same thing.

The old accounting system meant that the Wall Street numbers of "earnings per share" are not trustworthy. This made a big difference for many companies that appeared to be hugely profitable in terms of earnings per share.

When investors try to compare companies they look at things like price-to-earnings ratios (price of one share divided by earnings per share). If you require companies to expense stock options, meaning you require them to reduce their profit by the amount that they diluted the shareholders by issuing new shares, you make it so that companies will report the same earnings per share whether they used Scenario 1 or 2, which is more honest to the shareholders and allows two companies to be accurately compared in terms one another. It means that stock analysts don't have to figure out, themselves, based on the dilution of shares caused by employee stock options, how to compare company #1 and company #2; they can just look at the earnings and know that employee stock options aren't causing them to take a big dilution hit for one company versus another. In the bad old days, the only way to compare the earnings per share of two companies honestly was to dig through the annual reports, figure out the dilution cause by stock options, and try to recalculate the "earnings" yourself based on that information, which was often incomplete or late. Needless to say, stock analysts didn't really bother; of course the Motley Fool crowd went along happily comparing PE ratios of companies without realizing that employee stock options meant the earnings figures were distorted in unpredictable ways.

Expensing stock options is a way to make sure that the dilution caused by issuing stock to employees is fairly accounted for in the earnings per share and thus give the shareholders a better picture of the performance of the company per share.

Q I apologize if this has been raised before, but what do you think will happen to Microsoft when everybody has 100Mbit broadband straight into their house and office?

There would be no need for Windows or Office for the majority of users as the web would be quick enough to run whatever Web App is required. And they wouldn't have to use Microsoft software either.

For example: I already use Hotmail for my email and if I had a fast enough link with remote storage I might use an online word processor or spreadsheet too. That way my data would be available wherever I happen to be. Just like Hotmail.

—Roy

A Whoa there, cowboy! You're extrapolating like crazy from a small trend.

First of all, I highly doubt you would want to spend very much time using a word processor delivered to you in the form of a web page, especially given the state of HTML. User interfaces designed for IE 6.x are clunky and slow. This is not entirely an accident—I don't think Microsoft *wants* it to be possible to develop great user experiences in HTML form.

Second, lots of people do have very high bandwidth connections, and I have yet to meet the person who does their word processing and spreadsheeting in a web browser. The Microsoft Office business is doing fine, thank you very much.

Even if it were to be threatened by hypothetical web-browser-delivered productivity tools, you can bet Microsoft would get into that business too.

In the early 1990s, everybody thought IBM was going to disappear because they just didn't understand PCs and could not get over their mainframe mentality. What people forgot is that a large, successful company has a *long* way to fall, and during that fall they have *years* to regain their footing. Microsoft is the same way now. Whatever fanciful theory you come up with about how Microsoft is going to be wiped out (web apps, broadband, Linux, antitrust law, or black helicopters) can't change the fact that Microsoft has enough cash to keep operating for something like five years even if their revenue suddenly plummeted to zero without laying off one programmer. And their revenue is not going to zero tomorrow; even in their worst nightmare scenario, you might expect their revenue to drop, say, 20 percent a year, so now they can probably hang around for ten years before they have to start contemplating the first round of layoffs.

So it's not enough to come up with some reason why Microsoft will be threatened by a change in technology: you also have to assume that they would fail to respond to such a change for years and years.

INDEX

COLOPHON

This book's cover is modified from the famous frontispiece first used in the 1632 (fourth) edition of Robert Burton's *The Anatomy of Melancholy*. Our version is from a facsimile of the 1652 edition that we scanned at 400 dpi on an Epson Perfection scanner. We must confess to modifying Burton's frontispiece to suit our modern sensibilities. We used Adobe Photoshop 7 on a Mac G4.

Burton's *Anatomy of Melancholy* is one of those glorious works of seventeenth century English literature, written by a polymath in some of the most beautiful prose imaginable. However, it is very, very long, and few, if anybody, now reads it in its entirety—none of us have.

Still, it is worth browsing. As Hugh Cahill points out at http://www.kcl.ac.uk/depsta/iss/library/speccoll/bomarch/bomoct.html, in places it is introspective with an ironic twist:

I write of melancholy, by being busy to avoid melancholy.

and in many other places it is just plain brilliant and so true even today:

To say truth, 'tis the common fortune of most scholars to be servile and poor, to complain pitifully, and lay open their wants to their respective patrons... and... for hope of gain to lie, flatter, and with hyperbolical elogiums and commendations to magnify and extol an illiterate unworthy idiot for his excellent virtues, whom they should rather, as Machiavel observes, vilify and rail at downright for his most notorious villainies and vices.

Arguably, Burton's book is the first modern work in psychology (he uses the word *melancholy* as we would use the word *depression* today); he analyzes the causes and cures for depression with such insights that many parts of the book remain of great interest to both novelists *and* psychologists. And, of course, *all* parts of it remain of interest to lovers of great prose.

We hope therefore that you will see why, when we were trying to conceive a cover worthy of Joel, we felt that Burton's was appropriate!